Law's Picture Books

Anno primo Henrici vj^ti

A Parlement tenuz a Westm' le lundy procheyn devant le fest de Seint Martyn lan del regne du Roi Henry sisme puis le conquest primer mesme le Roi de ladvys & assent des seignurs espirituelx & temporelx & a les especiales instance & requeste des Coës venuz en mesme le parlement ad fait faire ordeiner & establier diverses ordinances & estatutz en la fourme qensuyt.

En primes ordine est pur la profit du Roi & lease de son poeple qe les seignurs de counseil du Roi pur le temps estoiantz averont assigne par auctorite du dit parlement maistres & ouvrers a faire monoie dor & dargent & tenir les eschaunges du monoie auxi bien en la Citee Deverwik come en la ville de Bristuit & auxi en tantz des lieux come semblera as ditz seignurs bon & necessarie selonc lour bones advys & discrecions ascun estatut ou ordinance fait au contrarie non obstant. **Item** qe toutz les estatutz & ordinances faitz des purveiours & achatours & nient repellez soient gardez & executz en toutz pointz & auxi proclamez en toutz Countees parmy le Roialme par mandement du Roy. Et qe chescun visconte venuz apres ceo qil avera resceu les ditz estatutz par eux faire proclamacion par tiel mandement les face proclamer chescun an quatre foitz parmy sa baillie sur peyne de paier au Roi a chescun foitz qil ent faille C s. et qe sur mesme la peyne chescun des ditz viscontz face delivrance du dit mandement a son successour immediat par endentures entre eux affaire pount il poet faire semblable proclamacion pur le temps qil estoise en son office pur lease & remedie de le poeple & qe chescun tiel successour apres tiel mandement par luy resceu face auxi tielx proclamacions quatre foitz par an & auxi tiel delivrance du dit mandement ferra a son successour come desuis sur la peyne avantdit. **Item** pur tant qe

Law's Picture Books

The Yale Law Library Collection

Michael Widener
Mark S. Weiner

Clark, New Jersey
2017

Catalogue of an exhibition at the Grolier Club, New York City
September 13 – November 18, 2017.

ISBN 978-1-61619-160-3

TALBOT PUBLISHING
AN IMPRINT OF
THE LAWBOOK EXCHANGE, LTD.
33 Terminal Avenue
Clark, New Jersey 07066-1321

Please see our website for a selection of our other publications and fine facsimile reprints of classic works of legal history: www.lawbookexchange.com.

Library of Congress Cataloging-in-Publication Data

Names: Widener, Michael. | Weiner, Mark Stuart. | Lillian Goldman Law Library.
Title: Law's picture books : the Yale Law Library collection / Michael Widener and Mark S. Weiner.
Description: Clark, NJ : Talbot Publishing, an imprint of The Lawbook Exchange, Ltd., 2017. | Includes bibliographical references.
Identifiers: LCCN 2017027066 | ISBN 9781616191603 (pbk. : alk. paper)
Subjects: LCSH: Law--Bibliography--Exhibitions. | Illustrated books--Exhibitions.
Classification: LCC K38 .L394 2017 | DDC 096.1074/7468--dc23
LC record available at https://lccn.loc.gov/2017027066

Front cover: item 1.04. Rear cover: item 8.04. Frontispiece: item 10.05.

This catalogue was made possible with the support of the Charles J. Tanenbaum Fund, Yale Law School, and a generous gift from the Pine Tree Foundation.

Permissions

Image from *Vollstandige Faksimile-Ausgabe im Originalformat des Wolfenbütteler Sachsenspiegels* (Akademische Druck- und Verlagsanstalt , 2006) [item 2.01] reproduced with permission of the publisher.

Images from *Illiustrirovannyi Trudovoi kodeks Rossiiskoi Federatsii.* (Moscow: Izdatelstvo "Mann, Ivanov i Ferber", 2014) [item 2.11] and *Illiustrirovannyi ugolovnyi kodeks Rossiiskoi Federatsii* (Izdatel'stvo "Mann, Ivanov i Ferber", 2013) [item 9.17] reproduced with the kind permission of the illustrator, Alexei Merinov.

Image from *Quick search manual* (1926) [item 3.07] reproduced with the kind permission of Thomson-Reuters.

Image from Eric Hilgendorf, *Dtv-Atlas Recht* (Deutscher Taschenbuch Verlag, 2003) [item 3.15] reproduced with the kind permission of the author.

Image from Clark Stoeckley, *The United States vs. Pvt. Chelsea Manning* (OR Books, 2014) [item 5.12] reproduced with the kind permission of the publisher.

Image from Syl Sobel, *The U.S. Constitution and you* (Barron's Educational Series, 2001) [item 8.11] reproduced with the kind permission of the publisher.

Image from Yuki Nakamichi & Yamanaka Masahiro, *Osaru no tomasu keiho o shiru* (Tarojiroshaeditasu, 2014) [item 8.12] reproduced with the kind permission of the publisher.

Image from *Bound by law? Tales from the public domain* (Duke Center for the Study of the Public Domain, 2006) [item 8.14] reproduced with the kind permission of the publisher.

Images from Nathaniel Burney, *The illustrated guide to criminal procedure* (Ivers Morgan, 2014) [item 8.17] reproduced with the kind permission of the author.

Images by Joseph Hémard from *Code penal* (Editions Littéraires de France) [items 9.00 & 9.05], and from *Code général des impôts directs et taxes assimilées* (Editions Littéraires et Artistiques, 1944) [item 9.03] © 2017 Artists Rights Society (ARS), New York / ADAGP, Paris.

Image by Albert Dubout from *Code de la route* (Maurice Gonon, 1956) [item 9.04] © 2017 Artists Rights Society (ARS), New York / SABAM, Brussels.

Cover from Kathi Linz, *Chickens may not cross the road and other crazy (but true) laws* (Houghton Mifflin, 2002) [item 9.13], illustrated by Tony Griego; jacket art copyright © 2002 by Tony Griego. Used by permission of Houghton Mifflin Harcourt Publishing Company. All rights reserved.

Image from Batton Lash, *Supernatural law*, no. 35 (Exhibit A Press, July 2002) [item 9.14] reproduced with the kind permission of the author / illustrator.

Images from *Unabridged graphic adaptation iTunes terms* (Birdcage Bottom Books, 2015) [item 9.15] reproduced with the kind permission of the illustrator, Robert Sikoryak.

Image from Allen Ginsberg, *Chicago trial testimony* (1975) [item 9.16], permission pending from The Permissions Company on behalf of City Lights Books.

Image from *The defense of Gracchus Babeuf before the High Court of Vendôme* (Gehenna Press, 1964) [item 10.08] reproduced by permission of the Estate of Leonard Baskin. © Estate of Leonard Baskin. Courtesy Galerie St. Etienne, New York. Portrait by Thomas Cornell reproduced with the kind permission of the Estate of Thomas Cornell.

Table of Contents

Collecting Yale Law Library's Picture Books

Michael Widener
Yale Law Library

Although I have spent virtually my entire career in academic law libraries, I am not trained as a lawyer. In some way I remain an outsider to the discipline of law. I have compensated by taking an interest in law books as objects. It was this interest that led me to law books with illustrations.

As the great American legal scholar Charles Alan Wright once wrote, "The only tool of the lawyer is words. ... Whether we are trying a case, writing a brief, drafting a contract, or negotiating with an adversary, words are the only things we have to work with."[1]

If you ask most people, including lawyers, to summon an image of law books, that image will be of words, words, and words, of monotonous reams of dreary words about equally dreary topics. Lawyers themselves look on their law books as tools of the trade, and don't pause to consider their physical aspects. A law book is one of the last places most people would expect to find illustrations. Modern law books might have some rather plain artwork on the cover. Early law books might have an author's portrait, or decorative initials. But even decoration seemed to become increasingly rare with time. Perhaps it was seen as frivolous, or distracting, or useless.

That was certainly the image I had of law books when I began my career as a rare law book librarian, some twenty-five years ago at the University of Texas Law Library. That is, until a legal historian, the late Professor Hans W. Baade, asked the library to acquire the first edition of Battista Aimo's treatise on riparian water rights, *De alluvionum iure universo* [4.03]. When the book arrived, I was surprised and fascinated by the many woodcuts. I readily perceived that it made sense to use illustrations. The images provided clear explanations of complex issues involving topography, water flow, and the law, explanations that would have been much more difficult to understand with text alone.

I began to wonder, how many other law books have illustrations? There couldn't be many, I thought. However, I began to look, and once I began to look I found more and more examples. I discovered that they were not all that uncommon. I found illustrations used to explain, or teach, or argue, or criticize.

One of the most common images is the tree of consanguinity. It diagrams degrees of relationship by blood, which are important factors in family law, inheritance, and other legal issues. The tree of consanguinity is an image that describes legal concepts. It serves as a teaching aid, and a memory aid. The tree motif was adapted to illustrate other legal concepts, such as property law.

Allegorical images are another common type, images used to symbolize the law. Lady Justice is the most common of these images. The Judgment of Solomon is another. These images provide insight into ideas about the nature of law and justice, and also about the image of the law and the legal profession, in the eyes of

1. Charles Alan Wright, *Townes Hall Notes* (Spring 1988), 5.

the profession itself and the general public.

It's clear that, when these allegorical images appear as frontispieces to law books, they should be seen, or rather read, as integral to the author's text. They were often conceived, and even paid for, by the author.[2] The powerful frontispiece to Beccaria's *Essay on Crimes and Punishment* [6.09] is the leading example, but not the only one.[3] Dismissing these images as mere decoration is a mistake.

In some cases, images have been used to describe individual laws and legal procedure. Joost de Damhoudere's guide to the practice of criminal law has dozens of images depicting crimes and procedure [2.00, 2.03, 2.04, 2.05, 6.03]. Recently, descriptive images are again coming into use as teaching aids [8.17, 8.18].

In the more recent past, law books have made forensic use of images, deploying them to advance arguments over guilt or innocence, or liability. Images have also been employed as sharp and effective tools for poking fun at the law, and for making serious critiques of the law.

I discovered not only law books that include illustrations, but also law books that qualify as illustrated books. By this I mean books where the illustrations are prominent and essential elements.

2. See Margery Corbett & Ronald Lightbown, *The Comely Frontispiece: The Emblematic Title-Page in England 1550-1660* (London: Routledge & Kegan Paul, 1979).

3. Franco Venturi, *Utopia and Reform in the Enlightenment* (Cambridge: Cambridge University Press, 1971), 105-106.

The earliest of these is the *Sachsenspiegel*, or "Mirror of the Saxons," a compilation of Saxon law composed in the thirteenth century. In the early fourteenth century four illustrated manuscripts of the *Sachsenspiegel* were created, known as the *codices picturati* [2.01]. They remain unsurpassed in legal literature for their intimate integration of text and image. Clothing, gestures, and objects make up a rich visual vocabulary.

The first systematic codification of a branch of law – in this case capital crimes – was the work known as the *Bambergensis* [6.01]. It was adopted for the Diocese of Bamberg, but became the model for the criminal code of the Holy Roman Empire. You wouldn't know by looking at the illustrations, but the *Bambergensis* actually placed new limits on torture. Most of its twenty woodcuts include brief verses of legal folk wisdom.

The printed law book in our collection with the most illustrations is the three-volume edition of the *Corpus Juris Canonici* published in Venice in 1514 [2.06]. The *Corpus Juris Canonici* served as the basis the basis of the Catholic Church's canon law from the Middle Ages until 1917. The 2,000 pages of this 1514 edition contain 442 woodcuts. The larger woodcuts are typical ones: tree diagrams, images from the Bible, book presentation scenes. The extraordinary ones are the 425 smaller woodcuts, one for almost every papal decree and law case. The simple, vigorous lines and cartoonish, almost abstract human figures in these woodcuts make them among my favorites.

The most successful illustrated book of law was Joost de Damhoudere's *Praxis Rerum Criminalium* [2.00, 2.03, 2.04, 2.05, 6.03]. It first appeared in 1554 and went through 37 editions in four languages, 23 of these with a series of about five dozen woodcuts. We know that the illustrations were Damhoudere's idea, because in an addendum to the earliest editions he wrote that the lack of illustrations for some of the chapters was the fault of lazy artists who missed their deadlines.[4] The book became the standard authority on the criminal law of northern Europe and was still cited in court in the eighteenth century. The images depict both criminal procedure and the crimes themselves, ranging from homicide to sex crimes, grave robbing, property crimes, and even environmental crime. They reveal a wealth of details about life in early modern society.

Probably the most bizarre of these illustrated books, to modern eyes, are the Roman law textbooks of Johannes Buno [8.07]. Their curious images are part of a complex system designed to help students memorize the *Corpus Juris Civilis*.

The funniest of these books are the French codes illustrated by Joseph Hémard, one of the most prolific French book illustrators of the twentieth century. With apologies to tax lawyers, a tax code is probably one of the most boring books one could think of, but not in the hands of Joseph Hémard [9.03]. He delights in making visual jokes about the tax laws. The images are always playful, even the ones that complain about taxes. They would not be nearly as funny without the serious bureaucratic language of the tax laws at their side. The tax code is especially interesting because it was published in 1944, in German-occupied Paris, on fine paper and with an expensive illustration process, *pochoir*. Hémard also illustrated the French penal code [9.00, 9.05] and the family law section of the Code Civil. He had many imitators in France, but no equals.

A recent phenomenon is legal textbooks modeled on graphic novels. The criminal law textbooks by Denise Cardia Saraiva in Brazil [8.18] and Nathaniel Burney in the U.S. [8.17] are two examples.

I learned about many of these books in my time at the University of Texas Law Library, but it was at the Yale Law Library that I received the resources and the support to begin collecting them in a serious fashion.

For me, book collecting is an art, and much of the art resides in the decisions about the scope of a given collection. Even a seemingly straightforward collection such as a collection of a given author requires many decisions about scope. Will you include the author's articles in periodicals or only his books? What about variants? Translations? Autographed copies? How about works about the author, or reviews of his works? What about manuscripts? Letters? Photographs? Works that influenced the author? Books that the author owned?

There are no "right" answers to any of these questions. Both institutional and individual collectors will answer these questions based on resources (money, space, time), on the purpose of the collection, and often on what delights or interests the collector. For an institutional library, its mission and existing strengths come into play, as well as potential use for research or teaching.

4. Joost de Damhoudere, *Enchiridion rerum criminalium* (Louvain: Etienne Wauters & Johan Bathen, 1554), 526.

I developed my own answers by picking apart the phrase "law books with illustrations." Let's begin with the term "book." Here we are dealing with the scope of the collection in terms of physical format. I decided to limit the collection to books and book-like genres because books are the lawyer's tools, and because books are what law libraries are good at collecting. I included broadsides because text is their primary component. I included ephemeral pamphlets because many of them contain detailed descriptions of legal events such as trials. I included manuscripts of legal texts with law-related illustrations, because they are hand-written books.

After an early foray into prints, I decided to exclude them, partly because they have little or no text, partly because library catalogers find them a nuisance, partly because they are difficult to store, and partly because the two major art collections at Yale were much better equipped to collect them.

What constitutes a "law" book? Books *of* the law, such as statutes, case reports, and legal treatises, obviously qualify as law books. I believe the same can be said for documents prepared by litigants, and textbooks for law students. Books *about* the law are more problematic: satires of the law, law-related children's books, popular accounts of trials, legal history. I have tended to include most of these, because they document public attitudes and ideas about the law.

What qualifies as an "illustration"? In Yale's case, I have limited them to illustrations with some kind of legal content. I have generally excluded coats of arms, because they are so common. One could argue that a coat of arms is a symbol of a text's legal authority, but that is a bit too tenuous of a connection for me. Some books of heraldry could be considered law books, in the sense of regulating the legitimacy of coats of arms and the qualifications for conferring them. Other kinds of images are similarly problematic: books of maritime law with plates of naval flags; guides to commercial law with plates of coins; facsimile reproductions of ancient documents or legal inscriptions.

I have excluded books where the only illustration is the author's portrait, but I have included collections of portraits of legal figures. However, one could make an interesting collection of law books with author portraits. What could you learn from such a collection? You won't know until you try.

What about decorative items? I have excluded them unless they have some kind of legal content. This legal content often consists solely of the figure of Lady Justice [for example, 10.03]. I have acquired many law books solely because they contain an image of Lady Justice.

I have not imposed chronological or geographic limits to our collection. In the modern works once can see continuities with works from long ago, as is the case with textbooks.

There remain some difficult choices. For example, is a diagram an illustration? Am I biased against new diagrams in favor of old ones? None of the many choices I have made are necessarily the *right* choices. They are only *my* choices.

To be accurate, my choices have also been the Yale Law Library's choices. I have been spending Yale's money, not my own. After reading an earlier draft of this paper, my wife pointed out the obvious fact that I am a librarian, not a collector, and that it would be nice for me to speak as a librarian, about use. I must add that my library has been extraordinarily supportive and tolerant.

Of what use is Yale's illustrated law book collection? When I first became interested in illustrated law books, back in Texas, I wasn't thinking about their use. I was simply curious and fascinated.

By the time I began collecting illustrated law books at Yale, I had to justify the effort. I saw that on the most basic and prosaic level, a collection of law-related images would be a useful resource for authors, publishers, and other "content creators," satisfying a demand for eye-catching and evocative images for dustjackets, images to illustrate historical events, images for teaching aids, images as mere decoration. These are all legitimate uses. I have supplied images for dustjackets,[5] scholarly monographs,[6] the library's annual holiday cards, and even a reality TV show.[7]

An illustrated law book collection fits well with a university like Yale that excels in the humanities, and in a law school, the Yale Law School, that has historically prided itself on interdisciplinary studies, innovation, a contrarian streak, and a sense of fun. The very building the Yale Law School occupies is covered with law-related imagery, some of it drawn from law books.

5. José Cárdenas Bunsen, *Escritura y Derecho Canónico en la obra de fray Bartolomé de las Casas* (Madrid: Iberoamericana-Vervuert, 2011).

6. James Epstein, *Scandal of Colonial Rule: Power and Subversion in the British Atlantic During the Age of Revolution* (Cambridge, U.K.: Cambridge University Press, 2012); *The Formation and Transmission of Western Legal Culture: 150 Books that Made the Law in the Age of Printing* (Serge Dauchy et al. eds.; Switzerland: Springer, 2016).

7. *Deadly Women*, Season 9, Episode 12 (30 Oct. 2015), "Girl on Girl."

One obvious use for the collection is the growing field of legal iconography. By happy coincidence, two Yale Law School professors, Judith Resnik and Dennis Curtis, were in the midst of a legal iconography project when I arrived at the school. I worked with them on their award-winning book *Representing Justice: Invention, Controversy and Rights in City-States and Democratic Courtrooms*.[8] Among the questions their book raises is how the figure of a woman, draped, holding scales and sword, has remained so widely recognized as a symbol of the law for more than 500 years, and what it says about the law. Our collaboration included an exhibition at Yale that we co-curated in the autumn of 2011, "The Remarkable Run of a Political Icon: Justice as a Sign of the Law."

Images of Lady Justice, or Justitia, have been a major focus of our illustrated law collection. I have purchased many books simply because the frontispiece or title page includes an image of Lady Justice. The library's Flickr site now includes over 600 images of Lady Justice published in printed books.[9] In essence, it is a data set of legal iconography, enabling researchers to test any number of hypotheses. It has supported research by scholars throughout the U.S., Europe, and Latin America, scholars who include legal historians, art historians, and historians of print culture.

Beyond iconography, the images in law books are important source material for a wide variety of inquiries. They show how the legal profession, legal publishers, and critics of the profession have attempted to

8. Judith Resnik & Dennis Curtis, *Representing Justice: Invention, Controversy and Rights in City-States and Democratic Courtrooms* (New Haven: Yale University Press, 2011).

9. https://www.flickr.com/photos/yalelawlibrary/albums/.

shape the profession's public image. We find evidence of the actual physical settings of law practice: about law offices, recordkeeping systems, law libraries, clients, even how lawyers dressed. Images of early courtrooms help us understand the rituals of litigation and lawmaking. We see intersections between law and technology, law and politics, law and society. We see how visual imagery has been employed or avoided in a largely textual discipline. We can see how legal literature has both embraced and forsaken the visual, and then ask why. A collection like this, which cuts across traditional boundaries, has the potential to raise new questions and to provide new answers to old questions.

There is no way to predict all the uses for a collection such as this. As the English historian S.F.C. Milsom wrote in his classic book, *Historical Foundations of the Common Law*: "Legal history is not unlike that children's game in which you draw lines between numbered dots, and suddenly from the jumble a picture emerges: but our dots are not numbered."[10]

In a sense, our illustrated law collection is a version of Milsom's jumble of unnumbered dots. I see a few pictures emerging from our jumble. In English law books, illustrations are relatively rare. The two English examples of allegorical title pages that I know are, ironically, in books by supposedly iconoclastic Puritans [1.10, 1.14]. Allegorical images appeared most prominently in German law books, up until the late eighteenth century [1.03, 1.05, 1.12]. Complex technical drawings appeared in many seventeenth- and eighteenth-century German law books on property law [4.07], mining law, environmental law [10.01, 10.02], and even criminal law [6.05]. Illustrated books on water law and property law were an Italian *forte*, beginning in the Middle Ages with essays by Bartolus of Sassoferato [4.01], continuing with Francesco Pecchio's multi-volume treatise on the law of aqueducts in the seventeenth century [4.00], and Luigi Piccoli's works on servitudes (or easements) in the early nineteenth century [4.08]. The English gift for biting satire is evident in a few early works on law reform [9.11, 9.12]. However, the best legal humorists were the French book illustrators of the twentieth century, led by Joseph Hémard [9.00, 9.03, 9.05]. The outstanding early U.S. examples of legal illustration are forensic images connected with litigation [7.00, 7.06, 7.09. 7.10, 7.11].

I am especially intrigued and charmed by the engraved title pages on a number of Dutch law books from the seventeenth and eighteenth centuries [5.02]. They have images of courtrooms, in some cases actual courtrooms that you can still visit today. I have collected ten examples, and the intriguing detail that all of them share is that there is always a dog in the foreground.

If a collection of illustrated law books is intended to support research, then there is no substitute for collecting the originals. The images are integral parts of the books they inhabit, and they cannot be fully understood or appreciated on a computer screen. One need not be an art historian to appreciate the importance of viewing these images in their original context.

This leads to my final rationale for collecting law books with illustrations: it is a collection focus that emphasizes the importance of the original artifact.

10. S. F. C. Milsom, *Historical Foundations of the Common Law* (2nd ed.; London: Butterworths, 1981), 8.

Why maintain and build a rare book and manuscript collection if the items I acquire have no significance as physical objects? "Isn't everything important already online?" This is a question many library directors and university administrators are asking, and it behooves us in special collections to have answers. For special collections librarians, as well as private collectors and our colleagues in the book trade, artifactual value plays an increasingly important role.

Academic special collections are playing a growing role in supporting teaching, as well as research. In the hands of students, our books and manuscripts wield an impact, a magic, that a PowerPoint slide or an online image can never approximate. Our institutions spend lots of money these days on smart classrooms, projectors, and digital infrastructure. I argue that special acquisitions are comparable investments in instructional technology.

With this emphasis on artifactual value, special collections increasingly take on the aspect of museums, of book and manuscript museums. When I began my career in special collections some twenty-five years ago, I announced that I was not going to run a "museum," by which I meant a forbidding "treasure room" where books and manuscripts were kept locked away for the exclusive use of "serious" researchers. I still don't believe in treasure rooms, but as my collections have become increasingly employed in teaching, I have come to embrace an entirely different kind of museum as a model. It is a children's museum I have in mind, an "exploratorium."

Special collections such as ours are increasingly valuable in helping an academic library, especially a law library, set itself apart from its peers. A collection like illustrated law books, which crosses traditional boundaries of genre and subject area, presents opportunities for promoting interdisciplinary research, an endeavor many law schools are keen to promote, and also for the law library to build alliances and cooperative ventures with other campus libraries.

In a 2001 magazine article about an American book collector, the rare book dealer William Reese articulated what he called the "Critical Mess Theory":

> You don't start off with a theory about what you're trying to do. You don't begin by saying, 'I'm trying to prove x.' You build a big pile. Once you get a big enough pile together – the critical mess – you're able to draw conclusions about it. You see patterns. ... People who have the greatest intuitive feel for physical objects start from a relationship with the objects and then acquire the scholarship, instead of the other way around. The way to become a connoisseur is to work in the entire spectrum of what's available – from utter crap to fabulous stuff. If you're going to spend your time looking only at the best, you're not going to have a critical eye.[11]

Another way of describing Reese's "critical mess" is collecting as pure research. The Yale Law Library's collection of illustrated law books is an example of collecting as pure research. It requires a leap of faith to begin a collection with no clear idea of where it will end. Unlike collecting an author, or a jurisdiction, or a well-known genre, there is no list or standard bibliography to go by. It forces you to look for the unexpected, for the book you didn't know you

11. Mark Singer, "The Book Eater: Michael Zinman, obsessive bibliophile, and the critical-mess theory of collecting," *The New Yorker* (5 Feb. 2001), at 66.

were looking for until you saw it. It forces you to seek out the help of book dealers, scholars, and students. It makes collecting a social activity.

Easily more than half of our illustrated law collection consists of items that the library acquired long before I arrived. A collection like this, which cuts across boundaries of time, format, and jurisdiction, presents the librarian with an opportunity to look at the library's existing holdings with fresh eyes.

Such collecting also requires a tolerance for imperfection, for the "utter crap" that William Reese mentioned. I am not building a fine art collection. I am building a research collection. Thus, I collect all the examples I can find, not only the pretty ones.

Ultimately, this sort of collecting promotes a sense of wonder and play, things that can be in short supply in today's world. It is this sense of wonder and play that has given me satisfaction and reward. If I do nothing else than instill a sense of wonder and play in those who visit and use the collection, I feel I have done something useful. I hope it does the same for you.

Reflections on an Exhibition

Mark S. Weiner

Rutgers Law School

Working with Mike Widener on "Law's Picture Books" was a great pleasure for me. We're a bit of an unlikely pair, the two of us, at least on the outside: Mike a soft-spoken, flowing-haired librarian from Laredo nearing retirement, and me a midcareer, talkative constitutional law professor from Los Angeles. Yet when we met nearly twenty years ago, at the University of Texas-Austin, where Mike long worked as the law school's rare book librarian before coming to Yale, we instantly appreciated our affinity. Our mutual love of books was part of that recognition. But more deeply we sensed a common approach to public education: a shared willingness to present legal history in a posture of open-ended playfulness; a desire to speak to people where it matters to them, and in an accessible voice, even while prompting deeper questions; a love of going out on a limb now and then; and a commitment to exploring the humanities in a spirit that's humane. Neither of us were surprised that our two-year collaboration was uniformly free and easy, filled with positive creative energy.

Most of our work took place in the Paskus-Danzinger Rare Book Room at the Yale Law Library, where Mike guided me through the unique collection of illustrated law books that he's curated and developed over the past decade.[1] What a marvelous place! Mike and I often wandered back and forth between the room's wide, elegant wooden tables and the neighboring stacks, or "vault," to retrieve books for review, rolling them into the reading room on a squeaky cart – and then spreading them eagerly on a tabletop. *What a beautiful frontispiece! Look here on page 10! Should we include it in the exhibit? What if we put* this *volume next to* that *volume?* This work moved me more and more as our preparations progressed. One of the special things about law books *as books* is that they were often published as aids to legal practice. They are like carpenters' tools. Many of the books in the Yale Law Library vault haven't been wielded for hundreds of years, since they last lay in the workshop of an actual carpenter of human affairs – which is to say, a lawyer. Still, when they were originally published, they were meant to help people solve practical problems. This use-value gives the books a special "human appeal," in the words of one of the giants of law librarianship, former Yale law librarian Frederick Hicks.[2] And, in fact, a spirit of humanity pervades the Yale collection, visible in all the signs that indi-

1. For an earlier foray into legal imagery at Yale, see Morris Cohen, *Law: The Art of Justice* (New York: H. Lauter Levin Associates, 1992). For a key work that includes images *of* law books, including those with illustrations, see Law Library of Congress, *Library of Congress Law Library: An Illustrated Guide* (Washington, D.C.: Library of Congress, 2005) (co-authored by Jolande Goldberg and Natalie Gawdiak). See also *The Formation and Transmission of Western Legal Culture: 150 Books that Made the Law in the Age of Printing* (Serge Dauchy et al. eds.; Cham, Switzerland: Springer, 2016).

2. Frederick C. Hicks, *Men and Books Famous in the Law* (Rochester, New York: Lawyers Cooperative Publishing, 1921), 15.

vidual lawyers actively used the books in their work. The books convey an aesthetic of worldly particularity. Looking at one of them is like gazing at a hammer with a deeply worn and stained grip, with scratches on its face and peen, left at rest long ago on a bench.

From the start of our collaboration, Mike and I conceived of our exhibit as something for the public, not only for specialists. In that spirit, the exhibit isn't meant to make a specific intervention in a scholarly debate; nor is it especially "thesis driven." It's meant most of all to delight and inspire. But it does have a strong organizing principle that we hope will help visitors engage with legal literature in a more sensitive way. The exhibit is organized functionally around some of the purposes that law book illustrations can serve. In arranging the volumes, we asked ourselves the seemingly simple question: what do the images in these books *do*? What *goals* are the illustrations intended to achieve? We ultimately divided the illustrations into ten different functional categories. In the process, we also came to appreciate something more abstract. We recognized that each purpose we identified helped us understand not only the illustrations themselves, but also the books in which they appear, because each purpose distinctively shapes the relation between the images in that category and their accompanying text. The functional role of an image shapes where it appears in the book, what part of the text it supplements, and how it reflects *back* on the text – and vice versa. To put it in grand terms, we came to embrace our functional organization both for itself and in the service of highlighting a dialectical relationship.

Our ten purposes are indicated in the titles of the cases: symbolizing the law, depicting the law, diagramming the law, calculating the law, staging the law, inflicting the law, arguing the law, teaching the law, laughing (and crying) at the law, and beautifying the law. These categories aren't reified; they just fit what we were seeing. And one could easily have added a number of additional categories. My notes from when Mike and I were first imagining the exhibit contain numerous potential case titles such as "charting the law," "mapping the law," and "advertising the law." Nothing would give us greater pleasure as curators than future exhibits or studies that investigate our categories and propose others. In the meantime, we present our divisions as a common sense way of organizing a large body of work and as a heuristic device for understanding the complex relation between text and image.

Take our first case, "Symbolizing the Law." These books contain figurative images used to represent abstract ideals – the most prevalent and best-known of which is the image of Lady Justice.[3] These illustrations tend to appear at the beginning of books, in frontispieces, where they herald and embody the principles of the entire text that follows – they "epitomize the book."[4] By contrast, consider our second case, "Depicting the Law." In these illustrations, figurative images illustrate specific passages of text and particular legal rules. They depict not the symbolic, but the concrete. The earliest such illustrations are represented by the thirteenth-century *Sachsenspiegel*,

3. On the iconography of Lady Justice, see Judith Resnik and Dennis Curtis, *Representing Justice: Invention, Controversy, and Rights in City-States and Democratic Courtrooms* (New Haven: Yale University Press, 2011).

4. Margery Corbett and Ronald Lightbrown, *The Comely Frontis-*

which we feature in a limited edition facsimile [2.01]. In this largely unsystematic document, the drawings in the margins of the book serve as index markers, while also clarifying the actions discussed in the neighboring text. The book remains unsurpassed in legal literature for its seamless integration of words and images.

Our case on legal diagrams focuses on the development of what for centuries was the most common illustration in law books: a tree depicting relations of consanguinity and affinity in inheritance law.[5] By depicting legal relationships in spatial terms, trees represent those relationships more efficiently than is possible through words alone. They stand beside their text in yet a third way – neither as allegories of the spirit of the whole nor as illustrations of a specific part but rather as concise charts of an extended structure of analysis. A fourth image-text relationship: "Arguing the Law" displays very precise illustrations used as courtroom evidence or to influence public opinion. They're the least symbolic, most literal type of law book image. Finally, a fifth – and a favorite: "Laughing at the Law." These illustrations gently – or, at times, forcefully – lift readers above the legal texts in which they appear, placing them in a critical relationship to legal rules and the language of the law. Mike is a particular fan of the French artist Joseph Hémard's illustrated French tax code, and I have become one too.[6]

Our functional organization will not be to everyone's taste, but there are important reasons supporting it. The first reason is curatorial, the second is historiographic. I spell out each purpose in the following paragraphs, in the process assuming a more academic tone and purpose – forewarned is forearmed!

The curatorial reason for our organizing principle is significant for museum visitors and their experience. Functional categorization tends to tie parts to wholes, as in the functionalist tradition in sociology, which conceives of society as composed of multiple interdependent, interlocking parts.[7] By organizing our exhibit in functional terms, we hope to encourage visitors to appreciate a number of unities they might otherwise overlook. The most important unity,

---

piece: The Emblematic Title-Page in England, 1550-1660 (London: Routledge & Kegan Paul, 1979), 46. For an earlier Grolier Club exhibit on symbolic illustrations, see Robin Raybould, *Emblemata: Symbolic Literature of the Renaissance: From the Collection of Robin Raybould* (New York: Grolier Club, 2010).

5. On the development of trees in western legal literature, see Hermann Schadt, *Die Darstellungen der Arbores Consanguinitatis und der Arbores Affinitatis: Bildschemata in juristischen Handschriften* (Tübingen: E. Wasmuth, 1982). On the legal context, see James A. Brundage, *Law, Sex, and Christian Society in Medieval Europe*(Chicago: University of Chicago Press, 1990) and John Witte, Jr., *From Sacrament to Contract: Marriage, Religion, and Law in the Western Tradition*, Second Edition (Westminster: John Knox Press, 2012 [1997]). On tree symbolism, see Gerhart B. Ladner, "Medieval and Modern Understanding of Symbolism: A Comparison," in *Images and Ideas in the Middle Ages: Selected Studies in History and Art*, Storia e Letteratura 155 (Rome: Edizioni di Storia e Letteratura, under the auspices of the Center for Medieval and Renaissance Studies, UCLA, and the Kress Foundation, 1983), 239-282. For an influential argument within cultural studies opposing "arborescent thought," see Gilles Deleuze and Félix Guattari, *A Thousand Plateaus*, trans. Brian Massumi (Minneapolis: University of Minnesota Press, 1987).

6. See Farley P. Katz, "The Art of Taxation: Joseph Hémard's Illustrated Tax Code," *The Tax Lawyer* 60 (1) (Fall 2006), 163-76.

7. See, e.g., Emile Durkheim, *The Division of Labor in Society* (1893) and Talcott Parsons, *The Social System* (Glencoe, Ill.: Free Press, 1951).

to which I've alluded already, is that of each book as an object – an object of which the image on display is just one part. The images Mike and I admired after we retrieved them from the vault are beautiful or interesting in themselves, but they generally weren't experienced independently of the books in which they appeared. We think that books and illustrations should be viewed together today, too, in order to appreciate their full significance and interest, including – though not limited to – the dialectical relationship between image and text.[8] Our exhibit would have been very different had we simply reproduced the images on display in perfect, high-resolution photographs and displayed them on the wall. It also would have been a different animal altogether had we exhibited law-related art generally, for instance if we had displayed books along alongside paintings or statuary.[9]

The unity of each individual book isn't the only coherence we hope our functional organization will help visitors appreciate. We also wish to foster a recognition of the aesthetic unity of the books as a group. Specifically, the books all stem from the same intellectual and professional field – law – and because the functional goals of their illustrations all relate to that common body of knowledge and action, they also share common sets of design principles and motifs. A functional organization highlights this fact – which, in turn, brings a variety of curatorial benefits. Most important, we believe, it encourages visitors to "see commonalities between some books of the past ... and those of today," and so to see their own era as part of an ongoing historical story.[10] If those visitors are themselves involved with the legal profession, this recognition extends to their own work.

The second reason supporting a functionalist organization is a bit more analytic. As a historiographic matter, organizing an exhibit in functional terms allows us to supplement the conceptual dualism through which illustrated books are often intuitively understood, what the eminent book historian David Bland called the alternating "stresses" of "illustration" and "decoration."[11] Some images prioritize explanation, while others privilege ornament. This is a powerful framework, and it makes instant sense. Yet it is not the end of the story (nor did Bland suggest it was). In the realm of legal publishing, there is an additional set of alternating stresses to which a functional organization helps draw our attention: between the generality and abstraction of law as a field of knowledge on the one hand and the real world of people and things to which it applies on the other. Call it the alternating stresses of abstraction and particularity.

8. In this respect, the exhibit also recognizes "the information about the relationship between form and text that can be gleaned from a book's design." Linda Nix, "Early medieval book design in England: the influence of manuscript design on the transmission of text," in *A Millennium of the Book: Production, Design & Illustration in Manuscript & Print*, 900-1900, ed. Robin Myers and Michael Harris (Winchester: St. Paul's Bibliographies, 1994), 1-21, 1. Naturally, this information can shed light on the larger development of law.

9. For a recent exhibit on law-related art generally, see *De Kunt van het Recht. Drie Eeuwen Gerechtigheid in Beeld (The Art of Law: Three Centuries of Justice Depicted)*, cur. Vanessa Paumen and Tine Van Poucke, Groenigemuseum, Bruges, Belgium (28 October 2016-5 February 2017).

10. Michael Twyman, "The emergence of the graphic book in the 19th century," in *A Millennium of the Book*, 135-80, 136.

11. David Bland, *The Illustration of Books* (New York: Pantheon Books, 1952), 11-18. Notably, Bland viewed the terms as "complementary and not opposed," 11.

This tension lies at the heart of law itself. As part of our effort to navigate the world, humans create general legal principles in words, and we then seek to apply those principles to particular situations – that's the dynamic, the direction, of most legal professional activity. Yet there are some things about the world that pictures capture better than words and general concepts. This limitation has given rise to a figurative impulse in legal literature. Some things – things with legal significance – can swiftly be achieved through pictures, even when they cannot be accomplished through words. Just what those things are – what images can *do* for law better than words – is revealed through our ten functional categories. As Judge Learned Hand put it, "words are utterly inadequate to deal with the fantastically multiform occasions which come up in human life."[12]

"Law's Picture Books" is a book exhibit, but in a larger sense it is an exhibit about the relation between law and visual culture. The subject has generated much lively scholarship over the past twenty years, and I wish to note just where this exhibit fits into that body of work.[13] Taking a very broad historical perspective, one can say that the development of the western legal tradition out of the pre-modern world depended on the increasing differentiation of law from other social fields. As law grew into an autonomous discipline, with its own distinct way of knowing, it became institutionally and culturally separate from religion, from ritual, from social custom, and from a range of other ideas, institutions, and practices with which it formerly overlapped or was coterminous.[14] Law became a thing apart. Unlike ancient Celtic peoples, for example, we no longer live in a world in which laws take the form of poetic maxims held in the memory of clerics who are also responsible for narrating the history of their people and mediating their relation to the sacred. In this respect, law takes part in the transformation of society over many centuries from what Durkheim called organic to mechanical solidarity. No longer integrated by a unified fellow-feeling, modern societies are integrated instead by a functional interdependency of roles. As this functional differentiation and complexity grew, social fields – including law – drifted away from each other like the Earth's tectonic plates.

12. Learned Hand, "Thou Shalt Not Ration Justice," 9 *NLADA Briefcase* 4 (April 1951), 3-5, 5.

13. See Anne Wagner and Richard K. Sherwin, eds., *Law, Culture and Visual Studies* (Dordrecht: Springer, 2014). There has been an especially systematic and sensitive approach to the subject in Germany and Austria. See, e.g., the journal *Signa Iuris: Beitrage zur Rechtsikonographie, Rechtsarchäologie und Rechtlichen Volkskunde*, eds. Gernot Kocher, Heiner Lück, Clausdieter Schott; Eric Hilgendorf, eds. *Beitrage zur Rechtsvisualisierung* (Berlin: Logos Verlag, 2005); Gernot Kocher, *Zeichen und Symbol des Rechts: Eine historische Ikonographie* (Munich: Beck, 1992); Franziska Prinz, *Der Bildgebrauch in gedruckten Rechtsbüchern des 15. bis zum Ausgang des 18. Jahrhunderts*, LIT Verlag, 2006; and Klaus Röhl, "Bilder in gedruckten Rechtsbüchern," in *Recht vermitteln: Strukturen, Formen und Medien des Kommunikation im Recht*, ed. Kent D. Lerch, (Berlin: Walter de Gruyter, 2005), 267-347.

14. See Harold J. Berman, *Law and Revolution, I: The Formation of the Western Legal Tradition* (Cambridge, Mass.: Harvard University Press, 1985).

Scholars of law and visual culture have suggested that this transformation brought with it a devaluation of the aesthetic within the realm of law (by the aesthetic, they tend to mean the sphere of culture governed by the non-propositional principles of beauty, form, and design). Most notably, it fostered a rejection of "visuality," as some theorists put it, and a turn in law toward the unvarnished written word as the exclusive vessel of law's meaning. As the western legal tradition developed, explain Peter Goodrich and Valérie Hayaert, law "was increasingly deemed to be a purely textual enterprise," and, consequently, "a degree of blindness ensued," a rejection of the deeply ceremonial, theatrical aspects of law's visual presence, both in the courtroom and in the rituals of everyday life.[15] Many scholars decry this growing logocentrism, associating it with "the modern cult of the abstract norm in juridical positivism"; with psychological repression; and perhaps most of all with a profound lack of political self-consciousness.[16]

One of the goals of scholars of law and visual culture has been to call attention to the various ways in which law's public presence still makes itself felt visually. Another of their projects – relevant to this exhibit – has been to engage in acts of historical recovery. They seek out the hidden history of law and the visual obscured by its modern separation, and trace the movement of the tectonic plates of law and the aesthetic during their centuries of drift.

Their project is motivated by a number of aims. At its most basic level, scholars seek to use a recovered past to foster contemporary sensitivity to law's aesthetic dimension. Lawyers, they argue, should "know the appearances of their profession and should be erudite in the images that they manipulate and transmit" – and studying the visual past of law is essential to that skill.[17] Other scholars look back on the legal transformation from "rites" to "rights" and hope to use the history of law's visuality to link the latter more closely with the former.[18] Some scholars look to the visual to develop what literary scholar Caleb Smith, in a recent work on the poetics of justice, calls forms of "nonrational persuasion" – that is, "modes of address and affirmation which involve not the critical evaluation of propositions but the affective and aesthetic response to justice's performative

15. Peter Goodrich and Valérie Hayaert, eds., *Genealogies of Legal Vision* (New York: Routledge, 2015), i; Peter Goodrich, *Legal Emblems and the Art of Law:* Obiter depicta *as the Vision of Governance* (Cambridge: Cambridge University Press, 2014), 8. Tellingly, in early modern Europe, art was often removed from courtrooms, and judicial robes became unadorned and black. Bernard J. Hibbitts, "Making Sense of Metaphors: Visuality, Aurality, and the Reconfiguration of American Legal Discourse," 16 *Cardozo Law Review* 229 (1994).

16. Martin Jay, "Must Justice Be Blind? The Challenge of Images to the Law," in Costas Douzina and Lynda Nead, eds., *Law and the Image: The Authority of Art and the Aesthetics of Law* (Chicago: The University of Chicago Press, 1999), 19-35, 25. See, e.g., Peter Goodrich, *Oedipus Lex: Psychoanalysis, History, Law* (Berkeley: University of California Press, 1995) and *Legal Emblems and the Art of Law*.

17. Goodrich, *Legal Emblems and the Art of Law*, 11. In the realm of law book publishing, an important development in this regard is John H. Langbein, Renée Lettow Lerner, Bruce P. Smith, History of the Common Law: The Development of Anglo-American Legal Institutions (New York: Aspen, 2009), a richly-illustrated book that brings visual culture into the study of legal history.

18. Resnik and Curtis, *Representing Justice*.

invocation."[19] Others implicitly go much further still: they imagine Pangaea.

Our exhibit can be understood as a contribution to any and every one of these projects – we take no position on them, at the same time that we encourage them all. Yet on one issue we do hold a strong view. We think it's significant that the illustrations on display appear in books. Each volume in our exhibit, each carpenter's tool of human organization, possesses a unique physical presence, and thus a special beauty. One might even say this beauty, an aesthetic of bibliographic particularity, was central to the development of western law. Illustrations – in books – participated in the formation of our foundational legal ideas. We hope that visitors will be as moved by this aesthetic as we are while they gaze upon some of the extraordinary tools that helped build modern society – and as they marvel at the images those books contain.

19. Caleb Smith, *The Oracle and the Curse: A Poetics of Justice form the Revolution to the Civil War* (Cambridge, Mass.: Harvard University Press, 2013), 9.

Ars Memoria in Early Law: Looking Beneath the Picture

Jolande E. Goldberg
Law Library of Congress

When considering the splendid assemblage of illustrated books on jurisprudence presented in this catalogue and in the exhibition "Law's Picture Books": be enchanted, but be patient and curious. Ask yourself: what are the layers *beneath*? This essay is a vignette of one of those layers, the medieval history of the *ars memoria*: techniques (*ars*) for the processing, storing, and the recall of complex data from the storage called "memory," an ancient subject of philosophical, spiritual, religious, and medical speculation.

The subject of memory craft has a prestigious pedigree – and great contemporary relevance. Its practice and teaching has long been a means to transmit and preserve cultural traditions and maintain collective social memory, especially in large, oral societies. Tellingly, Roman upper-class education since the fourth century prominently included the fields of "rhetoric" and systematic memory training. As Mary Carruthers notes in *The Book of Memory*, scholars thus "have always recognized that memory necessarily played a critical role in pre-modern Western civilization ... a world of few books."[1]

The ancient past provides us with a rich buffet of examples from a variety of fields. For instance, memory was a subject of serious investigation for ancient philosophy and medicine – which, notably, early recognized the importance of images for its tool box. Aristotle's *On Memory and Recollection* (*De memoria et reminiscentia*) portrays "memory as image," the final product of that which is perceived through the senses.[2] Aristotelian ideas and philosophical-medical studies in the eleventh to thirteenth centuries were also extensively commented upon in the Arabic and Hebrew traditions, foremost by Avicenna (980-1037), in his *On the Soul* (*De anima*), and Averroës (1126-1198), in his commentary on Aristotle's *On the Soul*. In the same track follows, somewhat later, Albertus Magnus (the German; 1193-1280) with his work *On the Soul* and an important commentary on Aristotle's *On Memory and Recollection*.

Likewise, following Aristotle's work, many later thinkers in antiquity, such as Tullius Cicero, entertained the notion that "double motions feed memory: talking and hearing," and that "visual images are retained easier than concepts." For best results, wrote Cicero in *On the Orator* (*De oratore*), "the auditory should be supported by visual images."[3]

In our own day, educated speculation and study in medicine and psychology generates the greatest

1. Mary Carruthers, *The Book of Memory: A Study of Memory in Medieval Culture* (2nd ed.; Cambridge: Cambridge University Press, 2008), 9.

2. Carruthers presents us with an excellent summary of the evolving field of "neuropsychology," grounded on Aristotle and further developed by his Hebrew and Arabic commentators. Ibid., 57-64.

3. Ibid., 91.

amount of literature on the subject. The study of the brain and its functions is among the fastest growing branches of life sciences, and "artificial memory" or memory systems are major topics for investigation in psychology and neuropsychology. How does the brain process the visual and the spoken, or the simultaneous inflow of aural and visual information? Current theory distinguishes between "three basic stores: sensory, long term and short term memory," and it distinguishes as well between "visual or iconic memory and auditory or echoic memory" – ideas with early roots, though we tend to forget that history.[4]

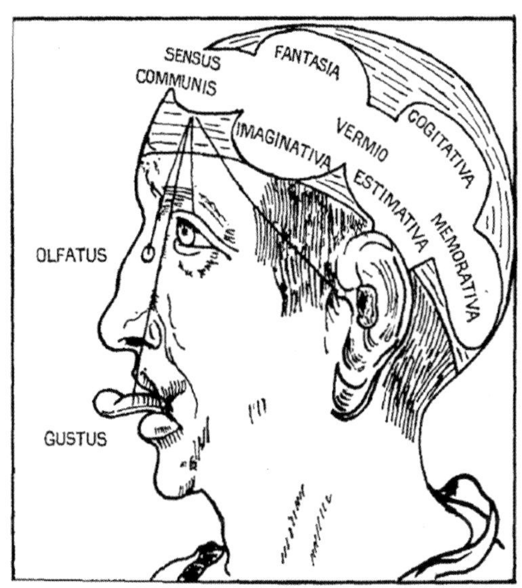

Johann Horst von Romberch, Congestorium artificiose memorie (Venice, 1533). Library of Congress

And the middle ages themselves? And medieval *legal* studies? As Carruthers notes, "Medieval culture was fundamentally memorial, to the same profound degree that modern culture in the West is documentary."[5] Medieval memory craft was mostly "tied to the monastic traditions" of meditation, prayer, and concentrated study of the Bible. Only after 1280, *memoria* made a strong appearance as a discipline of broader application in early universities or faculties, including in the changing field of law. Here, images were put to use in developing and transmitting a subject that began to flourish, in Italy, beginning in the late eleventh or early twelfth century.

A Tale of Two Laws

To appreciate the growth of medieval legal culture that made use of the *ars memoria*, we need to contemplate two great works – and two groups of commentators on those works – in juxtaposition. The first work is the *Corpus iuris civilis* of Justinian, Emperor in the East (ca. 537), a five-part compilation, restatement, and commentary on existing Roman law – the civil law. The second work is the *Decretum* of Gratian (ca. 1140), a scholarly, harmonized collection of early sources of religious law – the canon law – entitled *Concordance of Discordant Canons* (*Concordia discordantium canonum*). Both works present a system of law which settle, eventually, in tandem and separately, the forms and standards for law across Europe.

The *Corpus iuris civilis* (ca. 537) ordered by Justinian (483?-565) was, with the later addition of the Twelve Tables (541-450 B.C.), a testament to almost

4. Ronald T. Kellogg, *Fundamentals of Cognitive Psychology* (3rd ed.; Los Angeles: Sage [2016]), 107-109.

5. Carruthers, *The Book of Memory*, 9.

a thousand years of legal development, incorporating centuries of Roman imperial pronouncements, the fifth-century Theodosian code, and the third-century Hermogenian code. During the tumultuous events accompanying the decline of the Roman Empire, however, this monumental work was lost. For hundreds of years, Roman law survived only in adaptations of the customary law of the Visigoths, the Breviary of Alaric (*Lex Romana Visigothorum*, 506); the *Lex Romana Burgundionum* (before 516) and the *Leges Romanae Barbarorum* (Roman law of the German nations).

Sometime at the end of the eleventh or the beginning of the twelfth century, the *Digest* of Justinian, one part of the *Corpus iuris civilis*, reappeared in Pisa – when and under which circumstances remains unclear. This extraordinary event initiated the slow process of return, revival, and serious study of Roman law and, in time, the development of western jurisprudence.

The first center of its study was the city of Bologna. Between the eleventh and thirteenth centuries, the earliest European universities started out as free "associations" of magisters and students for particular disciplines. The "university" of Paris became a center for philosophy and theology. Salerno became a center for the study of medicine. And Bologna became a center for the study of law. Two of its great early jurists were Pepo (of Bologna, fl. 1075-1099) and Irnerius (1085-1125), the latter a philologist literate in grammar and logic – which explains the methods of the emerging jurisprudence.

Notably, Bologna also had a flourishing school for the *ars memoria* some time before and after the founding of the university in 1130. One important name stands out in its history in this regard: Boncompagno da Signa (ca. 1170-after 1240), who worked as a teacher for rhetoric there from the mid-1190s to maybe the 1230s, an ideal environment for rhetoric and memory training of jurists.

Within its shifting tides of politics and law, the city was set for the arrival of Gratian's *Concordance of Discordant Canons*, the *Decretum Gratiani*, written probably between 1130 and 1140. Gratian's work is a harmonized compilation of canon law from a pool of early sources, with an especially important treatment of marriage law in general and clerical marriage in particular – the Church over time had firmly established jurisdiction over marriage and inheritance. Its analysis draws on materials from a world apart, including apostolic canons, the work of the Sixth Ecumenical Council (the Third Council of Constantinople, 680-81), and the *Panormia* of Ivo, Bishop of Chartres (ca. 1040-1116). Although the *Decretum* was never recognized by Rome as an "official" compilation, it was adopted as the first section in Pope Gregory IX's (1227-1241) compilation of *decretales*, or ecclesiastical decrees, the first of a growing set of Papal *decretales* which for centuries were the principal sources of law for the Catholic Church.

Gratian? We really can only speculate on the status of the man behind the *Decretum*. Whether he was a monk, a scholar, or a teacher in Bologna, is not as important for our purpose as the question: Was he already familiar with Roman law? A critical comparative exploration by Anders Winroth of the first and second critical edition (*recensio*) of the *Decretum* seems to suggest that his knowledge of Roman law was originally rudimentary.[6] He appears, however, to be more on solid ground by the second edition. Scholarship focuses on the "original" Gratian, who is buried in a mound of accumulated editions, probably 150 manuscripts alone, and in a wealth of early print editions between 1471 and 1600 from printing houses in Mainz, Nuremberg, Strasbourg, Basel, Paris, and Lyons, and of editions from 1600 on to 1879. As always, educated conjecture fill the lacunae of history where the actual sources fall short of answers.

From the end of the twelfth to the beginning of the thirteenth centuries, we see the law school in Bologna reaching out for the star power of the emerging elite of jurists. These stars include men such as Accursius (1182-ca.1260), the Four Doctors (Quattuor Doctores: Bulgarus, d. 1166; Martinus Gosia, d. ca.1166; Hugo, de Alberico, d.1171; Jacobus, d. 1178); Bartolus of Sassoferato (1313-1357), who was considered the most important and influential scholar at the height of fourteenth-century jurisprudence; and his contemporary Baldo degli Ubaldi (1327?-1400). They all were known as "glossators," and later as "post-glossators," or commentators – writing the glosses and commentaries – on Roman civil law. At the same time, on the religious, ecclesiastical side of the law, the canon law, we find the *decretists* and *decretalists* – commentators on the *Decretum* of Gratian. Prominent names include Tancredus Bononiensis (ca.1185-1236?); Damasus (active 1210-1215); Bernard of Pavia, and Giovanni d'Andrea (ca.1270- 1348).

6. Anders Winroth, *The Making of Gratian's Decretum* (Cambridge: Cambridge University Press, 2000), 146-148, 156-168.

An outstanding group of these jurisprudents dealt equally in *both* disciplines, contributing to the evolving canonical jurisprudence and to the medieval Roman, civil law at once. Their work – a steadily increasing stock of comparative legal literature which addressed the differences between Roman and canon law in areas of family and marriage, teaching of the sacraments, and so forth – is considerable. It also reveals their working method: an abstracting, harmonizing and approximating process of adapting the rules, stemming from the Justinian Roman law, canon law, and Italian statutory and customary law, to the society of the late-twelfth to the fifteenth centuries.

These jurists and canonists alike were the pivotal force in the development of jurisprudence that bore the hallmark Bologna, not only in distilling the Justinian Roman law, but at the same time in preparing for the *ius commune*, later to be known as the common law of Europe.

Beginning in the fourteenth century, the curricula for study and the development of law and canonical jurisprudence expanded dramatically. The jurists and canonists were dealing with increasing amounts of complex legal stuff in the crafting of doctrine, and all who were in the business of public lectures, disputation, or examinations needed materials for teaching and for public debate.

In response to this development, from the mid-fifteenth century on – the beginning of book printing – the supply of broad categories of "auxiliary works" and teaching and learning aids begins to flow. Printing houses in Europe supplied broad categories of texts in answer to the expanding curricula of the university, or to satisfy the needs of the ecclesiastical or civil administrations, the courts, and the practitioners. The list is long and includes *Lectura*, *Repertoria*, *Brocarda* (case books, especially for canonical process), *florilegia* and *margarita*, *vocabularia*/dictionaries, encyclopedias, bibliography, formularies and *tabulae*, indexes, translations, and a host of how-to manuals. Many of these works were related to the *ars memoria*.

Mnemonic Aids: The Tool Box for Teaching and Studying Law

In his work on *memoria*, *Phoenix* [*seu De artificiosa memoria*] (1491/2), the noted legal scholar Petrus Ravennas (ca. 1448-1508/09) remarked that he would rather rely for his lectures on his memory than on a book. The translation of this work into English by Robert Coplande (1548), and its wide and long circulation, indicate the popularity of such books in the industry – books aimed at developing the craft of memory. Such books contained a wide variety of mnemonic devices.

Early memory aids were "indexing mnemonics," designed as a locating aid to text and as an aid to fix it to memory. These mnemonics were alphabet systems (e.g., Greek, Latin. Hebrew, Coptic), and numbering systems, which were widely disseminated in France and Italy from the thirteenth century on. Interesting is the division of a text into individual chapters which are alphabetized, numbered, or both. For example, Ravennas orders the text by alphabet, the letters being the "first set of keys" and then by "keywords" (subjects or topics) of the alphabetized text sections, which in turn are themselves arranged topic-by-letter, very much in the fashion of an alphabetical subject index.

Once the rare book vaults for early works on the law open, we surely will come across interesting textual features, as well as a plethora of figurative elements that have been applied for centuries to illustrate, describe, or teach historical or legal facts and acts. The thirty-nine woodcuts which illustrate two chapters of the *Consilia, quaestiones et tractatus of Bartolus* [4.01] – *On Alluvium* (*De fluminibus seu Tiberiadis: De alluvione*) and *On Islands* (*De insula*) – were graphic aids for a discourse on land rights of riparian owners, including notes on land surveying.

On closer examination, most of the textual and visual features of both works reveal themselves as a

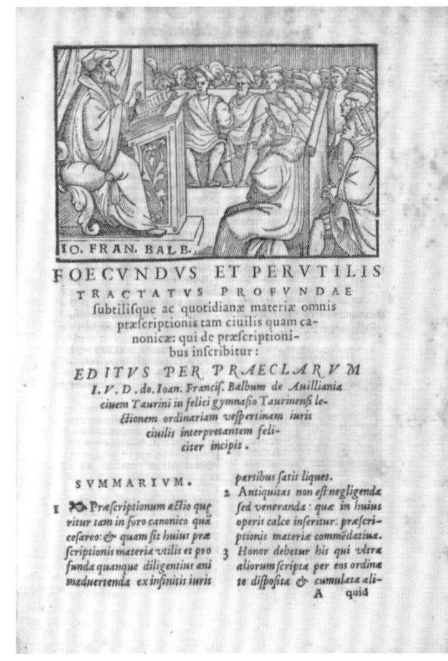
IO. FRAN. BALB.

FOECVNDVS ET PERVTILIS
TRACTATVS PROFVNDAE
ſubtiliſque ac quotidianæ materiæ omnis
præſcriptionis tam ciuilis quam canonicæ: qui de præſcriptionibus inſcribitur:

EDITVS PER PRAECLARVM I. V. D. do. Ioan. Franciſ. Balbum de Auilliania ciuem Taurini in felici gymnaſio Taurinenſi lectionem ordinariam veſpertinam iuris ciuilis interpretantem feliciter incipit.

SVMMARIVM.

1 *Præſcriptionum actio quęritur tam in foro canonico quā cęſareo: & quam ſit huius præſcriptionis materia vtilis et profunda quanque diligentius animaduertenda ex infinitis iuris partibus ſatis liquet.*

2 *Antiquitas non eſt negligenda ſed veneranda: quæ in huius operis calce inſeritur: præſcriptionis materiæ commēdatiua.*

3 *Honor debetur his qui vltra aliorum ſcripta per eos ordinate diſpoſita & cumulata ali-*

A quid

Giovanni Francesco Balbo, *Tractatus de praescriptionibus* (Venice, 1568). Law Library of Congress.

kin of the *ars memoria*. Applied to classroom situation, students, by prescribed exercises, used them to gain the skills, or art, to commit to memory structures of complex concepts – the architecture of multi-layered composition of a text (the *lectura*), which was read to them by a lector. The vignette from Balbo's *Tractatus de praescriptionibus* tellingly shows students listening and memorizing a text section-by-section.

It is a timeless practice for students and scholars alike to write in the margins of the texts they study, offering random observations, definitions, and references to a particular "spot" in such a text. As Carruthers notes, "[m]arginal notations, glosses, and images are an integral part of the *painture* of literature, addressing the ocular gateway to memory and meditation."[7] These supplemental marginal notes to a text

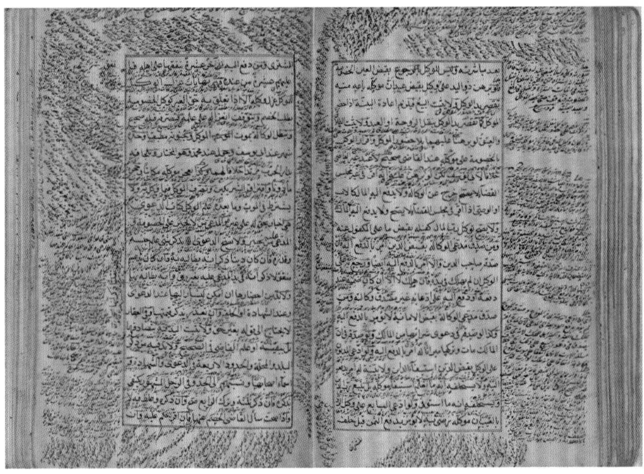

Ibrāhīm ibn Muhammad Halabī, *Multaqá al-abhur*. Manuscript, 1517. Law Library of Congress.

are classified as "textual memory devices." Eventually compiled, edited, and better organized or standardized by known scholars, the gloss became known as *glossa ordinari*, the ordinary gloss. The production and dissemination of glossed texts or publication of the glosses or glossating *apparatus* independent from the text is generally related to the growth of the universities and new demands by an ever-broadening community of users.

In the neighboring example, we can discern how, for memory sake, gloss and main text are visually linked with "visual hooks," as *memoria* scholars refer to them. The *glossa* is linked to the main text by a key word, a red line, a letter or number, often emphasized

Digestum Novum seu Pandectarum iuris civilis tomus tertius (Venice, 1592). Law Library of Congress.

in color. The example of the glossed *regulae iuris* edition shows the visual flowing-together of gloss and main text (interestingly, though, the *regulae iuris*, or shorthand legal rules, were a mnemonic device in themselves!).

7. Carruthers, *The Book of Memory*, 314.

Mnemonic tabulae or plates are another form of "ocular gateway" to memory. Adopted by many disciplines, they appear as various schemes, such as charts, and textual arrangements, some as simple tables or verbal schemes, reminiscent of classification. These materials can be memorized in a visual manner for learning a language (grammar tables) and ordering/classifying subjects, and they function as tabular listings of legal rules.

This chart of John Selden (1584-1654), eminent lawyer and Christian Hebraist in seventeenth-century England, was very much part of the debate on the future of the Church of England. His observations weigh in on questions of a new organization of the Church, but also on the controversial questions of reforming marriage and divorce, then still governed by canon law. The chart used by Selden outlines

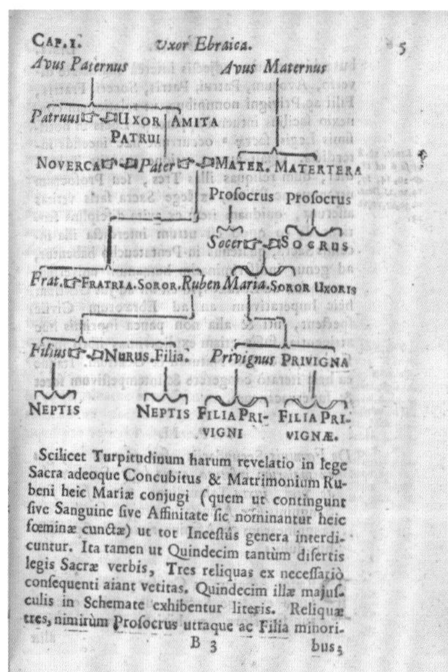

Cap. I. *Uxor Ebraica.* 5

Avus Paternus *Avus Maternus*

Patruus UXOR PATRUI | AMITA

NOVERCA *Pater* MATER. MATERTERA

Prosocrus Prosocrus

Socer SOCRUS

Frat. FRATRIA. SOROR. *Ruben Maria.* SOROR UXORIS

Filius NURUS. Filia. *Privignus* PRIVIGNA

NEPTIS NEPTIS FILIA PRIVIGNI FILIA PRIVIGNÆ.

Scilicet Turpitudinum harum revelatio in lege Sacra adeoque Concubitus & Matrimonium Rubeni heic Mariæ conjugi (quem ut contingunt sive Sanguine sive Affinitate sic nominantur heic fœminæ cunctæ) ut tot Incestûs genera interdicuntur. Ita tamen ut Quindecim tantùm disertis legis Sacræ verbis, Tres reliquas ex necessariò consequenti aiant vetitas. Quindecim illæ majusculis in Schemate exhibentur literis. Reliquæ tres, nimirùm Prosocrus utraque ac Filia minori-

B 3 bus;

John Selden, *Uxor Ebraica* (London, 1646). Law Library of Congress.

visually the traditional verbal listing of the fifteen "forbidden" women, highlighted in capital letters. The text relates to Leviticus and Deuteronomy of the Pentateuch with the organization of relationships and incest.

Another wonderful example is Johannes Buno's (1617-1697) plates for students of Roman law, reproduced elsewhere in this catalogue [8.07]. Born in Germany, Buno studied philosophy and theology at the University of Marburg. There, he was also introduced to the various mnemonic techniques which later enabled him to develop his own memory system while teaching in various finishing schools for aristocratic youth. In the history of teaching, Buno's school textbooks are believed to be the most advanced and important works of this kind at the end of the seventeenth century, when the German Gymnasium began to teach lessons on history. His first publication was a mnemonic history book (1647), a Latin grammar, and a mnemonic bible.

Training students to memorize the mass of Roman law was a particular challenge. His *Memoriale codicis Justiniaenei*, featured here, represents the most successful of the teaching methods of its time. It consists of fourteen woodcut mnemonic plates to support the learning and memorizing of the main points of the *Codex* of the *Corpus iuris civilis*.

Confluence of Art and Law

It has been long since established by the core of *memoria* specialists that manuscript and book illustrations may not only function as the pictorial transcript of the written text in aid of a prevalent oral society, but as "visual contemporary interpretation"and information.[8] For historico-legal research, this fact is important, because art and art history as auxiliaries for law seem to have been generally neglected. The reason? Legal historical research relies primarily on the written text of sources. This is part of the answer why law is not included in the mainstream of the very active research field *memoria*. The other part was the prevailing sentiment in the *memoria* camp that law is too narrow or too specialized a field, as Carruthers notes, which addresses "much broader and varied audiences and concerns." Thus, memory in law has remained more a subject for learned discourse in a comparatively small circle of legal-historical orientation.

Of course, we are accustomed to the notion that the medieval manuscript and Renaissance book culture made extensive use of all the media of art, whether in the field of philosophy, the Bible, books of liturgy and prayer books, works on meditation, and works of *Minnesang* and epic. Illuminations, illustrations, and diagrammatic presentations are penned, inked, etched, and painted in a quite arresting variety, fancy in color and gold. It is unfortunate that not only has legal iconography been neglected by art history, but that the *figurae legis*, the wealth of the schemata and diagrammatic illustrations, are either unknown or dismissed by *memoria* specialists.

Yet a systematic review of canon law, and of the Reformation and common law period in Europe, reveals that the legal literature – literally every known genre – with its decorative richness and diagrammatic visuals, can share the ranks with its elegant *cousins réligieux* and is very much part of the medieval and Renaissance manuscript/book culture. A significant industry of artists/illustrators, scribal shops, and so forth, contracted by the growing number of incunabular presses and by printing houses of the sixteenth to eighteenth centuries, supplied memory devices which were added to printed legal texts. Artists included the likes of Hans Holbein (1497-1542) in Basel, Hans Baldung "Green" (1484-1545) in Strassburg [8.02], and the madly talented Albrecht Dürer (1471-1528) [10.06], eventually the European "master supreme" for woodcut and etching techniques.

This confluence of art and law can be seen especially in diagrams with mnemonic functions, such as formae or figurae. These were originally geomet-

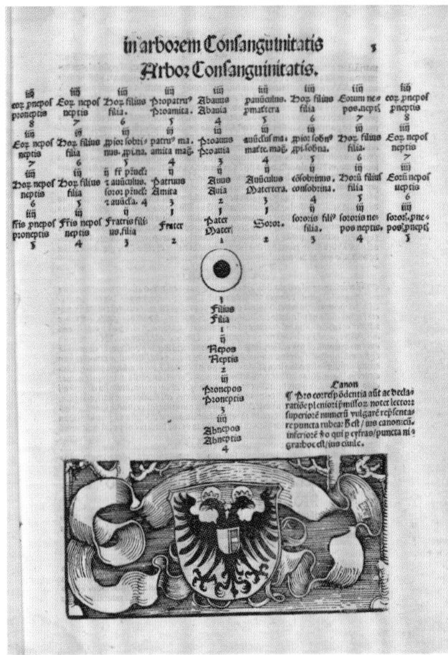

Johannes Lindholz, *Arbores consanguinitatis, affinitatis, cognationis spiritualis atque legalis* (Strassburg, 1516). Law Library of Congress.

8. Milena Bartlová, "*In memoriam defunctorum*: Visual Arts as Devices of Memory," in *The Making of Memory in the Middle Ages* (Lucie Doležalová, ed.; Leiden/Boston: Brill, 2010), 473.

ric shapes such as circles and triangles, the so-called "stemmata," appearing in manuscripts of the twelfth to thirteenth centuries as hand-drawn forms.

With the introduction of a figurative ornamental element – for example, a figure which presents such a stemma, like a teacher, known as a "presentation figure," or other central structures, such as a tree or stairs, to which symbols or coded content could be attached – the term *schema* was applied.

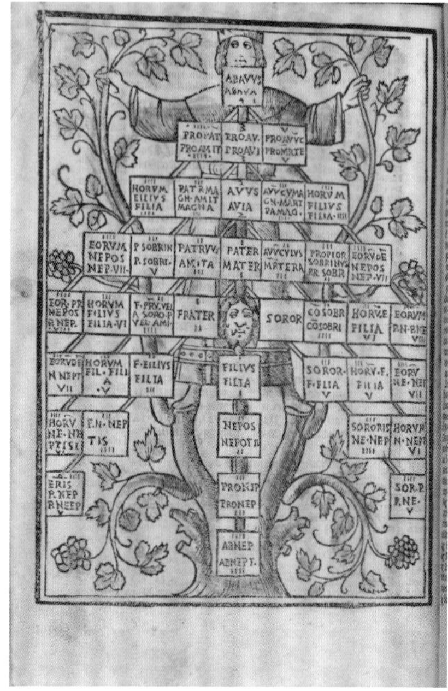

Instituta novissime recognita aptissimisque figuris exculta (Venice, 1516). Law Library of Congress.

Sketches like these can clarify at a glance the inherent liability of acts and facts and the resulting legal actions. Their visual presentations are ideal for the classroom. They explain (1) a system of rules and (2) subject relations. One could describe them as tools for pictorial delivery of detailed verbal information contained in a text, thus functioning as an ocular navigation tool to memory.

Among the diagrams of special importance are those treating the subject of marriage and inheritance. This is, to date, still a complicated and confusing matter for all who must deal with it. To bring across the various levels of relationships in Roman law and canon law, particular diagrams were introduced very early to substitute for lengthy or hard-to-grasp verbal discourse, which often fell short of precision of clarity. We can distinguish two groups of such diagrams, which represent the degrees of inter-generational relationships: the Roman *scala* and the canonical *arbor*.

Canonical arbores

This figurative group of "trees" had an enormous running time to the end of the nineteenth century, among them the *arbores consanguinitatis*, *affinitatis* and *arbores legales* and *spirituales*, as well as *arbores* as organization devices for particular subjects. By the twelfth century, the contentious debate over the forbidden degrees of marriage in the Church had subsided. With the First Lateran Council (1123), relationships to the seventh degrees down the blood line – the so called canonical generation count – were firmly set. Within these seven degrees, the marriage impediments were harbored. It is thought that the decision of the Council had now made space for the *arbor* – which appeared for the first time in Gratian's *Decretum*, featuring seven degrees of relationships, inserted in marriage law. Although Gratian did not require the addition of a diagram, it began to be included in the *Decretum*

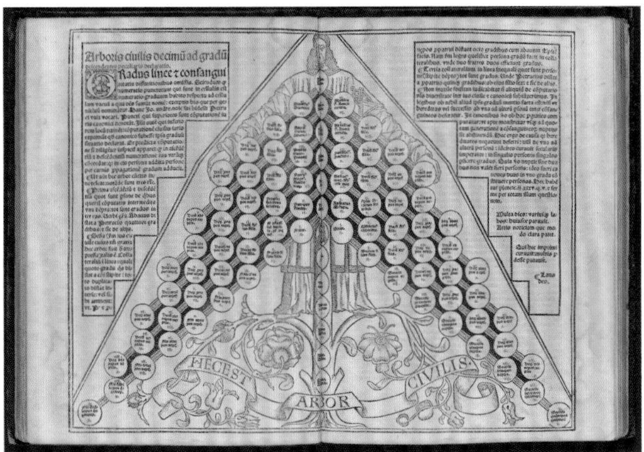

Institutiones imperiales (Lyon, 1513). Law Library of Congress.

as a pictorial aid which was long and widely used as a textbook or teaching manual on canon law.

During the Renaissance, we see the *arbor*, particularly in the West, crossing over into Roman law as the *arbor civilis*. Justifiably, "Law's Picture Books" devotes an entire case to such diagrams – one easily could have devoted an entire exhibition to them. [See Section 3, Diagramming the Law]

The term *arbor* itself had a long and varied past. Initially, only parts of the tree are introduced in the learned discourse, such as root (*radix*), trunk (*truncus*), or branch (*brassum*). Eventually, the word served, without dependence on illustrative matter, as the definitive terminus for subject arrangements, particularly in the field of genealogy. The strong tree image with roots, trunk, and branches, in many cases adorned with blossoms, leaves, and fruit, is an organic entity. It also lends itself to systematic arrangement of content – we still use the terms "branches" of the law, "roots" of a concept, and so forth.

Research on artistic and figurative presentations in medieval biblical and scholastic works point to the symbolism of the *arbor vitae* of paradise. Vignettes of Adam and Eve, which are added to many presentations of the *arbores*, signal marital relations. In particular, they point to the sacred quality or sacramentality of marriage, the root of canonical teaching.

Over time, the arbor achieved figurative flexibility, opening the way for systematic arrangements in fields other than marriage and inheritance, making detailed ranking of topics and subjects, and their relationship to one another, clearly visible – in artistic form [3.00, 3.07, 3.08, 3.09, 3.11].

Yet the concepts and workings of the *ars memoria* are in principle not different from the aim of modern information and library science to provide the best options for search, discovery, and retrieval of text, images, or other "value added data," for example, classification data. I have over the years developed my own tool box – templates of classification which are really nothing else but templates of *memoria* for teaching and memorizing law classification!

Law's Picture Books and the History of Book Illustration

Erin C. Blake
Folger Shakespeare Library

When I was invited to write this essay, one that would situate "law's picture books" within the history of book illustration, I wondered what would happen if I took the assignment literally. Would it be possible to survey the history of European printed book illustration using only the books in this exhibition? Beginning with the major illustration techniques of the hand press period, I decided to try it.

Over the first hundred years or so of book printing, the vast majority of illustrations were printed in relief, usually from a woodcut, on the same kind of press as printed text. By about 1550, increasing numbers of book illustrations came to be printed in intaglio, on a rolling press, separately from printed text (usually from engraved and etched copper-based plates). These two techniques dominated book illustration until the nineteenth century, when lithography came into use.

To make a woodcut illustration, you start by transferring your design onto a hardwood plank. Then you cut away everything except your design lines. In other words, black lines are made by gouging out the white space on either side, while white lines are made by gouging a single line into the surface. The fish on pages 649 and 650 of *Landrecht, Briceÿ-, Gerichts-, Malefitz- und andere Ordnungen des Fürstenthumben Obern und Nidern Baÿrn* [10.01] provide a perfect side-by-side example. Compare the pectoral and pelvic fins of the left-hand fish with the pectoral and pelvic fins of the right-hand fish. The left-hand fish's fins are black lines on a white background; the right-hand fish's fins are white lines on a black background. Notice, also, how the woodcutter used straight lines (horizontal on top, vertical below) for the scales for one fish, and curved lines and cross-hatching for the scales of the other. But keep in mind, this is a woodcut, so the cross-hatched lines aren't actually made by cross-hatching; they are made by cutting out the little squares and diamonds between the black lines.

Printing woodcut book illustrations is quite straightforward, since the standard height of a woodblock matches the standard height of moveable type. That means that image and text can be printed together on a common press. The illustration is basically a single very large piece of wooden type that gets inked and printed along with the rest of the type in a forme. This makes woodcuts naturally suited to book illustration, unlike intaglio illustrations, which have to be printed under heavy pressure, on a rolling press.

Intaglio illustrations are made by transferring a design onto a metal plate, then cutting into the plate along on those lines, hence the name intaglio, which is Italian for "carving" or "cutting into." Before the nineteenth century, most intaglio plates were copper or copper alloy, so the printing surfaces as well as prints made from them are commonly referred to as copperplates. They are better suited to reproducing fine lines and great detail than woodcuts, which are naturally limited by wood's fragility. If you make a woodcut line too thin, it will break. It's no surprise that the information-packed images in Johannes Buno's *Memoriale Institutionum juris* [8.07], for example, are copperplate illustrations. It's also no surprise that you're seeing four highly detailed pictures crammed onto a single plate rather than separate, larger images for each. Copper was an expensive medium, so it paid to use as little as possible, and intaglio printing is a much slower process than relief printing, so having fewer plates greatly sped up production.

Inking and printing an intaglio plate is a complicated process. First, you have to heat the plate to make it more receptive to the ink. Then you slather thick ink all over the surface, massaging it into the cut lines. Next, you remove the excess ink in several stages, ending with a final wipe using the flat of your hand. After the final wiping, the only substantial ink left will be the ink held inside the cut lines, below the surface of the plate. Meanwhile, your printing paper has been thoroughly dampened. Running the inked plate and the dampened paper face-to-face through a high-pressure rolling press squeezes the paper into the cut lines, where it comes in contact with the ink. When you peel the paper off the plate, the ink comes with it.

Lorenzo Mascambrone's *Degli asili de Christiani ragionamento* [10.03] shows relief and intaglio techniques together on the same page. The decorative initial containing a small townscape and a giant letter "S" was printed from a relief block that was locked into the forme alongside the ordinary type, with a blank spot left where the engraved headpiece would go. The headpiece was then added by dampening the partially-printed sheet and running it through a rolling press, under high pressure. The "plate mark" around the image is especially distinct in this example, clearly showing the size of the metal plate by the impression it left behind. In *Statuta Hospitalis Hierusalem* [10.04], the two techniques also appear on the same page, but this time they combine to create a single full-page illustration, with an engraving carefully placed in the blank space left inside a frame made of woodblocks.

Most intaglio book illustrations were made by a combination of etching and engraving – often more etching than engraving – but are nevertheless referred to as "engravings" because they do not typically show the freedom of artistic expression associated with etching. With an engraving, lines are cut into the plate with sharp tools. With an etching, lines are scratched into a layer of protective varnish to reveal the bare metal, then cut into the plate by acid that eats away at the exposed metal. In the world of fine prints, etching is considered a more elevated art form than engraving because the lines you see were actually drawn by the artist, not cut by a professional engraver copying an artist's design. In the world of book illustration, though, the hierarchy is reversed. Etchings and engravings were both made by professional craftsmen, with etching being quicker and cheaper than engraving. Etched plates also wore out faster. "Entirely engraved in line" was a selling point for an illustrated book, not a detraction.

The earliest illustrated books tended to have highly stylized woodcuts, with an emphasis on outline, like the tree of blood relationships in Giovanni d'Andrea, *Super arboribus consanguinitatis et affinitatis*, from about 1473 [3.02], and the author portrait in Paolo Attavanti, *Breviarium totius juris canonici*, from 1479 [10.07]. Neither has much in the way of shading, and in both the image is pressed up against the "picture plane." That is, the images seem to sit on the surface of the paper rather than receding into space. Paolo's hands might be in front of his bookshelf, but he could easily touch the bookshelf's far left edge with the tip of his nose.

Later illustrations show the influence of Renaissance artistic theories, where creating a naturalistic illusion of space becomes important, as if the reader is looking through the page into another world. In the case of *Praxis rerum criminalium* [2.03], the artist took great pains to show us that the amorous couple and the lone man are not only in real space, they are in the same building at the same time. Because the wall between them only stretches part way to the ceiling, and remains one floor tile too short to reach the surface of the page, there is no mistaking this for two different instances of the same space, like the diagrams of property division in *De alluvionum iure universo* [4.03], or side-by-side depictions of unrelated spaces, like the frontispiece illustration in *Juristische Ergötzlichkeiten vom Jung-Gesellen Rechte* [8.05].

This isn't to say that a realistic sense of space has to have great depth. The great Albrecht Dürer willfully plays with spatial conventions in the full-page woodcut that follows the title page of a 1522 edition of the laws of Nuremberg [10.06]. There is no reason for coats of arms and symbolic figures to share the same space like this. Indeed, there's no reason for coats of arms to exist in three-dimensional space at all, since they are purely symbolic. Nevertheless, here they are all together. The angels in particular call attention to the oddity, twisting around to get a good look at the Imperial arms in the center instead of just holding up the crown. Justice is, literally, above it all, looking heavenward in the upper left.

Dürer's woodcut in *Reformacion der Stat Nüremberg* not only plays with conventions of space, it seems to be thumbing its nose at the technical conventions of woodcut illustration. The figures' clothing is shaded by parallel lines, as you would expect in a woodcut, where black lines are created by cutting out the white space between them. Instead of a woodcut's typical mostly-white background, though, or even an atypical (but technically reasonable) solid black background, this background design almost exclusively uses the dense cross-hatching normally associated with engraving. The one exception comes at the lower right edge. There, like a knowing wink to connoisseurs, the woodcut illustration goes even further into the vocabulary of engraving, with the white space chiseled out between the lines leaving short, tight curls that mimic the flick of an engraver's burin cutting into copper. The traditional narrative of book illustration history might present this as a highly skilled example of a cost-saving measure, where a woodcut is cleverly disguised to mimic an engraving. But in Dürer's case, it's easy to believe that he is simply showing off.

Generally speaking, engravings are more expensive than woodcuts. Copper costs more than wood; cutting an engraving takes more time and skill than cutting a woodblock; and printing an intaglio plate is a much slower and more labor-intensive process than printing a relief block. Engravings in books therefore carry a prestige value independent from their pictorial value. Consider the frontispiece engraving in *Maximae juris celebriores, deductae ex jure canonico, civili, glossa* [1.04], for example. The picture of richly dressed "Justitia" standing in a book-filled room does not aid in the literal understanding of the words that follow. Rather, it works in tandem with the costly two-color printing of the title page to prepare you for something important. It is the visual equivalent of a drum-roll or fanfare announcing the text's imminent arrival.

Engravings lend themselves to frontispieces for technical reasons, not just aesthetic ones. Because they have to be printed on a separate press from the book's text, they are usually printed independently from the text pages, so they won't naturally fall in the correct place when the sheets are gathered and folded for binding. Some books include printed instructions to the binder, listing which engraving should face which page. With engraved frontispieces, that information is already known: it goes at the front. Other engravings state their intended location on the print itself, like the example from *Iurisprudentia numismatibus illustrata* [5.04], which helpfully includes "ad pag. 162" in the upper margin, just inside the plate mark. It is also worth remarking that the illustration actually *is* bound at page 162. Just because the publisher intended it to go there doesn't mean it always ended up that way.

Comentarios a las ordenanzas de minas [4.04] provides an excellent example of how to get around the difficulty of fitting engravings into the exact spot in the text where they belong. Instead of placing each image as close as possible to the relevant paragraph, three large plates contain multiple images each. Numbers in the images correspond with numbered paragraphs in the text. Some copies of this book have the left edge of the folding plates bound into the gutter, so that even when the plate is unfolded, part of it is hidden by the text block, and you have to flip back and forth to match up image and text. The copy shown here is much more user-friendly, since the plate are bound as "throw outs," where the blank margin on the left is wide enough to throw the image clear of the text block when the plate is unfolded. The illustration remains fully visible as you turn the pages.

Until the nineteenth century, the relief printing and intaglio printing techniques described above remained the only options for printed book illustration. Then came lithography, which still dominates commercial printing in the form of offset lithography. Relief and intaglio printing both rely on a physical distance between the inked and un-inked parts of the surface; the ink is either applied on top of a raised surface (relief printing) or into the grooves of an incised surface (intaglio printing). Lithography, instead, relies on the fact that oil and water do not mix. Oily ink is applied across a smooth surface (planographic printing) but does not stick to the dampened parts of the surface, only to the design lines, which repel water but attract ink.

Lithography allows large images to be printed relatively inexpensively, and it quickly became the standard technique for maps and charts. In the nineteenth century and first half of the twentieth, text was rarely printed lithographically, so instructions for placement of illustrations often continued to be printed on the image, or provided within the text, as with intaglio plates. The *Order of reference of the Supreme Court of the United States, in the case of the State of Pennsylvania, complainant, against the Wheeling & Belmont Bridge Company and others, defendants* [7.11] includes unusually detailed "Directions to the Binder for Placing the Map and Plates." The eight lithographs are described not just by full title, but with the name of the person responsible for creating them. Let there be no mistake which one is which, and whose is whose. These illustrations aren't added to make the book more attractive, they are added as part of the evidence.

The role of illustration as evidence can also be seen in the books in this exhibition that make use of photography. A photograph has intrinsic connotations of direct eyewitness value. Light reflected off the actual surface of an actual object was directly captured to make the illustration. This isn't an artist's impression, it is the impression of the thing itself. Or is it? The book illustration is not itself a photograph (not usually, anyway), it is a photograph that has been re-photographed through a half-tone screen in order to translate the continuous tone into dots that would hold black ink: bigger dots for the darker areas, smaller dots (with more surrounding white space) for lighter areas. Even then, in the early years it required considerable hand work to bring out the contrasts enough to make a legible image emerge from a muddy half-tone. In *El crimen de Santa Julia*, published in 1899 [7.08], this is evident in the man on the left, whose hat and clothes appear to have been entirely painted. The illustration is a photograph not because the technique makes the clearest image, but because it inherently shows real people. Similarly, the photograph showing how people can be concealed in the tail of an airplane in *Textbook of aerial laws* [2.10] would have been easier to grasp as a hand-drawn technical illustration, but then it wouldn't have the same "truth value," so to speak.

At the other end of the creative spectrum from matter-of-fact photography comes the twentieth century fine press book, exemplified here by *The defense of Gracchus Babeuf before the High Court of Vendôme* from the Gehenna Press, with twenty-one etchings by Thomas Cornell [10.08]. These etched portraits are fine art in their own right, an expression of the artist's creative aesthetic and intellectual power, not illustrations that only make sense when they are part of a book. As such, they make an interesting contrast with earlier etched illustrations, like the scenes related to mining law in *Comentarios a las ordenanzas de minas* [4.04] or the dense mnemonic images in *Memoriale Institutionum juris* [8.07]. Those illustrations were etched because etching is quicker and easier than engraving, not because the publisher wanted to give free rein to artistic expression.

When I first started teaching the history of printed book illustration, I would finish up with fine press books, then pose the question of whether that was the end point of original book illustration for adults, or was it possible that sequential art, also known as graphic novels, might break into the mainstream. That is no longer a question. It was possible, and it did. The form is even used for law books, with Nathaniel Burney's *Illustrated guide to criminal procedure* [8.17] a fine case in point.

This returns me to my original question. Can illustrated law books be used to survey the history of book illustration? In broad strokes, I believe the answer is yes, though I have only been able to touch on a few aspects here. Many more can be seen in the exhibition, and you can be certain that some of the fine examples seen in this exhibition will be making an appearance in my survey course.

Maximae juris celebriores, deductæ ex jure canonico, civili, glossa: illustratae exemplis, rationibus, limitationibus, in usum juri utrique addictoram. Tyrnavia: Typis Academicis, S. Jesu, 1742.

Law's Picture Books
The Yale Law Library Collection

ILLUSTRATED LAW BOOKS? THE TERM MAY SEEM LIKE AN OXYMORON. After all, law is conceptual, analytic, and so very *wordy*. Yet the object of law is human life, and its practitioners mediate between abstract rules and the real world of people and things. This tension has given rise to a surprising figurative impulse in legal literature – to law's picture books.

The works on display here reveal and explore this tradition. They offer a beguiling diversity of images from Europe, Great Britain, Asia, and the Americas, from the Middle Ages to the present day. They were published for many audiences, including legal professionals, law students, and lay readers. Often they were meant to be used as tools in the workshops of legal practice.

The volumes all come from the collection of illustrated law books at the Yale Law Library, developed by rare book librarian Michael Widener. As a collector based in a university, Mike's goal has been to foster curiosity and experiment. Over the past decade, he has created a unique resource for researchers in a variety of academic fields.

This catalogue, like our exhibition, is organized around ten functional purposes that law book illustrations can serve. What goals can illustrations achieve that are difficult to realize through legal prose alone? What can images in law books *do*? Each purpose in turn shapes the dialogue legal illustrations have with their accompanying text – the conversation between word and image.

Some of the volumes in the exhibition were chosen because they played an important role in history. Other books exemplify a publishing genre, or present a fascinating intellectual puzzle, or are superlative examples of their kind. And some books simply capture the imagination with their unexpected loveliness.

In this book of criminal law from the Republic of Genoa, Lady Justice's eyes are wide open. Elsewhere in this section, they are covered with a blindfold. The image of Lady Justice, or Justitia, has remained remarkably stable across the centuries. Yet her gestures have often varied, as have the people and objects surrounding her. Lady Justice derives symbolic meaning from her context. What other differences do you see?

STATVTA CRIMINALIA
SER. REIP. IANVENSIS
GENVÆ SVMPTIBVS IOSEPHI BOTTARII BIBLIOPOLÆ SVB INSIGNI PVERI IESV. CVM PRIVIL.
Dominicus fiasel. Sarsan. Inu.
Ioseph Testana Scul.

GENOA (REPUBLIC). *Criminalium iurium serenissimae reipublicae Genuensis.* Genoa: Ioannes Baptista Tiboldus, 1669. Engraving by Giuseppe Maria Testana.

Symbolizing the Law 1

Allegorical illustrations are central to the history of law book publishing. As figurative images used to represent philosophical ideals, they often appear at the beginning of books, where they herald and embody the principles of the text that follows. This exhibition likewise begins with such images.

The most widespread and best known allegorical image of law is Lady Justice, who has become a trademark for the legal profession – its brand. But there have been many other visual allegories of law, some still familiar, others now obscure. In all their forms and varieties, such illustrations dance between figure and idea, just as law itself mediates between actual human life and the abstraction of rules.

1.01

Republic of Venice, Council of Ten.

Parte presa nell'Eccelso Conseglio di X ... in materia de banditi.

Venice: Rampazetto, 1609.

Many states have used the figure of Lady Justice, or Justitia, to symbolize their dominion. In this banditry law from the Republic of Venice, she stands between two sumptuous lions, which recall the winged lion of St. Mark, the best-known symbol of the city. As *Venetia,* she embodies both Justice and Venice itself.

2

PARTE
PRESA
Nell'Eccelſo Conſeglio di X.
1609. A' 31. Agoſto.
In materia di Banditi.

Stampata in Calle dalle Raſſe,
Per il Rampazetto.

Benedict Carpzov.

Verhandeling der lyfstraffelyke misdaaden en haare berechtinge, naar 't voorschrift des gemeenen rechts.

Rotterdam: Jan Daniel Beman, 1752. Volume 1 of 2. Engraving by Jan Punt.

1.02

VERKLARING
VAN DE
TYTELPRENT.

GOds Stedehounderes op aerde,
GERECHTIGHEIT, daelt van omhoog,
Beschenen door het *Alziende Oog*,
Met haren *Evenaer* en *Zwaerde*,
Opdat ze, op 't stevig *Rechtältaer*,
Haer *Wetten* stave en 't Recht bevoordeel',
Door haer *Voorzichtigheit* en *Oordeel*,
Verbeeld door 't geestryk *Kinderpaer*,
Dat alles afmeet, alle daden
Ten toets' in 't *Spiegelglas* vertoont;
Waerop BELOONING de Onschuldt loont,
De DEUGDT bekroont met *Lauwerbladen*,
De STRAF den TWIST, vol wrok en nydt,
Den MOORDT en andre helgedrochten,
Door angst in 't wroegend hart bevochten,
Met haer gestrenge *Zweep'* kastyd.
De *Schat* uit *Amaltheaes Hooren*,
't *Gebloemte*, 't *Ooft*, de *Palm* en *Kroon*,
Verbeeld der Deugden heilryk loon,
Om elk op 't heilpadt aen te sporen.
Dus strekt, ten schrikk' van 't Onbescheit,
De *Stapel Roeden*, *Koorden*, *Boeijen*
Om 't zaedt der Ondeugd' uit te roeijen,
Tot glory der GERECHTIGHEIT.

D. SMITS.

The books on the pedestal beneath Lady Justice are the *Corpus Juris Civilis*, or Roman civil code, the Bible, and the *Corpus Juris Canonici*, the ecclesiastical laws of the Church. The poem provides a verbal "explanation of the title engraving," carefully decoding its visual symbols.

1.03

Adam Friedrich Glafey.

Vollständigen Geschichte des Rechts der Vernunfft.

Leipzig: Christoph Riegel, 1739.

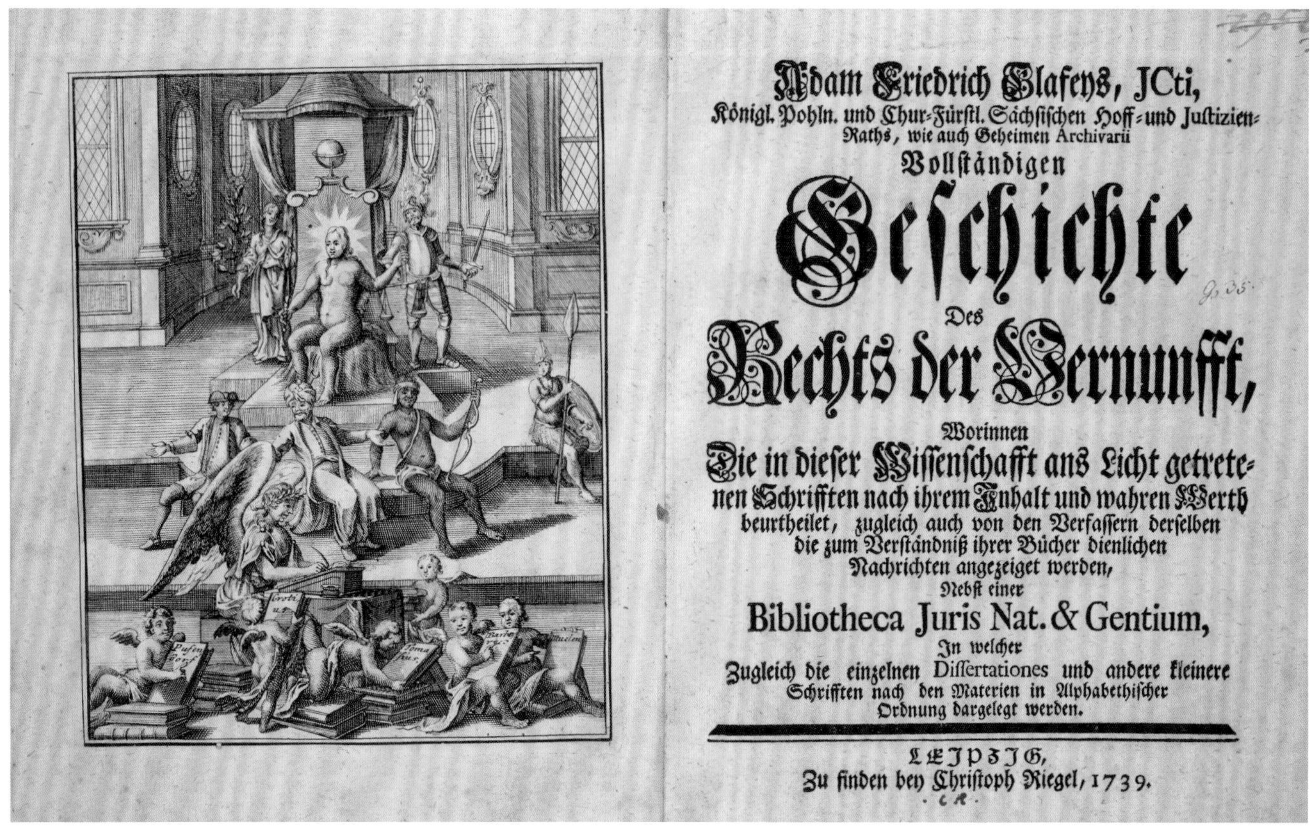

Adam Friedrich Glafeys, JCti,
Königl. Pohln. und Chur-Fürstl. Sächsischen Hoff- und Justizien-
Raths, wie auch Geheimen Archivarii
Vollständigen
Geschichte
Des
Rechts der Vernunfft,
Worinnen
Die in dieser Wissenschafft ans Licht getrete-
nen Schrifften nach ihrem Inhalt und wahren Werth
beurtheilet, zugleich auch von den Verfassern derselben
die zum Verständniß ihrer Bücher dienlichen
Nachrichten angezeiget werden,
Nebst einer
Bibliotheca Juris Nat. & Gentium,
In welcher
Zugleich die einzelnen Dissertationes und andere kleinere
Schrifften nach den Materien in Alphabethischer
Ordnung dargelegt werden.
LEIPZIG,
Zu finden bey Christoph Riegel, 1739.

The frontispiece of this bibliography of natural and international law – the two subjects are linked – shows a nude Justitia watching over figures representing Europe, Asia, Africa, and the Americas. An angel pens the writings of leading legal theorists in the field, their books lovingly held by putti.

Maximae juris celebriores, deductae ex jure canonico, civili, glossa.

Trnava: Typis Academicis, S. Jesu, 1742.

1.04

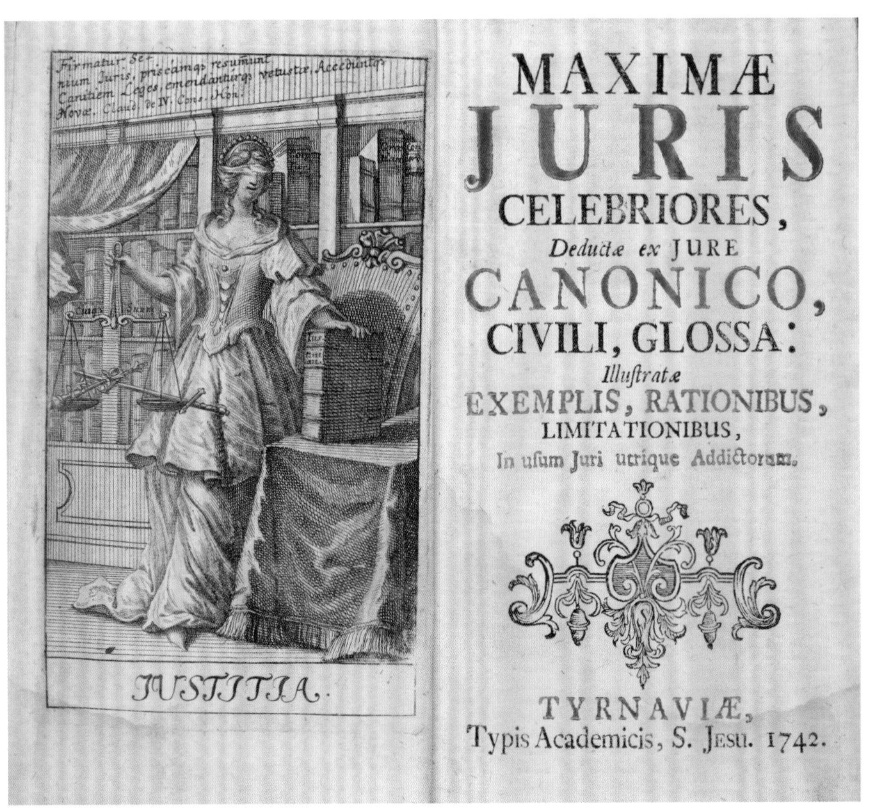

What's the relation of this book of legal maxims, published by a Jesuit press in present-day Slovakia, to those depicted on the library shelves in the frontispiece? Justitia's hand rests upon a volume of the *Corpus Juris Civilis,* while her scales balance civil and spiritual authority. The Latin motto reads: "Old customs are preserved; law has recovered its ancient sanctity through the amendment of former statutes and the addition of new ones."

1.05

Teutsches corpus juris publici & privati, oder, Codex diplomaticus.

Ulm: Johann Conrad Wohlers, 1717. Volume 1 of 2. Engraved frontispiece by Engelhard Nunzer.
German Law Collection of the Association of the Bar of the City of New York.

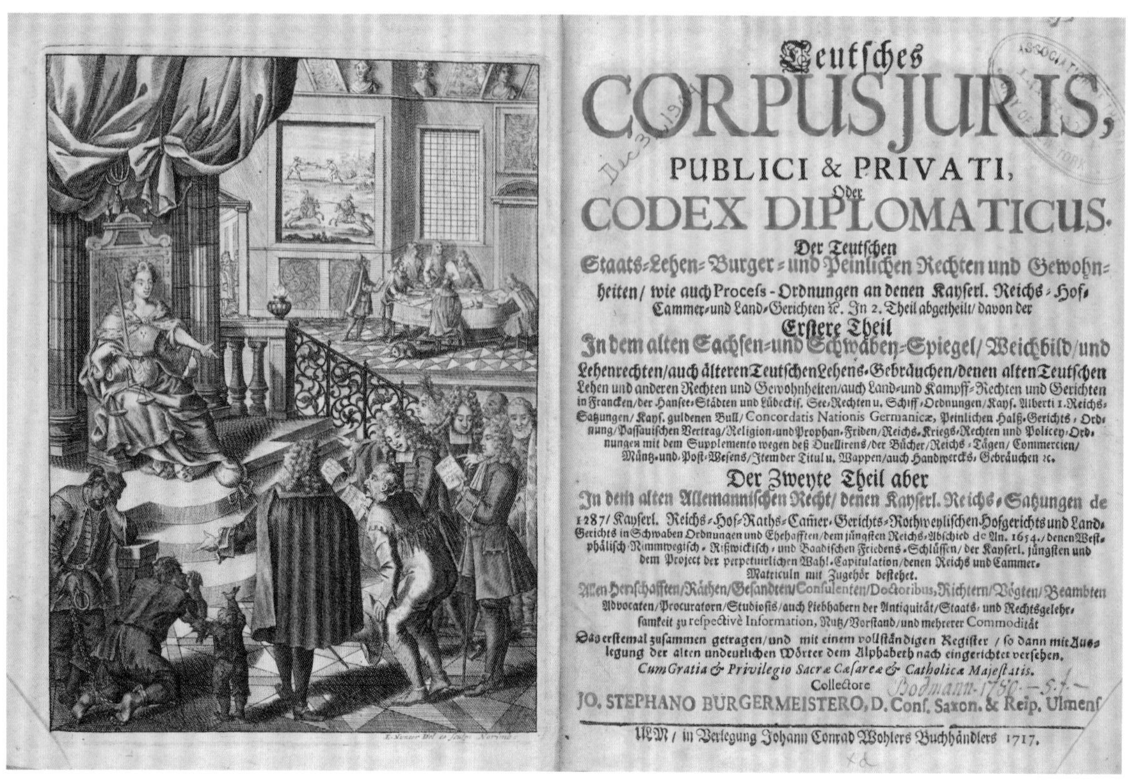

Teutsches
CORPUS JURIS,
PUBLICI & PRIVATI,
Oder
CODEX DIPLOMATICUS.
Der Teutschen
Staats-Lehen-Burger-und Peinlichen Rechten und Gewohnheiten/ wie auch Procefs-Ordnungen an denen Kayserl. Reichs-Hof-Cammer-und Land-Gerichten &c. In 2. Theil abgetheilt/ davon der
Erstere Theil
In dem alten Sachsen-und Schwaben-Spiegel/ Weichbild/ und Lehenrechten/ auch älteren Teutschen Lehens-Gebräuchen/ denen alten Teutschen Lehen und anderen Rechten und Gewohnheiten/ auch Land-und Kampff-Rechten und Gerichten in Francken/ der Hansee-Städten und Lübeckis. See-Rechten u. Schiff-Ordnungen/ Kays. Alberti I. Reichs-Satzungen/ Kays. guldenen Bull/ Concordatis Nationis Germanicæ, Peinlichen Halß-Gerichts-Ordnung/ Passauischen Vertrag/ Religion-und Prophan-Friden/ Reichs-Kriegs-Rechten und Policey-Ordnungen mit dem Supplemento wegen deß Duellirens/ der Bücher/ Reichs-Tägen/ Commercien/ Müntz-und Post-Wesens/ Item der Titul u. Wappen/ auch Handwercks-Gebräuchen &c.
Der Zweyte Theil aber
In dem alten Allemannischen Recht/ denen Kayserl. Reichs-Satzungen de 1287/ Kayserl. Reichs-Hof-Raths-Camer-Gerichts-Rothweylischen Hofgerichts und Land-Gerichts in Schwaben Ordnungen und Ehehafften/ dem jüngsten Reichs-Abschied de An. 1654./ denen Westphälisch-Nimmwegisch-Rißwickisch-und Baadischen Friedens-Schlüssen/ der Kayserl. jüngsten und dem Project der perpetuirlichen Wahl-Capitulation/ denen Reichs und Cammer-Matriculn mit Zugehör bestehet.
Allen Herschafften/ Räthen/ Gesandten/ Consulenten/ Doctoribus, Richtern/ Vögten/ Beambten Advocaten/ Procuratorn/ Studiosis/ auch Liebhabern der Antiquität/ Staats-und Rechtsgelehrsamkeit zu respectivè Information, Nutz/ Vorstand/ und mehrerer Commodität
Das erstemal zusammen getragen/ und mit einem vollständigen Register/ so dann mit Auslegung der alten undeutlichen Wörter dem Alphabeth nach eingerichtet versehen.
Cum Gratia & Privilegio Sacræ Cæsareæ & Catholicæ Majestatis.
Collectore
JO. STEPHANO BURGERMEISTERO, D. Cons. Saxon. & Reip. Ulmens.
ULM/ in Verlegung Johann Conrad Wohlers Buchhändlers 1717.

At first glance, this image seems simple enough: Justitia is dispensing justice to the poor and downtrodden, while lawyers make their arguments. But look closer. Who is the man skulking beneath Lady Justice's feet? And is she stepping on a bag ... of money? The ragged man in chains with his child: is he a criminal or a debtor? Is Justitia taking sides?

Wm. F. Wernse & Co.

Promotional brochure for the American digest and legal directory.

1.06

St. Louis: Wm. F. Wernse & Co., 1888. Acquired with the Charles J. Tanenbaum Fund.

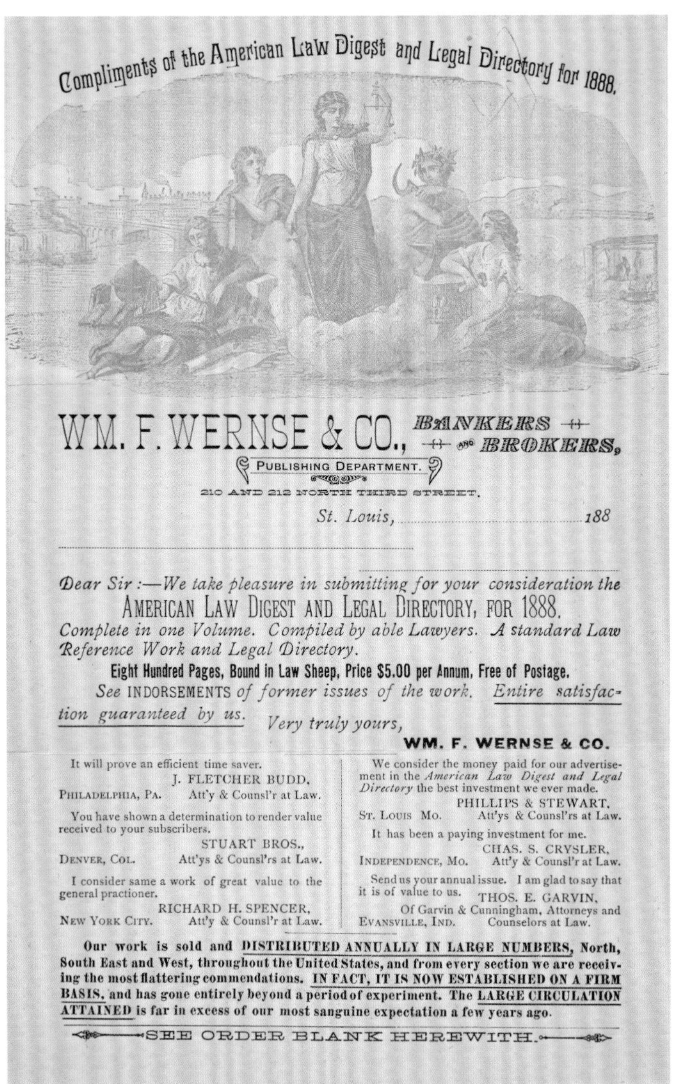

Compliments of the American Law Digest and Legal Directory for 1888.

WM. F. WERNSE & CO., BANKERS AND BROKERS,

PUBLISHING DEPARTMENT.

210 AND 212 NORTH THIRD STREET.

St. Louis, ... 188

Dear Sir:—We take pleasure in submitting for your consideration the

AMERICAN LAW DIGEST AND LEGAL DIRECTORY, FOR 1888.

Complete in one Volume. Compiled by able Lawyers. A standard Law Reference Work and Legal Directory.

Eight Hundred Pages, Bound in Law Sheep, Price $5.00 per Annum, Free of Postage.

See INDORSEMENTS *of former issues of the work. Entire satisfaction guaranteed by us.*

Very truly yours,

WM. F. WERNSE & CO.

It will prove an efficient time saver.
J. FLETCHER BUDD,
PHILADELPHIA, PA. Att'y & Counsl'r at Law.

You have shown a determination to render value received to your subscribers.
STUART BROS.,
DENVER, COL. Att'ys & Counsl'rs at Law.

I consider same a work of great value to the general practioner.
RICHARD H. SPENCER,
NEW YORK CITY. Att'y & Counsl'r at Law.

We consider the money paid for our advertisement in the *American Law Digest and Legal Directory* the best investment we ever made.
PHILLIPS & STEWART,
ST. LOUIS MO. Att'ys & Counsl'rs at Law.

It has been a paying investment for me.
CHAS. S. CRYSLER,
INDEPENDENCE, MO. Att'y & Counsl'r at Law.

Send us your annual issue. I am glad to say that it is of value to us.
THOS. E. GARVIN,
Of Garvin & Cunningham, Attorneys and
EVANSVILLE, IND. Counselors at Law.

Our work is sold and DISTRIBUTED ANNUALLY IN LARGE NUMBERS, North, South East and West, throughout the United States, and from every section we are receiving the most flattering commendations. IN FACT, IT IS NOW ESTABLISHED ON A FIRM BASIS, and has gone entirely beyond a period of experiment. The LARGE CIRCULATION ATTAINED is far in excess of our most sanguine expectation a few years ago.

SEE ORDER BLANK HEREWITH.

One of Lady Justice's modern roles is as a trademark for the American legal profession – and its books. Here, she has taken up residence in St. Louis, Missouri.

1.07

Justice is waiting.

[Los Angeles?] Mooney Defense of Southern California, 1930.

This pamphlet was used in the campaign to win freedom for the radical labor organizer Tom Mooney, who was framed on murder charges after a deadly 1917 bombing in San Francisco. Lady Justice plays a distinctively modern symbolic role – a polemical one. Despite the damning evidence in her lap, she waits in vain for the Governor of California to grant a new trial. And in reality, Mooney waited another nine years to be exonerated.

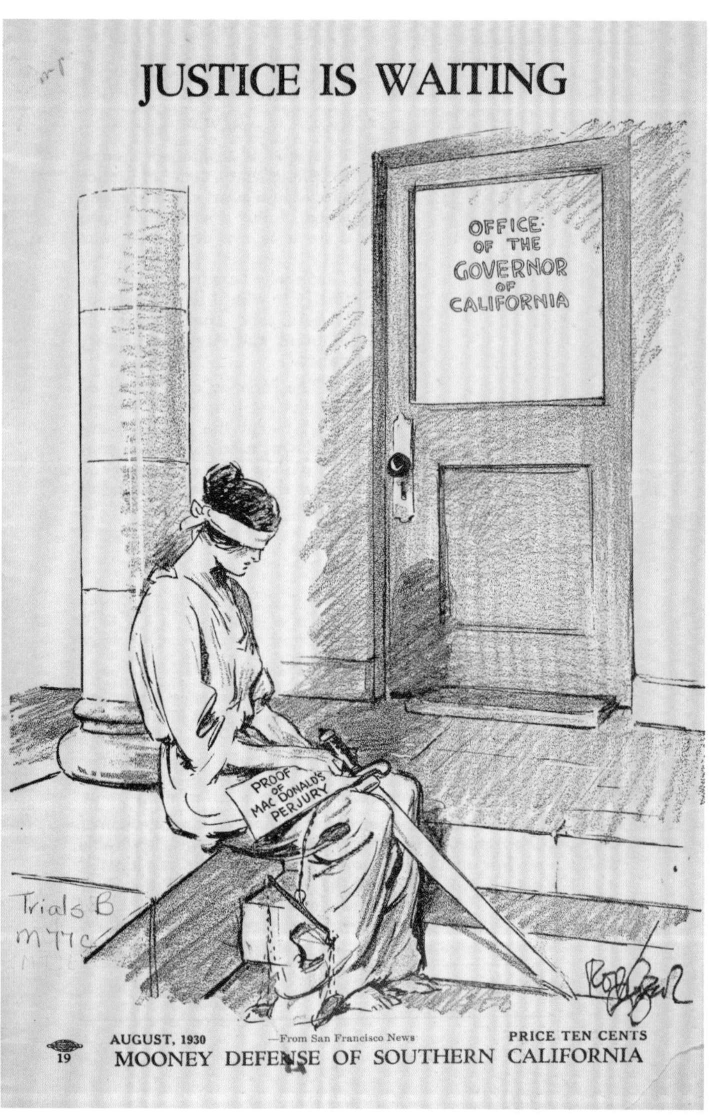

Ignaz Lehmann.

1.08

Amerika's Gesetze.

St. Louis, Mo.: C. Witter, 1857. Acquired with the Ralph Gregory Elliot Fund.

Lady Justice can serve as a symbol of aspiration and hope – hope for a life protected by the rule of law. While here she might resemble the Statue of Liberty, that statue was dedicated almost thirty years later, in 1886. What is Lady Justice holding in her left hand, even higher than her scales? What other works in this section link Lady Justice with books?

1.09

Joost de Damhoudere.

Practycke in civile saecken.

The Hague: Hillebrant Jacobsz van Wouw, 1626.

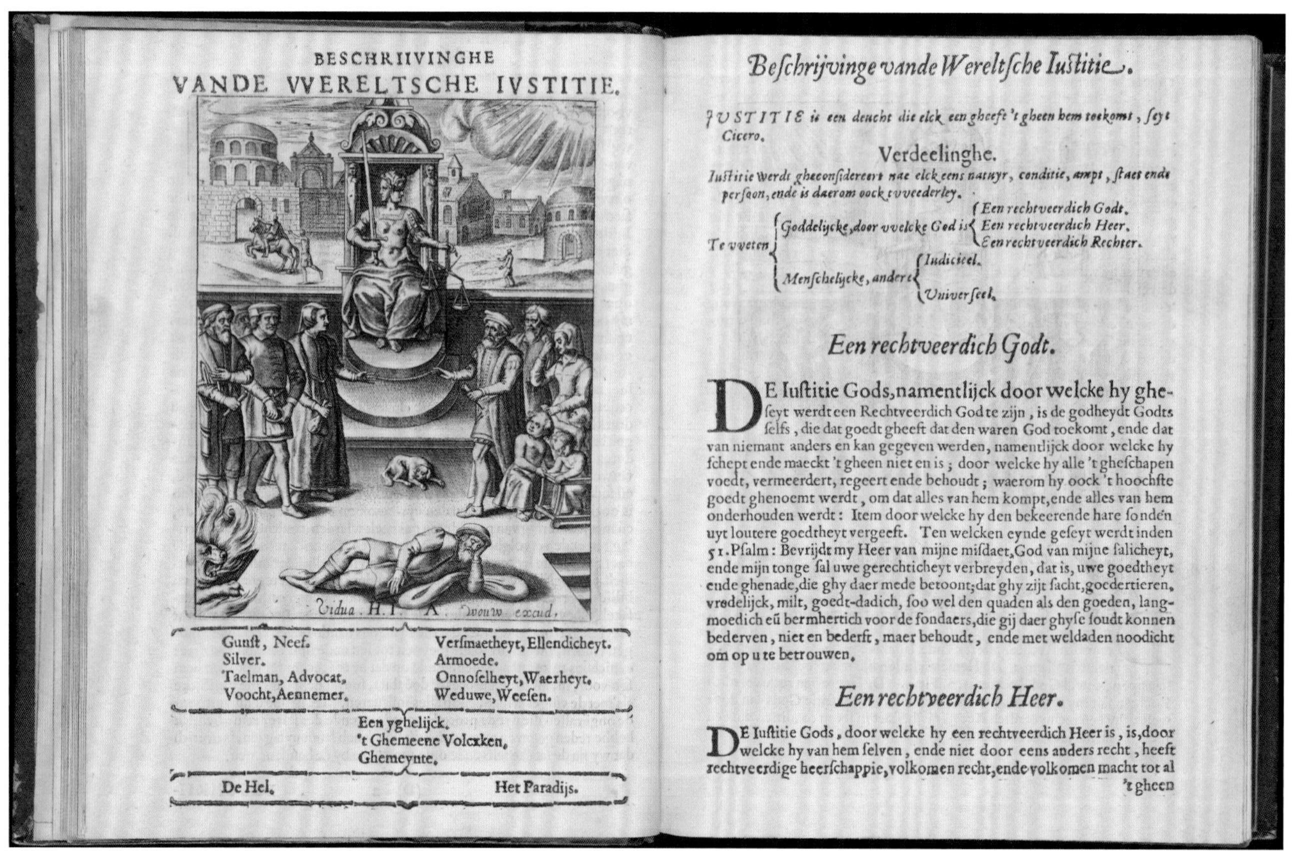

BESCHRIIVINGHE
VANDE VVERELTSCHE IVSTITIE.

Gunſt, Neef. — Verſmaetheyt, Ellendicheyt.
Silver. — Armoede.
Taelman, Advocat, — Onnoſelheyt, Waerheyt.
Voocht, Aennemer. — Weduwe, Weeſen.

Een yghelijck.
't Ghemeene Volcxken,
Ghemeynte.

De Hel. — Het Paradijs.

Beſchrijvinge vande Wereltſche Iuſtitie.

IUSTITIE is een deucht die elck een gheeft 't gheen hem toekomt, ſeyt Cicero.

Verdeelinghe.

Iuſtitie werdt gheconſidereert nae elck eens natuyr, conditie, ampt, ſtaet ende perſoon, ende is daerom oock tvveederley.

Te vveten
- *Goddelijcke, door vvelcke God is*
  - *Een rechtveerdich Godt.*
  - *Een rechtveerdich Heer.*
  - *Een rechtveerdich Rechter.*
- *Menſchelijcke, andere*
  - *Iudicieel.*
  - *Univerſeel.*

Een rechtveerdich Godt.

DE Iuſtitie Gods, namentlijck door welcke hy gheſeyt werdt een Rechtveerdich God te zijn, is de godheydt Godts ſelfs, die dat goedt gheeft dat den waren God toekomt, ende dat van niemant anders en kan gegeven werden, namentlijck door welcke hy ſchept ende maeckt 't gheen niet en is; door welcke hy alle 't gheſchapen voedt, vermeerdert, regeert ende behoudt; waerom hy oock 't hoochſte goedt ghenoemt werdt, om dat alles van hem kompt, ende alles van hem onderhouden werdt: Item door welcke hy den bekeerende hare ſonden uyt loutere goedtheyt vergeeft. Ten welcken eynde geſeyt werdt inden 51. Pſalm: Bevrijdt my Heer van mijne miſdaet, God van mijne ſalicheyt, ende mijn tonge ſal uwe gerechticheyt verbreyden, dat is, uwe goedtheyt ende ghenade, die ghy daer mede betoont; dat ghy zijt ſacht, goedertieren, vrødelijck, milt, goedt-dadich, ſoo wel den quaden als den goeden, langmoedich eñ bermhertich voor de ſondaers, die gij daer ghyſe ſoudt konnen bederven, niet en bederft, maer behoudt, ende met weldaden noodicht om op u te betrouwen,

Een rechtveerdich Heer.

DE Iuſtitie Gods, door welcke hy een rechtveerdich Heer is, is, door welcke hy van hem ſelven, ende niet door eens anders recht, heeft rechtveerdige heerſchappie, volkomen recht, ende volkomen macht tot al 't gheen

As its accompanying essay explains, the two faces illustrating this guide to civil law signify the corrupt nature of "worldly justice," which gazes favorably on the rich and powerful while remaining blind to widows, orphans, and the poor. Joost de Damhoudere (1507-1581) seems to suggest that *true* justice will only come in the afterlife, at the hands of a just God.

William Lawrence.

Marriage by the morall law of God vindicated against all ceremonial laws of popes and bishops.

[London: s.n.], 1680. Acquired with the John A. Hoober Fund.

1.10

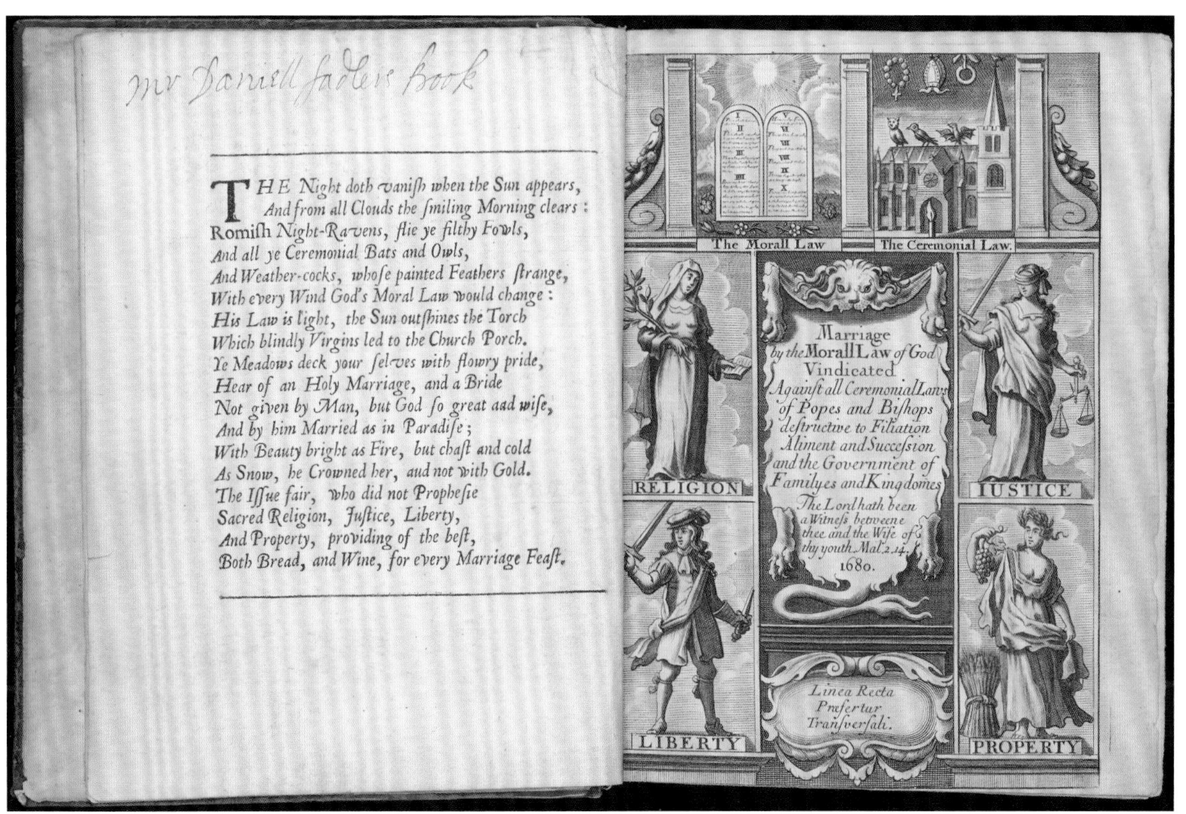

THE Night doth vanish when the Sun appears,
And from all Clouds the smiling Morning clears:
Romish Night-Ravens, flie ye filthy Fowls,
And all ye Ceremonial Bats and Owls,
And Weather-cocks, whose painted Feathers strange,
With every Wind God's Moral Law would change:
His Law is light, the Sun outshines the Torch
Which blindly Virgins led to the Church Porch.
Ye Meadows deck your selves with flowry pride,
Hear of an Holy Marriage, and a Bride
Not given by Man, but God so great aad wise,
And by him Married as in Paradise;
With Beauty bright as Fire, but chast and cold
As Snow, he Crowned her, and not with Gold.
The Issue fair, who did not Prophesie
Sacred Religion, Justice, Liberty,
And Property, providing of the best,
Both Bread, and Wine, for every Marriage Feast.

The Morall Law
The Ceremonial Law
Marriage by the Morall Law of God Vindicated Against all Ceremonial Laws of Popes and Bishops destructive to Filiation Aliment and Succession and the Government of Families and Kingdomes
The Lord hath been a Witness between thee and the Wife of thy youth Mal. 2.14.
1680.
RELIGION
IUSTICE
LIBERTY
PROPERTY
Linea Recta Præfertur Transversali.

A commentary on English marriage law, this volume was a salvo in favor of a Protestant heir to Charles II (1630-1685). The three animals atop the church in the upper-right corner are described in the accompanying poem, as is Lady Justice. It may be ironic that the author, an iconoclastic Puritan, published one of the most iconographic title pages ever to grace an English law book!

S · YVO PATRONORVM PATRONVS.
Pauperis et Viduæ adjutor tutorque Pupilli
Oppressis faueas Iuraque redde tuis.
I. le clerc. ex.

Heinrich Knaust. 1.11

De D. Ivonis juris consulti laudibus et vita oratio.

Cologne: Maternus Cholinus, 1574. Acquired with the Charles J. Tanenbaum Fund.

Saint Ivo of Kermartin (1253-1303), patron saint of lawyers and abandoned children, turns away from the wealthy and toward the poor. How might this symbol about law differ from that of Lady Justice in items 1.04, 1.08, and 1.09? Only four other copies of this hagiography are known to exist, all in European libraries, and none of them contain this striking, hand-colored image.

1.12

Ulrich Tengler.

Der neü Leyenspiegel.

Strassburg, 1514. Acquired with the John A. Hoober Fund.

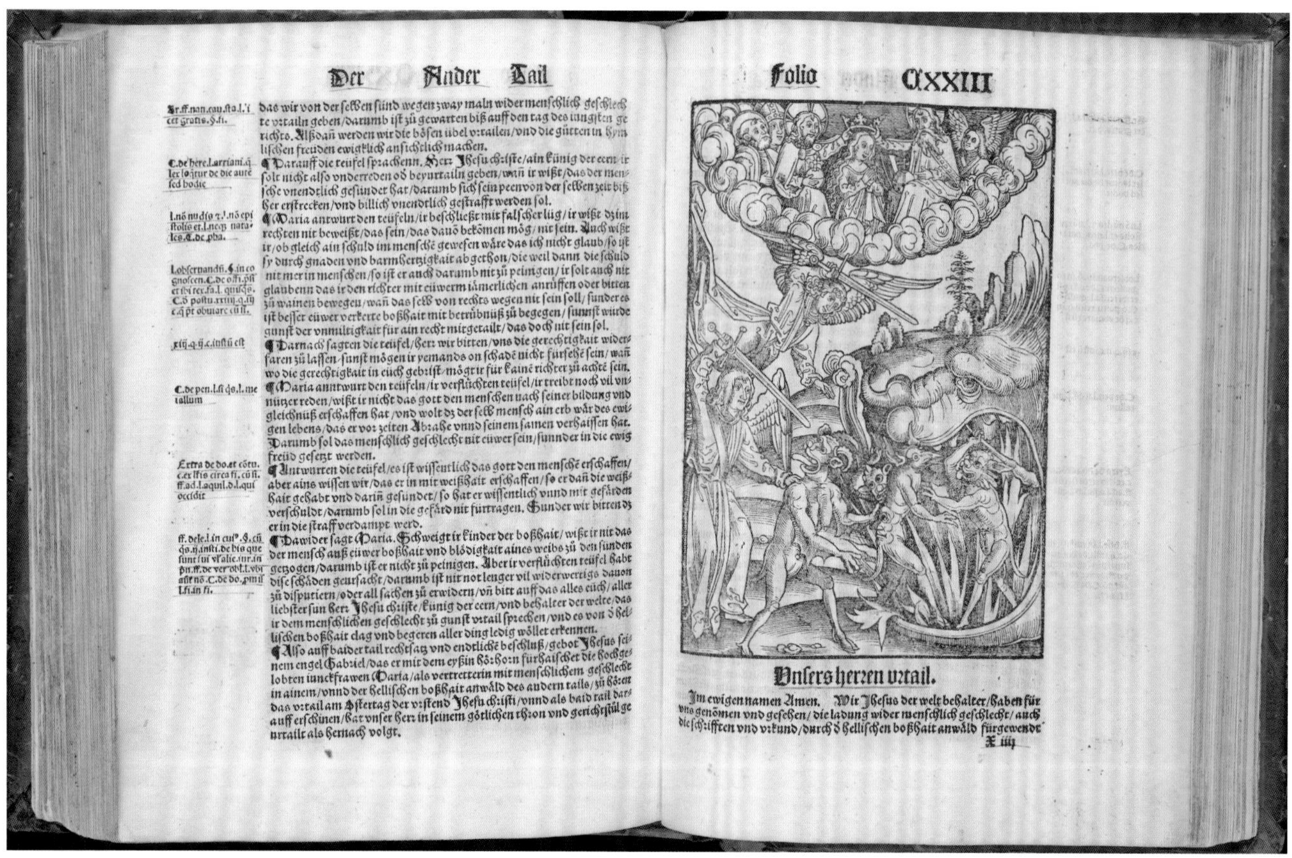

This symbol of judgment and justice appears in the first German-language treatise on Roman law. Celebrated for its introduction of basic principles of criminal law and procedure into the German states, the book also is notorious for its discussion of witches, magicians, heretics, and Jews. After over five hundred years, does this image retain its evocative power to divide worlds?

Antonius Matthaeus. 1.13

De judiciis disputationes septendecim.

3rd. ed. Amsterdam: Johannes Janssonius van Waesberghe, 1665. Engraving by Cornelis van Dalen. Roman-Canon Law Collection of the Association of the Bar of the City of New York.

The Greek historian Herodotus tells how Cambyses (d. 522), king of Persia, had the judge Sisamnes flayed alive for accepting a bribe. He then had the judge's skin stretched over a chair, and appointed Sisamnes's son to serve as his father's successor – "enjoining him to remember in what seat he was sitting to give judgment." Although now largely forgotten, the story was well known in early modern Europe, and adorns this analysis of seventeen legal cases.

1.14

William Sheppard.

A sure guide for His Majesties justices of peace.

London: John Streater for Henry & Timothy Twyford, 1663.

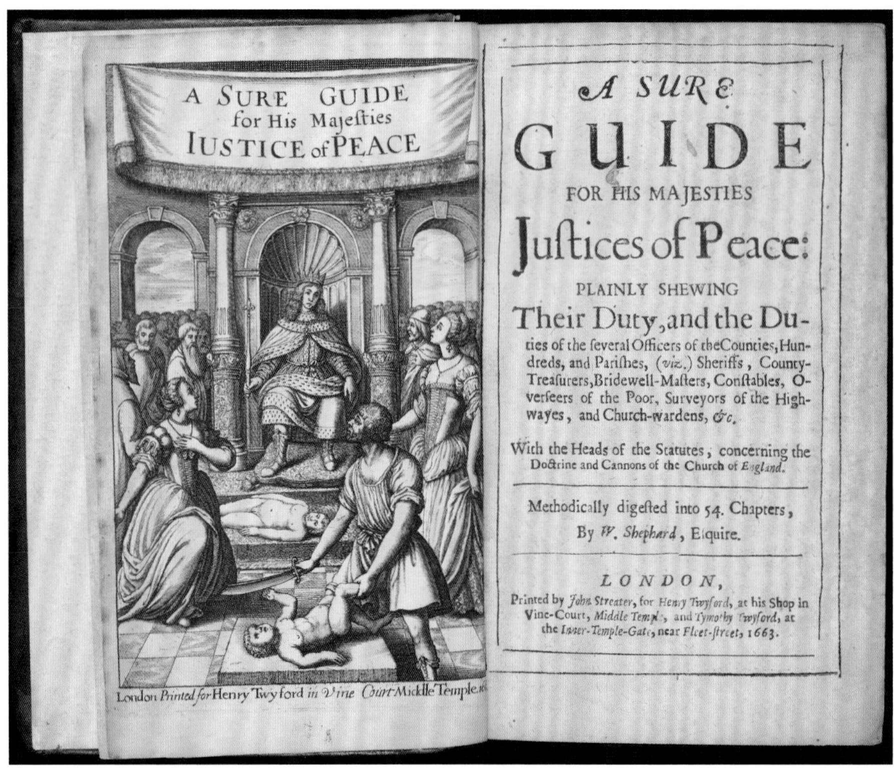

A SURE GUIDE
for His Majeſties
IUSTICE of PEACE

London Printed for Henry Twyford in Vine Court Middle Temple.

A SURE
GUIDE
FOR HIS MAJESTIES
Juſtices of Peace:
PLAINLY SHEWING
Their Duty, and the Duties of the ſeveral Officers of the Counties, Hundreds, and Pariſhes, (*viz.*) Sheriffs, County-Treaſurers, Bridewell-Maſters, Conſtables, Overſeers of the Poor, Surveyors of the Highwayes, and Church-wardens, *&c.*

With the Heads of the Statutes, concerning the Doctrine and Cannons of the Church of *England.*

Methodically digeſted into 54. Chapters,
By *W. Shephard*, Eſquire.

LONDON,
Printed by *John Streater*, for *Henry Twyford*, at his Shop in Vine-Court, *Middle Temple*, and *Tymothy Twyford*, at the *Inner-Temple-Gate*, near *Fleet-ſtreet*, 1663.

Another popular depiction of justice was the Judgment of Solomon. Like the author of *Marriage by the morall law of God* (item 1.10), the author of this volume was an English Puritan. An adviser to Oliver Cromwell, he wrote twenty-seven books, making him one of the most prolific legal authors of the seventeenth century.

Guillaume Le Rouillé.

Justicie atque iniusticie descriptionum compendium.

Paris: Claude Chevallon, 1520.

1.15

In this work of bookseller and printer Guillaume Le Rouillé (c. 1518-1589), a fearsome beast with both claws and cloven-hoofs symbolizes the origins of injustice. Each of its twelve legs represents one of injustice's foundations, such as "a lawless ruler." But some items wouldn't be considered sources of injustice today, such as "a woman without modesty," "a proud pauper," and "a disobedient child." Symbols of justice may lose their meaning as conceptions of justice change.

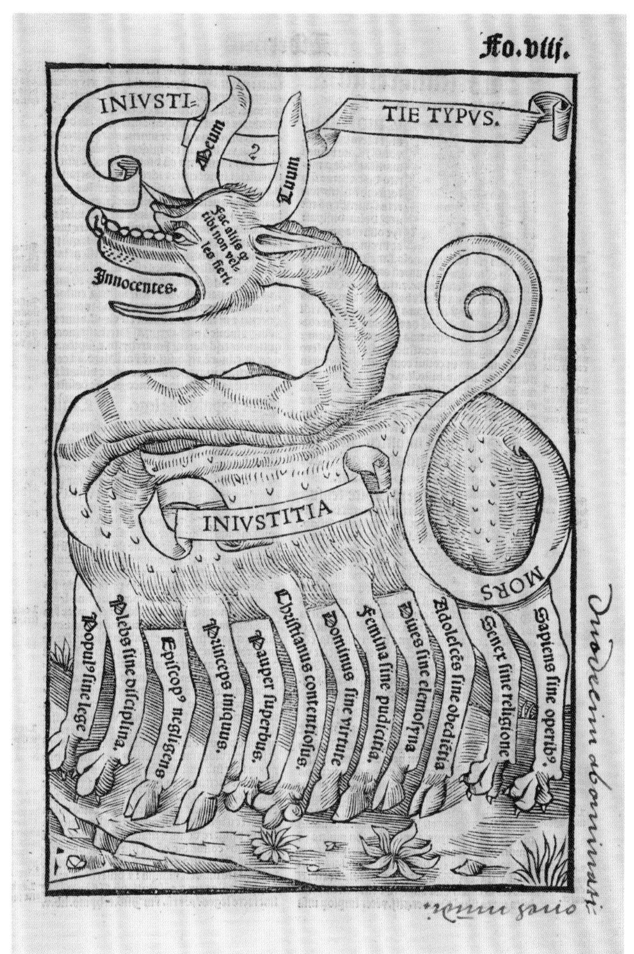

The works of the Flemish jurist Joost de Damhoudere (1507–1581) are among the most richly illustrated books in the history of legal literature. They were also exceedingly popular (see item 2.03).

Joost de Damhoudere. *Practycke in criminele saken.* Rotterdam: Pieter van Waesberge, 1650. Acquired with the Albert S. Wheeler Fund.

HET LXVII CAPITTEL.

Van Homicidie, dat gheheeten is doodt-ſlaghe.

't Begrijp.

1 Doodt-ſlagh, was het tweede Crime.
2 Adams ende Evaas inobedientie, was het eerſte Crime.
3 Doodt-ſlagh is deteſtable den Enghelen.
4 Doodt-ſlagh is alleen ghepunieert lijvelijck, in 't Gheeſtelijcke Recht.
5 Doodt-ſlaghs peyne, ſpruyten uyt der Wet van ghelijcken.
6 Doodt-ſlaghers, zijn ſchenders van 't menſchelijcke gheſlachte.
7 Doodt-ſlaghers wille, wanneerſe ghepunieert werdt.
8 Laghen uyt haer ſelven, zijn Crime.
9 d'Attentatie ſtaet voor 't faict.
10 Doodt-ſlagh is van Godt verboden.
11 Waerom den Menſche is d'edelſte Creatuer.

Den doodt-ſlagher hindert:
12 Godt, als Createur tweeſins.
13 Den Ghemeente, ende Prince.
14 d'Ouders, ende Gheſlachte van den verſlaghen.
15 Den verſlaghen boven al.

M 2 16 Op

Depicting the Law 2

A woman heedlessly dumps a chamber pot from a second-story window. A group of clergy physically block laity from assembling around an altar. A bearded man furtively moves a boundary stone. In illustrations such as these, figurative images illustrate specific passages of text and particular legal rules. They depict not the symbolic, but the concrete. What type of knives were prohibited in Genoa in 1646? Look to the image – there is the law.

Some illustrations are intended to instruct, others to delight, and others to critique. And, every now and then – because law is about life, after all – some images show a man and woman caught *in flagrante delicto.*

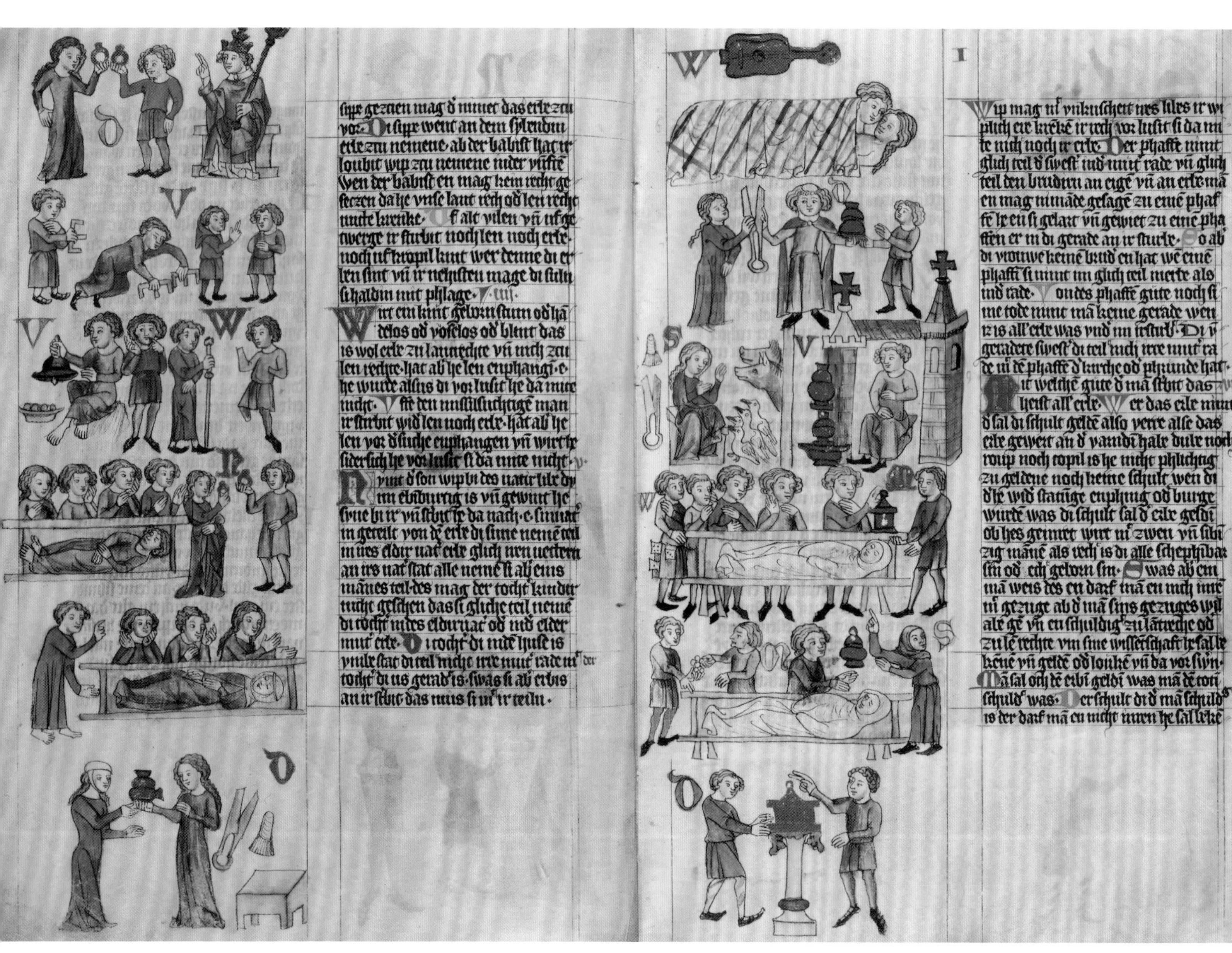

Eike von Repgow.

2.01

Vollstandige Faksimile-Ausgabe im Originalformat des Wolfenbütteler Sachsenspiegels [facsimile].

Graz: Akademische Druck- und Verlagsanstalt, 2006.

At bottom right, two men swear an oath on holy relics. At top right, a woman has lost her honor but not her inheritance by sleeping with – a lowly musician! A collection of German customary law from the thirteenth century, the *Sachsenspiegel* (the "mirror of the Saxons") remains unsurpassed in legal literature for its seamless integration of text and image. It contains an extraordinarily rich visual vocabulary of clothing, gestures, and objects.

2.02

Niccolò de' Tudeschi (Panormitanus).

Lectura super V libris decretalium.

Basel: Michael Wenssler, Berthold Ruppel & Bernard Richel, 1477. Volume 4 of 5. Acquired with the John A. Hoober Fund.

The rule so precisely illustrated in this important fifteenth-century commentary on canon law derives from the second Council of Tours of 567: "That the laity should be away from the altar when the holy mysteries are celebrated." Both the image and the blank space left for an introductory capital letter carry over design traditions from medieval manuscripts to the new medium of the printed book.

De vita et honestate clericorum.

De vita et honestate clericorum. Rub.

Omnipotentis dei postulato suffragio ut omnium in volumine ordinem fuisse servatum continuanda est prima rubrica ad precedentia que per decretum duobus modis continuatur et primo sic. Supra visum est de iudiciis et eius singulis partibus. sed quia clerici debent ab eis quantum possunt abstinere. nam decet servos dei parvo incommodo a strepitu iudiciorum esse quietos. c. unico. de sindico. Et quoniam non solum a iudiciis abstinere debent sed vita et honestate fulgere. Ideo post tractatum iudiciorum subicitur hec rubrica. hec tamen continuatio non est multum contexta cum precedentibus. unde forte ponitur secunda. Quia supra visum est de iudiciis et iudices maxime clerici non debent esse in peccato maxime cum iudicant. iii. q. vii. iudicet. Ideo post tractatum iuditiorum subicitur qualiter clerici debeant se habere in vita et honestate ut sic vitent omnem maculam peccati. Adverte tamen quia in hac continuatione decretum simpliciter dicunt quod existentes in peccato non possunt iudicare quod non est simpliciter verum. dic ergo quod ex mero iure iudicare alios non possunt sed ex potestate officii sic vide de hoc iii. q. vii. § fi. et in glo. sum. plene per Inno. in c. sciscitatus. § de Rep. et in c. cum venerabilis de excep. peccat tamen iudex alium iudicando si ipse peccator est. ut in c. iudicet. et in c. in grauibus. et c. qui sine. iii. q. vii. Et idem dic in sacerdotibus respectu fori penitentialis. peccant enim si existentes in peccato aliis penitentiam iniungunt licet absolutio teneat. deberet enim primo se corrigere saltem per contritionem et postmodum penitentiam aliis iniungere. et vide tex. cum glo. in v. iudicandus. de pe. dist. vi. c. i. glo. in dicto. c. in grauibus. Et utrum malorum sacerdotum preces noceant vel prosint illis pro quibus fiunt. vide tex. cum glo. in dicto. c. in grauibus. melius vide. xlix. di. in sum. Item adde et aliud quod licet malus sacerdos ita conficiat sicut bonus. i. q. i. multi. tamen facilius exaudiuntur boni sacerdotes quam mali. i. q. i. in c. ipsi sacerdotes. cum enim sint intercessores apud deum si displicent deo nedum exaudiuntur. sed potius deum ad iram provocant. unde tex. no. in d. c. in grauibus dicit quod si is qui displicet ad intercedendum mittitur irati animus ad deteriora provocatur. Nota illum tex. perpetuo pro ambasiatoribus destinandis ut eligantur hi qui sunt benivoli et accepti illi ad quem mittuntur. nam si displicent redibunt sine effectu. malus tamen sacerdos ex potestate officii etiam prophetare potest ut prophetavit cayphas. nam dicitur in euangelio prophetavit etc. Item fecit Saul dum prophetavit. David persequens. vide. i. q. i. dictum. et c. prophetavit Et utrum sancti et boni sacerdotes habeant semper spiritum sanctum. an vero recedat ad tempus. et que doctrina fuit inter sanctos et xpm respectu spus sancti vide tex. in c. querendum. de pe. di. ii. Tertio potest ordinari et aptius ut. § in prohe. continuatur. nam in primo libro dixit de

Joost de Damhoudere.

Praxis rerum criminalium.

Antwerp: Jean Beller, 1556.

2.03

362 PRAXIS

adijcere libuit, ipſos ſecundum iura ciuilia, nuſquam locorum eſſe liberos, ne in templis quidẽ, aut cæmeterijs, in Autẽt. de manda. Princip. §. quòd ſi delinquẽtes, colla. 3. verſicul. Neque gloſſa. in verb. Publicus latro, in cap. inter alia, extr. de immunita. Eccleſ.

De permiſsione adulterij. Cap. 90.

SVMMARIA.

Lenocinium mariti, puniendum exilio. 1.
Maritus ex vxore quæſtum faciens, punitur exilio. 2.
Clancularium vxoris adulterium, per maritum non eſt deferendum iudici. 3.
Signa manifeſti, & certi occulti & incerti adulterij. 4.
Coniectura adulterij elicitur ex loci qualitate, perſonarum qualitate, & actu, & modo. 5.
Mariti improba in vxoris adulterio conniuentia non eſt ferenda iudici. 6.
Francorum frequentia adulteria, vnde naſcantur. 7.
Franci de adulterio nullam ferunt ſententiam pœnalem iuris. 8.
Exemplum. 9.
Alterum exemplum. 10.

Sicut ex ſuperiori capite conſtat grauiter eſſe puniendos, qui turpiter adulteria cõmittunt: ita non minus puniendi ſunt qui vxoris adulteria cum illo ſatyrico dicente (non omnibus dormio) diſsimulanter ferunt, & vxores ſuas in ea turpitudine quaſi fouent, & alunt. Maritus
1 igitur, qui ſciens volénſque diſsimulat, & permittit vxorem adulterari, ita vt nec verbis, nec re vlla illi adulteranti obſiſtat, nec ipſam ab adultero retrahat, vel nec ipſam à ſe dimoueat, is ob vxorij adulterij diſsimulationẽ damnandus eſt exilio, aut alia ſimili pœna arbitraria Iudicis.
2 Multò igitur magis dictis pœnis, aut acrioribus eſt cõdẽnãdus, quoties ex vxoris adulterio vllũ ſibi quęſtũ parat, aut lucrum: hoc enim faciẽdo crimẽ pręterea committit lenocinij

RERVM CRIMINALIVM. 363

lenocinij, lege 2. §. lenocinij. ff. ad l. Iul. de adult. & l. 2. C. eod. titul. & ibi gloſſa. Verum hic ſciendum, ſi adulterium vxoris non fuerit manifeſtum, nihílque de eo certi habeatur in ore, & notitia vulgi, præter incertã ſuſpicionem & rumuſculum popularem, quem maritus facilè ſua prudentia, & probitate tueri poſſet & tegere, in eo caſu

Aa iij non

Today the situation illustrated here might today be called an "open marriage." In the sixteenth century, it was a felony. This handbook of criminal law is one of the most successful books in the history of legal literature, appearing in thirty-nine editions in four languages between 1554 and 1660. Its five dozen illustrations are prominent, indispensible features of the volume, making it not simply a book with illustrations, but rather a true "illustrated book."

2.04

Joost de Damhoudere.

La practique et enchiridion des causes criminelles.

Louvain: Etienne Wauters & Johan Bathen, 1555. Illustrations by Gerard de Jode.
Acquired with the John A. Hoober Fund.

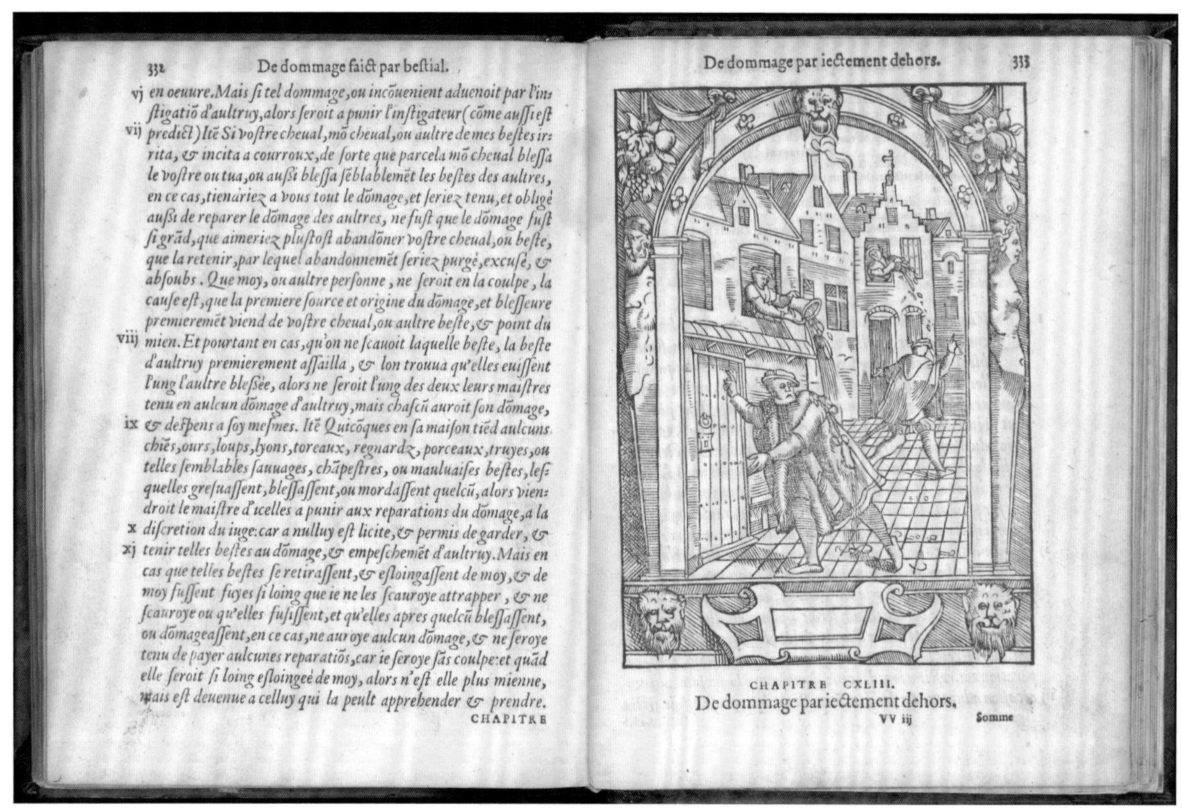

332 De dommage faict par beſtial.

vj en oeuure. Mais ſi tel dommage, ou incōuenient aduenoit par l'in-
ſtigatiō d'aultruy, alors ſeroit a punir l'inſtigateur (cōme auſſi eſt
vij predict) Itē Si voſtre cheual, mō cheual, ou aultre de mes beſtes ir-
rita, & incita a courroux, de ſorte que parcela mō cheual bleſſa
le voſtre ou tua, ou auſſi bleſſa ſēblablemēt les beſtes des aultres,
en ce cas, tiendriez a vous tout le dōmage, et ſeriez tenu, et obligé
auſſi de reparer le dōmage des aultres, ne fuſt que le dōmage fuſt
ſi grād, que aimeriez pluſtoſt abandōner voſtre cheual, ou beſte,
que la retenir, par lequel abandonnemēt ſeriez purgé, excuſé, &
abſoubs. Que moy, ou aultre perſonne, ne ſeroit en la coulpe, la
cauſe eſt, que la premiere ſource et origine du dōmage, et bleſſeure
premieremēt viend de voſtre cheual, ou aultre beſte, & point du
viij mien. Et pourtant en cas, qu'on ne ſcauoit laquelle beſte, la beſte
d'aultruy premierement aſſailla, & lon trouua qu'elles euiſſent
l'ung l'aultre bleſſée, alors ne ſeroit l'ung des deux leurs maiſtres
tenu en aulcun dōmage d'aultruy, mais chaſcū auroit ſon dōmage,
ix & deſpens a ſoy meſmes. Itē Quicōques en ſa maiſon tiēd aulcuns
chiēs, ours, loups, lyons, toreaux, regnardz, porceaux, truyes, ou
telles ſemblables ſauuages, chāpeſtres, ou mauluaiſes beſtes, leſ-
quelles greſuaſſent, bleſſaſſent, ou mordaſſent quelcū, alors vien-
droit le maiſtre d'icelles a punir aux reparations du dōmage, a la
x diſcretion du iuge: car a nulluy eſt licite, & permis de garder, &
xj tenir telles beſtes au dōmage, & empeſchemēt d'aultruy. Mais en
cas que telles beſtes ſe retiraſſent, & eſloingaſſent de moy, & de
moy fuſſent fuyes ſi loing que ie ne les ſcauroye attrapper, & ne
ſcauroye ou qu'elles fuſiſſent, et qu'elles apres quelcū bleſſaſſent,
ou dōmageaſſent, en ce cas, ne auroye aulcun dōmage, & ne ſeroye
tenu de payer aulcunes reparatiōs, car ie ſeroye ſās coulpe: et quād
elle ſeroit ſi loing eſloingeé de moy, alors n'eſt elle plus mienne,
mais eſt deuenue a celluy qui la peult apprehender & prendre.
CHAPITRE

De dommage par iectement dehors. 333

CHAPITRE CXLIII.
De dommage par iectement dehors.
VV iij Somme

Damhoudere's treatise on criminal law stood out from the competition for its lively depictions of specific crimes. The illustration shows pedestrians fleeing the falling household garbage – or worse – unlawfully thrown onto public streets. Scholars know that the illustrations were Damhoudere's idea – he railed against lazy and expensive illustrators for failing to provide images for some chapters.

Joost de Damhoudere.

Practycke in criminele saecken.

Rotterdam: Jean van Waesberge, 1628.

2.05

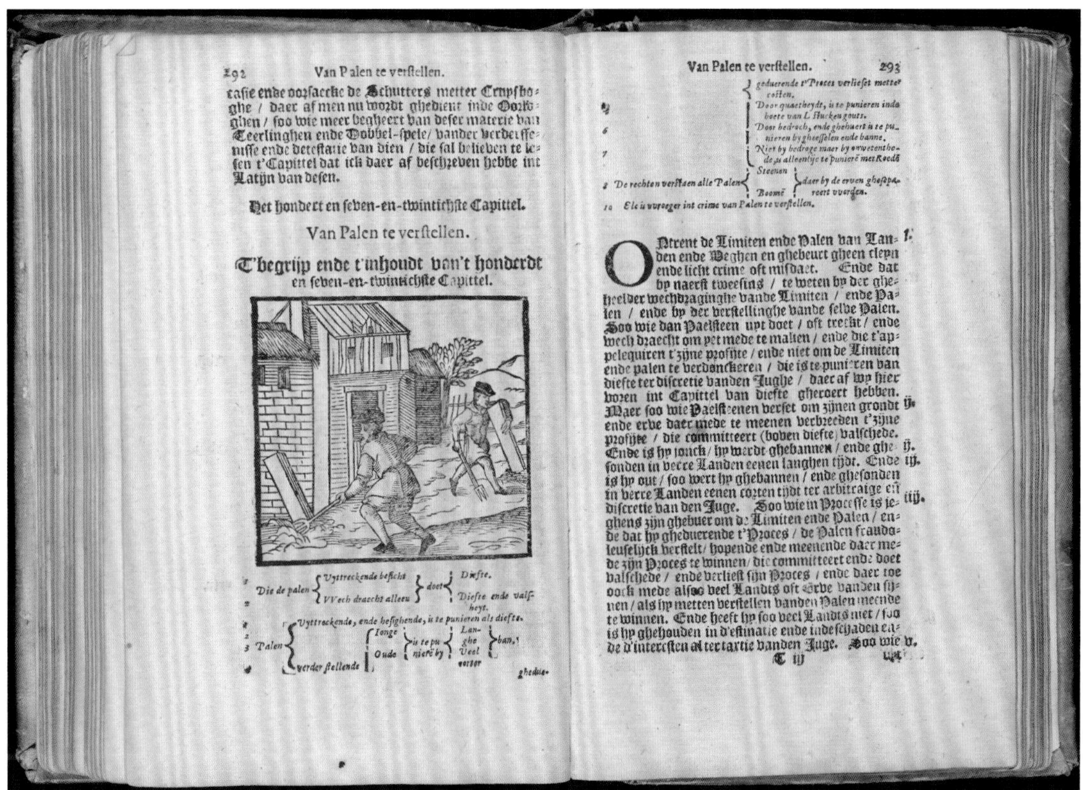

292 Van Palen te verstellen.

casie ende oorsaecke de Schutters metter Cruysboghe / daer af men nu wordt ghedient inde Oorloghen / soo wie meer begheert van deser materie van Teerlinghen ende Dobbel-spele / vander verderffenisse ende detestatie van dien / die sal believen te lesen t'Capittel dat ick daer af beschreven hebbe int Latijn van desen.

Het hondert en seven-en-twintichste Capittel.

Van Palen te verstellen.

T'begrijp ende t'inhoudt van't honderdt en seven-en-twintichste Capittel.

Die de palen { Uyttreckende besicht / VVech draecht alleen } doet { Dieste. / Dieste ende valsheyt.

Uyttreckende, ende besighende, is te punieren als dieste.

Palen { verder stellende { Ionge / Oude } is te punierē by { Langhe / Veel corter } ban.

Van Palen te verstellen. 293

geduerende t'Proces verlieset metter costen.

Door quaetheydt, is te punieren inde boete van L stucken gouts.

Door bedrogh, ende ghebuert is te punieren by gheesselen ende banne.

Niet by bedroge maer by onwetentheyde, is alleenlijc te punierē met Roedē

De rechten verstaen alle Palen { Steenen / Boomē } daer by de erven ghespareert worden.

Elc is vvroeger int crime van Palen te verstellen.

Omtrent de Limiten ende Palen van Landen ende Weghen en ghebeurt gheen cleyn ende licht crime oft misdaet. Ende dat by naerst tweesins / te weten by der gheelder wechdraginghe vande Limiten / ende Palen / ende by der verstellinghe vande selve Palen. 1.
Soo wie dan Paelsteen uyt doet / oft treckt / ende wech draecht om yet mede te maken / ende die t'appelequiren t'zijne profijte / ende niet om de Limiten ende palen te verdonckeren / die is te punieren van dieste ter discretie vanden Iughe / daer af wy hier voren int Capittel van dieste gheroert hebben.
Maer soo wie Paelsteenen verset om zijnen gronde ij.
ende erve daer mede te meenen verbreeden t'zijne profijte / die committeert (boven dieste) valschede.
Ende is hy jonck / hy werdt ghebannen / ende ghe- ij.
sonden in verre Landen eenen langhen tijdt. Ende iij.
is hy out / soo wert hy ghebannen / ende ghesonden in verre Landen eenen corten tijdt ter arbitraige en iiij.
discretie van den Iuge. Soo wie in Processe is jeghens zijn ghebuer om de Limiten ende Palen / ende dat hy gheduerende t'Proces / de Palen fraudeleuselijck verstelt / hopende ende meenende daer mede zijn Proces te winnen / die committeert ende doet valschede / ende verliest sijn Proces / ende daer toe oock mede alsoo veel Landts oft Erve vanden sijnen / als hy metten verstellen vanden Palen meende te winnen. Ende heeft hy soo veel Landts niet / soo is hy ghehouden in d'estimatie ende inde schaden ende d'interesten al ter tartie vanden Iuge. Soo wie v.

C iij

Illustrations were an enduring feature of Damhoudere's *Praxis Rerum Criminalium*, appearing in twenty-four of its thirty-nine editions. Later Dutch editions, like this one, reproduced the original illustrations in a more folksy style. The oblong posts depicted here are boundary markers. What are the two men doing with them?

2.06

Decretales Domini pape Gregorij noni.

Venice: Luca-Antonio Giunta, 1514. Acquired with the John A. Hoober Fund.

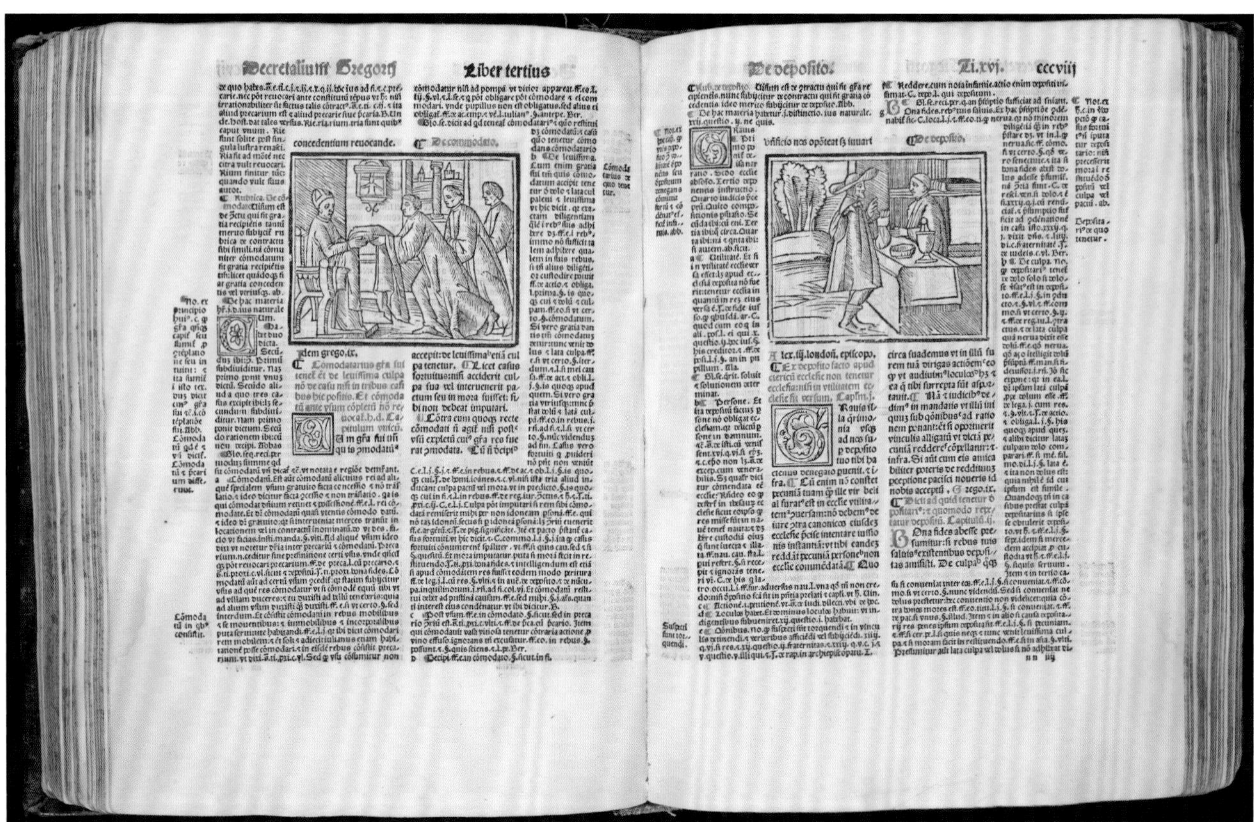
Decretalium Gregorij Liber tertius

De deposito. Ti.xvi. cccviij

One hundred and seventy-two woodcuts grace this essential text of canon law, the law book in the Yale collection with the greatest number of illustrations. *Commodatum* is a gratuitous loan of an item on fixed terms, for a specific purpose. In the discussion of *commodatum* at left, the image shows a man borrowing an item from a prelate – or, one hopes, returning it. The Catholic Church governed many aspects of life outside the strictly religious sphere.

Justinus Göbler.

Statutenbuch, Gesatz, Ordnungen und Gebrauch, keyserlicher, allgemeyner.

Frankfurt: Christian Egenolff, 1572.

2.07

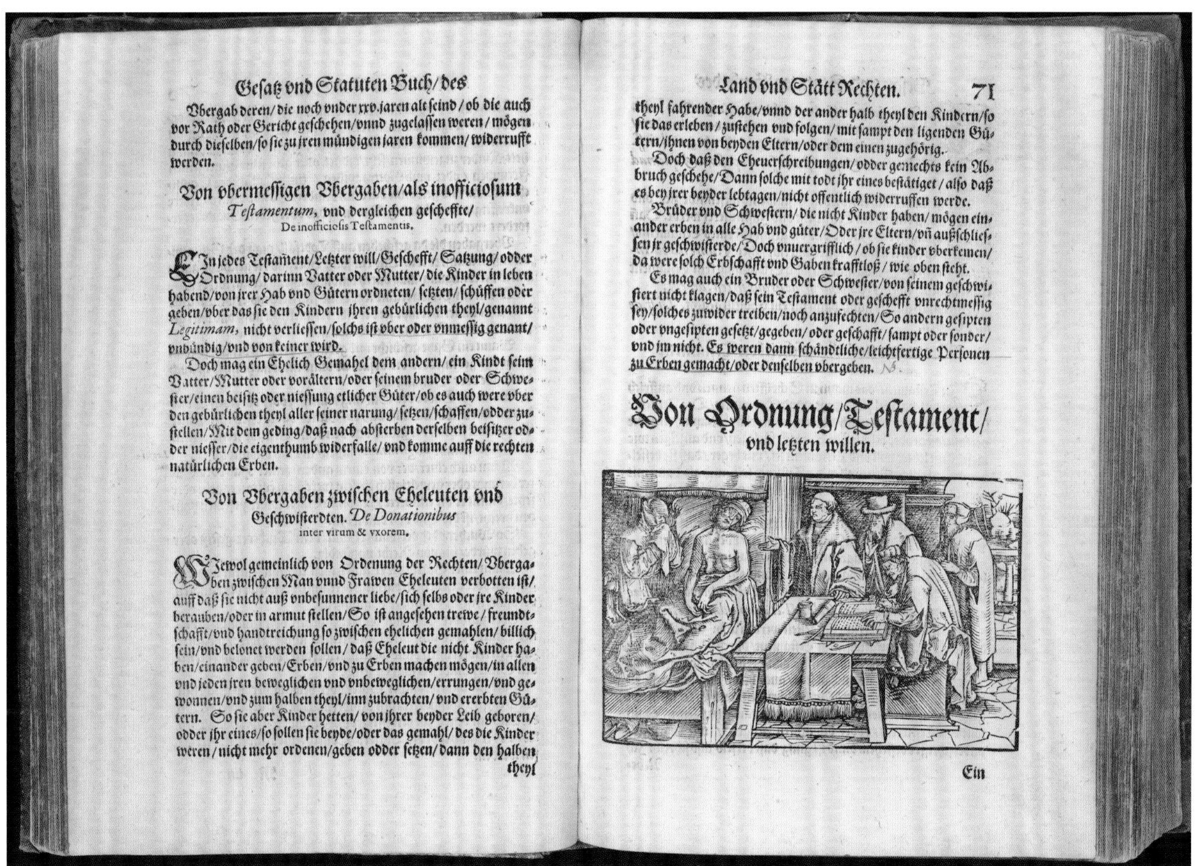

Gesatz vnd Statuten Buch/ des

Vbergab deren/ die noch vnder xxv. jaren alt seind / ob die auch vor Rath oder Gericht geschehen/ vnnd zugelassen weren / mögen durch dieselben/ so sie zu jren mündigen jaren kommen/ widerrufft werden.

Von vbermessigen Vbergaben/ als inofficiosum *Testamentum*, vnd dergleichen gescheffte/ De inofficiosis Testamentis.

EIn jedes Testament/ Letzter will/ Geschefft/ Satzung/ odder Ordnung/ darinn Vatter oder Mutter/ die Kinder in leben habend/ von jrer Hab vnd Gütern ordneten/ setzten/ schüffen oder geben/ vber das sie den Kindern jhren gebürlichen theyl/ genannt *Legitimam*, nicht verliessen/ solchs ist vber oder vnmessig genant/ vnbündig/ vnd von keiner wird.

Doch mag ein Ehelich Gemahel dem andern/ ein Kindt seim Vatter/ Mutter oder vorältern/ oder seinem bruder oder Schwester/ einen beisitz oder niessung etlicher Güter/ ob es auch were vber den gebürlichen theyl aller seiner narung/ setzen/ schaffen/ odder zustellen/ Mit dem geding/ daß nach absterben derselben beisitzer odder niesser/ die eigenthumb widerfalle/ vnd komme auff die rechten natürlichen Erben.

Von Vbergaben zwischen Eheleuten vnd Geschwisterdten. *De Donationibus* inter virum & vxorem.

WIewol gemeinlich von Ordenung der Rechten/ Vbergaben zwischen Man vnnd Frawen Eheleuten verbotten ist/ auff daß sie nicht auß vnbesunnener liebe/ sich selbs oder jre Kinder berauben/ oder in armut stellen/ So ist angesehen trewe / freundtschafft/ vnd handtreichung so zwischen ehelichen gemahlen/ billich sein/ vnd belonet werden sollen / daß Eheleut die nicht Kinder haben/ einander geben/ Erben/ vnd zu Erben machen mögen/ in allen vnd jeden jren beweglichen vnd vnbeweglichen/ errungen/ vnd gewonnen/ vnd zum halben theyl/ inn zubrachten/ vnd ererbten Gütern. So sie aber Kinder hetten/ von jhrer beyder Leib geboren/ odder jhr eines/ so sollen sie beyde/ oder das gemahl/ des die Kinder weren / nicht mehr ordenen/ geben odder setzen/ dann den halben theyl

Land vnd Stätt Rechten. 71

theyl fahrender Habe/ vnnd der ander halb theyl den Kindern/ so sie das erleben / zustehen vnd folgen/ mit sampt den ligenden Gütern/ jhnen von beyden Eltern/ oder dem einen zugehörig.

Doch daß den Eheuerschreibungen/ odder gemechts kein Abbruch geschehe/ Dann solche mit todt jhr eines bestätiget / also daß es bey jrer beyder lebtagen/ nicht offentlich widerruffen werde.

Brüder vnd Schwestern/ die nicht Kinder haben/ mögen einander erben in alle Hab vnd güter/ Oder jre Eltern/ vnd außschliessen jr geschwisterde/ Doch vnuergrifflich / ob sie kinder vberkemen/ da were solch Erbschafft vnd Gaben krafftloß / wie oben steht.

Es mag auch ein Bruder oder Schwester/ von seinem geschwistert nicht klagen/ daß sein Testament oder geschefft vnrechtmessig sey/ solches zuwider treiben/ noch anzufechten/ So andern gesipten oder vngesipten gesetzt/ gegeben/ oder geschafft/ sampt oder sonder/ vnd jm nicht. Es weren dann schändtliche/ leichtfertige Personen zu Erben gemacht/ oder denselben vbergeben.

Von Ordnung/ Testament/ vnd letzten willen.

Ein

An authoritative commentary on German law, this volume is illustrated with nineteen woodcuts, including many narrative engravings of legal processes – in this case, the taking of a last will and testament. Note the lawyer's tools spread across his desk, and the focused attention he maintains on his work.

2.08

Veit Guggenberger.

Ayd-Buch: warinnen findig das ayd, und ayd-schwur seyen, wie mancherley derselben gefunden.

Munich: Heinrich Theodor von Cöllen, 1738.

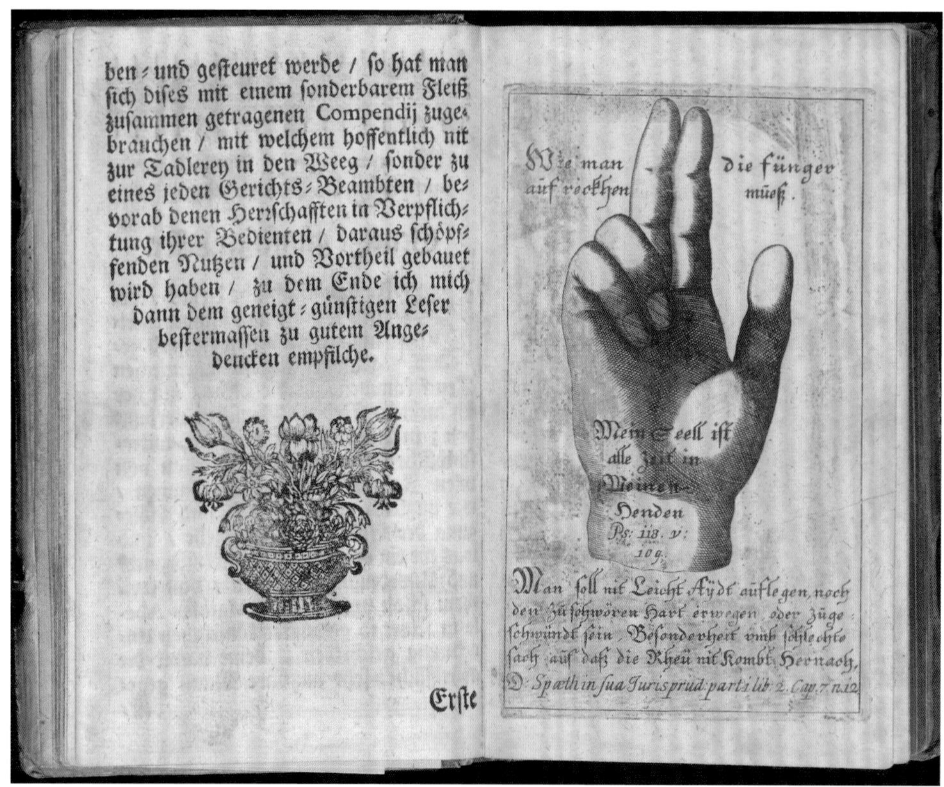
ben = und gesteuret werde / so hat man
sich dises mit einem sonderbarem Fleiß
zusammen getragenen Compendij zuge=
brauchen / mit welchem hoffentlich nit
zur Tadlerey in den Weeg / sonder zu
eines jeden Gerichts=Beambten / be=
vorab denen Herrschafften in Verpflich=
tung ihrer Bedienten / daraus schöpf=
fenden Nutzen / und Vortheil gebauet
wird haben / zu dem Ende ich mich
dann dem geneigt=günstigen Leser
bestermassen zu gutem Ange=
dencken empfilche.

Erste

This treatise on the administration of the oaths of different trades – including apothecaries, doctors, bakers, architects, and grave-diggers – includes this plate showing the proper hand gesture for oath-taking. The text written on the palm and wrist cites a passage from Psalms that translates as "My soul is continually in my hand, yet do I not forget your law."

2.09

Genoa (Italy).

Prohibitione de coltelli.

Genoa: Giovanni Maria Farroni, 1646.

PROHIBITIONE

DE COLTELLI

Essendo stata nuouamente introdotta à notitia de Serenissimi Colleggi vna forma di Coltelli stretti, e con punta talmente accuta, che euidentemente si vede dalla forma che si conserua in Palazzo, e che resta impressa in margine del presente proclama esser fatti totalmente per pungere, e non per tagliare, e circa la prohibitione di essi militano assolutamente tutte le ragioni, che già diedero motiuo di prohibire i Fuselli alla somiglianza de quali questi onninamente s'accostano. Volendo perciò i Serenissimi Colleggi riparare à gl'inconuenienti grãdi che possono succedere con l'vso di simili armi in pregiuditio del seruiggio publico, & della vita di particolari; hanno deliberato che se ne publichi la prohibitione con gl'ordini seguenti, cioè.

Che non possa qualsiuoglia persona di qual stato, grado, e conditione che sia compresi anco li Colonelli, Capitani e Soldati, Stipendiati della Republica, & ogn'altro che hauesse licenza d'armi, portare, tenire, fabricare, acconciare, contrattare, introdure, ne fare introdure, cõtrattare, o fabricare simile sorte di Coltelli sotto pena di anni cinque di relegatione nel Regno di Corsica, ò di tre anni di Galera à giuditio, & in arbitrio de Serenissimi Colleggi. Dalle quali pene respettiuamente possa essimersi chi v'incorrerà con pagare in Camera Illustrissima scuti cinquecento d'oro.

Che li relegati per il sudetto cõto siano obligati mandar fede autentica di sei in sei mesi dell'ossaruanza di detta relegatione, ò vero presentarle tutte insieme finita essa relegatione, altrimente non s'intenda che l'habbiano osseruata, ma debbano cominciarla di nuouo per tutti detti anni cinque.

Che li relegati come sopra debbano dar sigortà prima di vscir di Carcere d'approuarsi dal Serenissimo Senato, ò Serenis. Colleggi della somma di scuti due milla d'oro in oro, in osseruatione di detta relegatione, la quale sigortà non dandosi frà vn mese dal dì che gli sarà notificata la sentenza debba osseruarla in Galera à vogare, ò in carcere in arbitrio de prefati Serenis. Colleggi, a qual resti facoltà di moderar detta somma della sigortà in quella minore che loro parerà hauuto risguardo all'essere, e qualità del condannato.

Che tutti li Coltelleri, & ogni altri che hauessero appresso di loro, ò à loro dispositione coltelli della sudetta qualità debbano disfarsene frà il termine di giorni quindeci dal dì della publicatione della presente, acciò del tutto resti estirpata essa qualità d'Armi quali giorni spirati sia immediatamente luogo all'osseruanza di quanto sopra.

Del che tutto hanno lor SS. Serenissime decretato si facci la presente publica Grida, acciò ad alcuno non possa in verun tempo esserne pretesa ignoranza ne scusa.

Data in Genoua nel Palazzo Regale a 3. Ottobre 1646.

Nella Cancellaria del M. Horatio Dulmeta Cancelliere, e Segretario.

1646. adi 12. Ottobre,

SI è publicato il presente proclama à suono di tromba con alta, & intelligibile voce per me Marc'Antonio Bianco Cintraco publico in Piazza di Banchi, & per tutte le Piazze della presente Città, & nelli Borghi di Bisagno, & Borgo di S. Lazaro, e Lochi soliti, e consueti.

Detto Marc'Antonio.

IN GENOVA, Per Gio: Maria Farroni.

The Republic of Genoa left no doubt about precisely what kind of knife was prohibited in the city – it included an image of it in this proclamation. The words "costa" and "lama" appear on the blade in mirror image, indicating the spine and edge sides of the weapon. The broadside notes that these wicked blades were designed for stabbing, not cutting.

2.10

Henry Woodhouse.
Textbook of aerial laws: and regulations for aerial navigation, international, national and municipal, civil and military.
New York: Frederick A. Stokes, 1920.

These photographs from the infancy of air travel demonstrate the potential of aircraft as tools for smuggling people and goods. They are among the first photographs to appear in a legal treatise. The plane depicted at upper left is "equipped for overnight travel." The *Textbook of Aerial Laws* includes a dedicated space for reader notes. The author was an aviation enthusiast, not a lawyer, who later became notorious as a forger of historical documents.

How a third person can be smuggled in an apparent two-seater aeroplane. The type shown herewith is a Breguet aerial touring plane, equipped for overnight travel with upper and lower berths.

Checking the cargo of an aeroplane at an aerodrome to comply with the custom laws and prevent smuggling.

Face p. 47

Russia (Federation). 2.11

Illiustrirovannyi Trudovoi kodeks Rossiiskoi Federatsii.

Moscow: Izdatelstvo "Mann, Ivanov i Ferber", 2014. Illustrations by Alexei Merinov. Gift of William E. Butler, 2014.

ЧАСТЬ ТРЕТЬЯ | Раздел VI. Оплата и нормирование труда

Ст. 149

Статья 149. Оплата труда в других случаях выполнения работ в условиях, отклоняющихся от нормальных

При выполнении работ в условиях, отклоняющихся от нормальных (при выполнении работ различной квалификации, совмещении профессий (должностей), сверхурочной работе, работе в ночное время, выходные и нерабочие праздничные дни и при выполнении работ в других условиях, отклоняющихся от нормальных), работнику производятся соответствующие выплаты, предусмотренные трудовым законодательством и иными нормативными правовыми актами, содержащими нормы трудового права, коллективным договором, соглашениями, локальными нормативными актами, трудовым договором. Размеры выплат, установленные коллективным договором, соглашениями, локальными нормативными актами, трудовым договором, не могут быть ниже установленных трудовым законодательством и иными нормативными правовыми актами, содержащими нормы трудового права.

232

Глава 21. Заработная плата

Ст. 150

Статья 150. Оплата труда при выполнении работ различной квалификации

При выполнении работником с повременной оплатой труда работ различной квалификации его труд оплачивается по работе более высокой квалификации.

При выполнении работником со сдельной оплатой труда работ различной квалификации его труд оплачивается по расценкам выполняемой им работы.

В случаях, когда с учетом характера производства работникам со сдельной оплатой труда поручается выполнение работ, тарифицируемых ниже присвоенных им разрядов, работодатель обязан выплатить им межразрядную разницу.

233

"I had never expected the Labor Code to be such an interesting subject to illustrate in cartoons," explains Russian illustrator Alexei Merinov (b. 1959). "I've done it with a leftist slant: It's full of Soviet sickles and hammers, greedy fat cats and senior Russian bureaucrats." The image at right illustrates a paragraph of the code regulating compensation for work performed at varying qualification levels. "So who ordered fried chicken?!"

A Tree Grows in Bookland

Diagrams like this one trace their origin to geometric charts of Roman inheritance law. They begin to resemble trees in illuminated manuscripts around the twelfth century, when the church was systematizing its marriage law. Among the visual ways to depict kinship, the tree likely appealed to medieval concepts of organic order, and perhaps brought to mind the Tree of Jesse and the symbolic role of trees in Christian theology.

Liber sextus Decretalium D. Bonifacii Papae VIII.
Venice: Giunta, 1600.
Acquired with the John A. Hoober Fund.

240 Arbor. seu figura declaratiua tituli de iure patronatus.

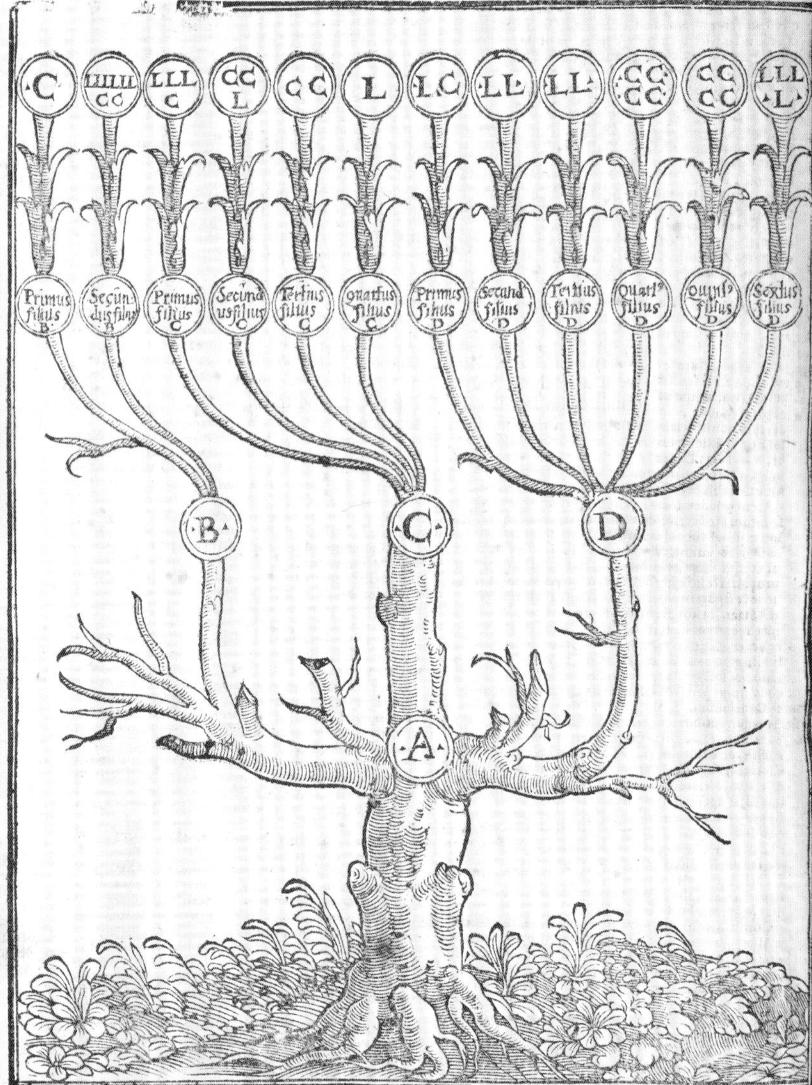

RO istius arboris declaratione, quã format glossa hic, præmitte q A patronus positus in radice siue in prima cellula istius arboris habuit tres filios, scilicet B.C.D. vt patet ascẽdẽdo ad tres cellulas sequentes, & duodecim nepotes, vt patet ascẽdẽdo ad duodecim cellulas immediate sequentes: & triginta & septẽ pro nepotes tã laicos quàm clericos, vt patet ascendẽdo ad duodecim vltimas cellulas. Et aduerte q in istis vltimis cellulis clerici significantur p istã litterã C. & laici.

Diagramming the Law

3

FOR CENTURIES, THE MOST COMMON ILLUSTRATION IN LAW BOOKS was a visual metaphor drawn from the natural world: the tree. As a graphic device used in legal textbooks and treatises, trees of consanguinity and affinity helped readers grasp the legal significance of kinship for marriage and inheritance. By depicting legal relationships in spatial terms, trees represent those relationships more efficiently than is possible through language. They stand beside their text neither as allegories of the spirit of the whole nor as illustrations of a specific part but rather as concise charts of an extended structure of analysis.

The metaphor of the tree long persisted as a beguiling way to depict kinship and its legal consequences. Its success also gave bud to new ways to crisply display legal and conceptual relationships.

3.01

Giovanni d'Andrea.

De arbore consanguineitatis et affinitatis.

Manuscript on vellum, Italy, 14th century. Acquired with the John A. Hoober Fund.

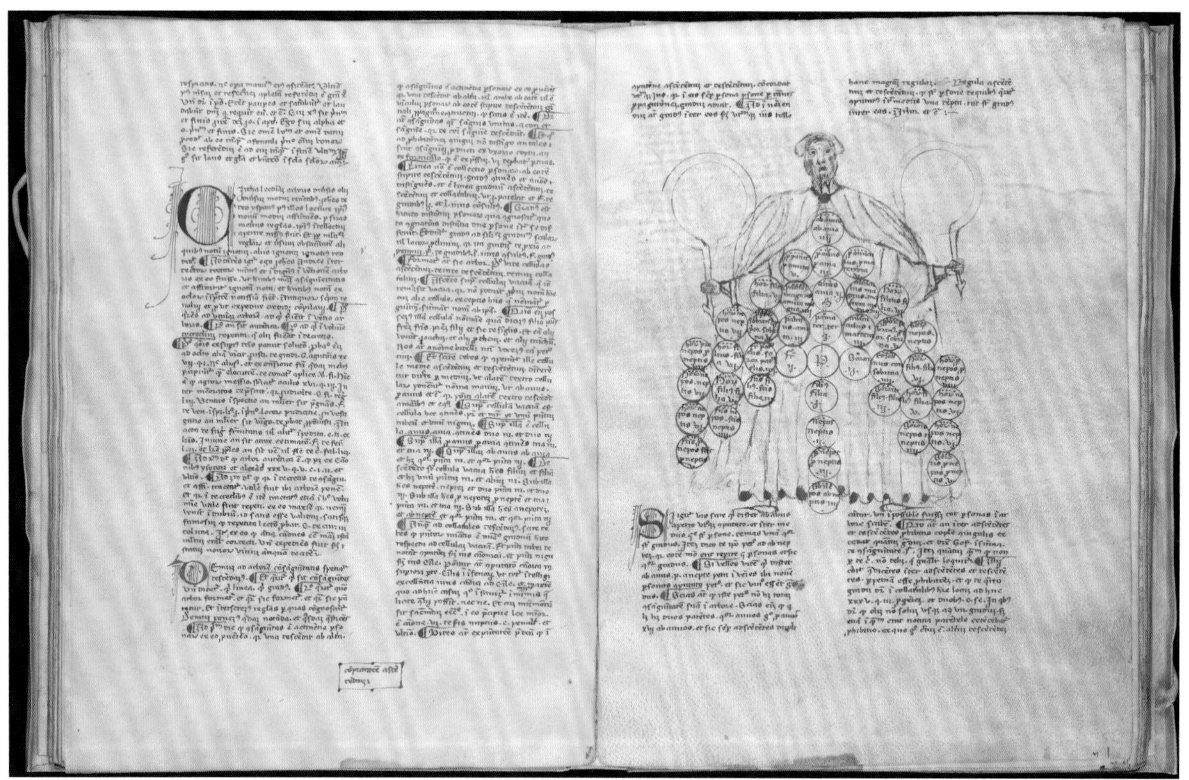

This "tree" diagrams inter-generational kinship relations to determine when a marriage is permissible based on ecclesiastical law. Each medallion represents a member of an extended family group, identified according its relation to a reference figure. The work of canon law scholar Giovanni d'Andrea (ca. 1270-1348), which formed the backbone of marriage law in Europe for centuries, follows marriage rules promulgated by the Fourth Lateran Council of 1215.

Giovanni d'Andrea.

Super arboribus consanguinitatis et affinitatis.

Nuremberg: Friedrich Creussner, ca. 1473. Acquired with the John A. Hoober Fund.

3.02

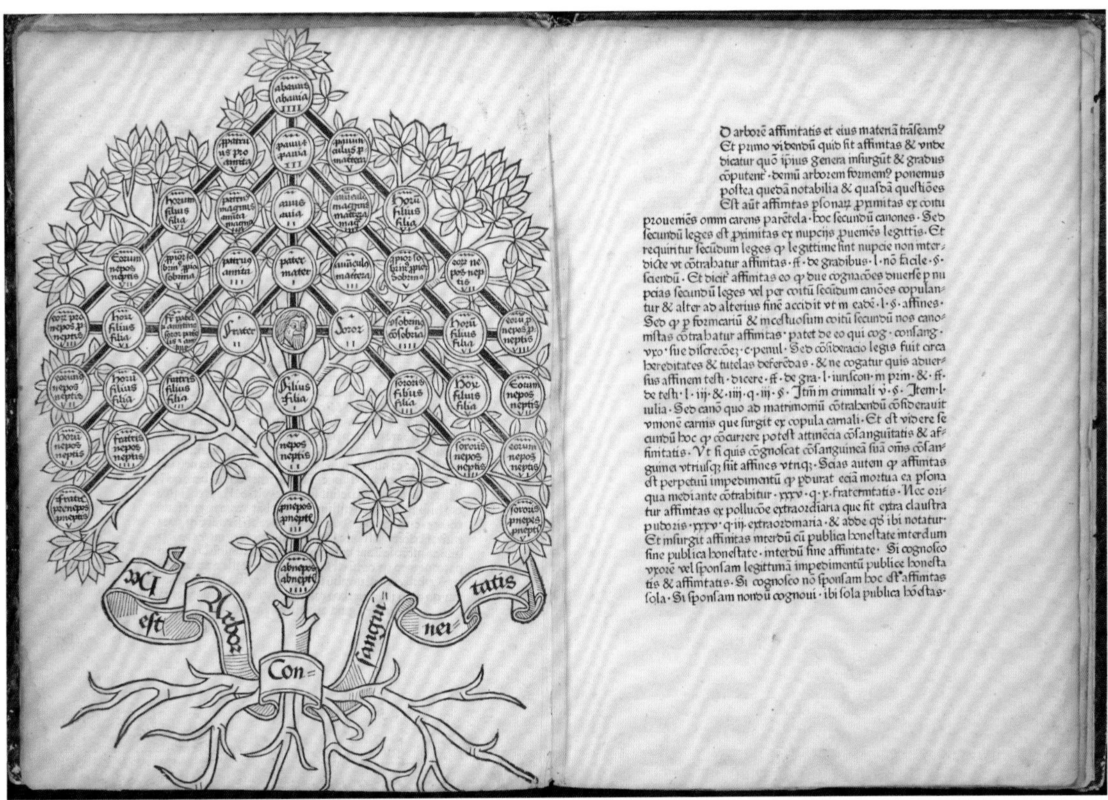

This image may very well be the first illustration to appear in a printed law book. Its reference medallion includes an image of a bearded man. Compare this illustration with that in item 3.01. Although published here as an individual item, Giovanni d'Andrea's essay was often included as an appendix in books of canon law.

3.03

De haereditatibus quae ab intestato deferunt.

Manuscript, Italy?, 17th century?

This copy of student notes from a course on the Roman law of inheritance and succession includes an exceptionally handsome tree, or *arbor*, of consanguinity. The chart appears to be set in a Tuscan landscape featuring hills, a villa, and a wild boar.

Barthélemy de Chasseneuz.

Le grant coustumier de Bourgogne.

Paris: Francois Regnault, 1534. Acquired with the John A. Hoober Fund.

3.04

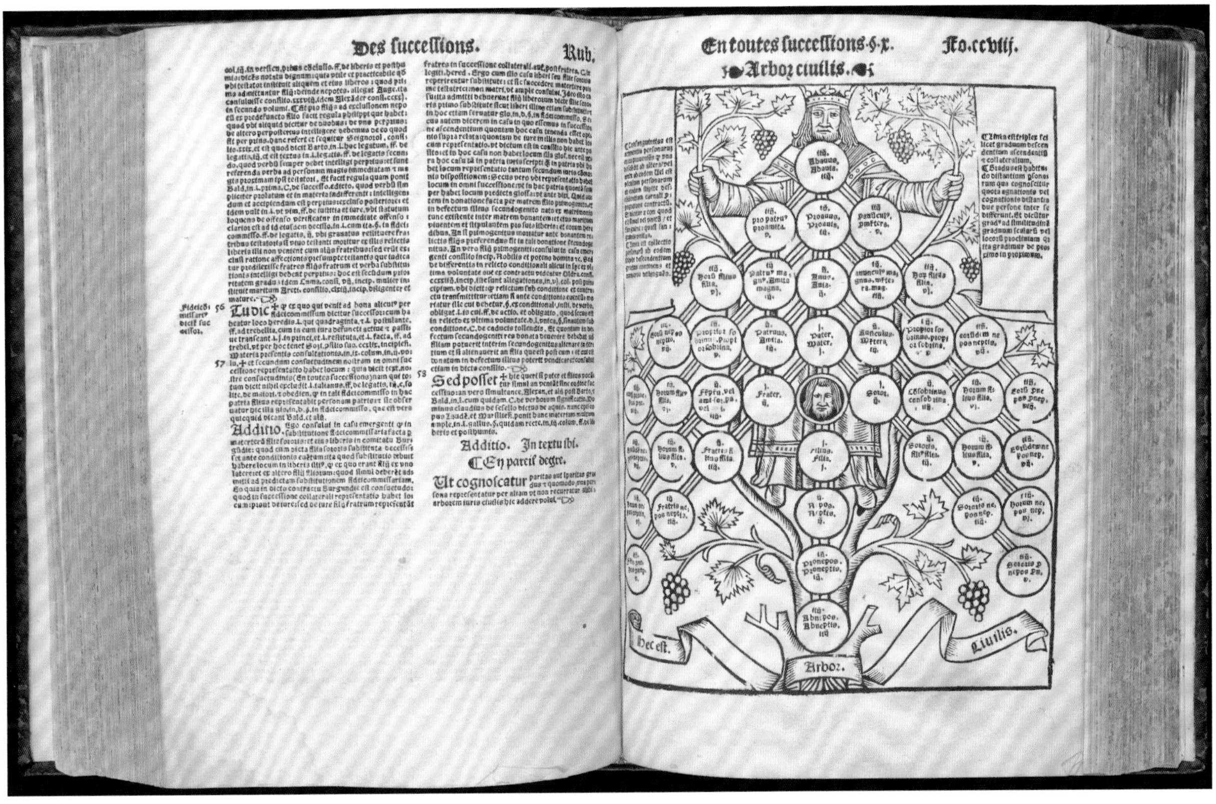

The diagram in this book of local and customary law incorporates fruit into its decorative elements.

3.05

CALIFORNIA.

The civil codes of the State of California.

Sacramento: T.A. Springer, State Printer, 1872.

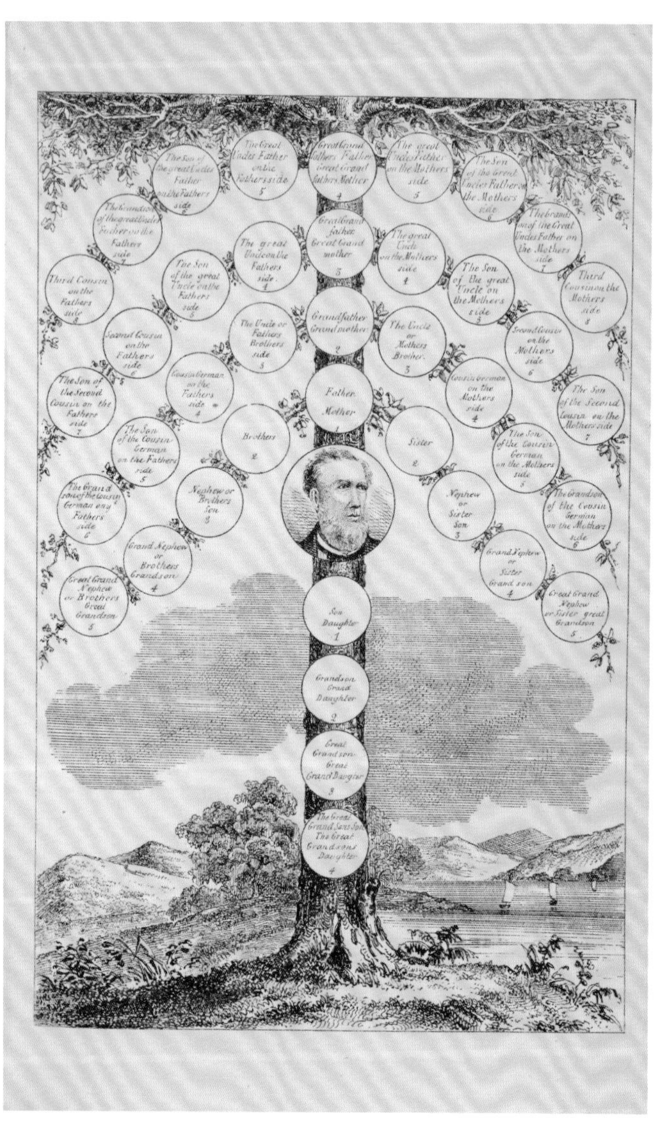

This image is a rare – and possibly unique – example of a tree of consanguinity in a book of American statutes. Fittingly, it is from California, which possesses a significant legal inheritance from Spain and Mexico. Its landscape backdrop appears to depict the northern part of the state.

William Blackstone.

An essay on collateral consanguinity.

London: W. Owen ... and R. Clements, in Oxford, 1750.

3.06

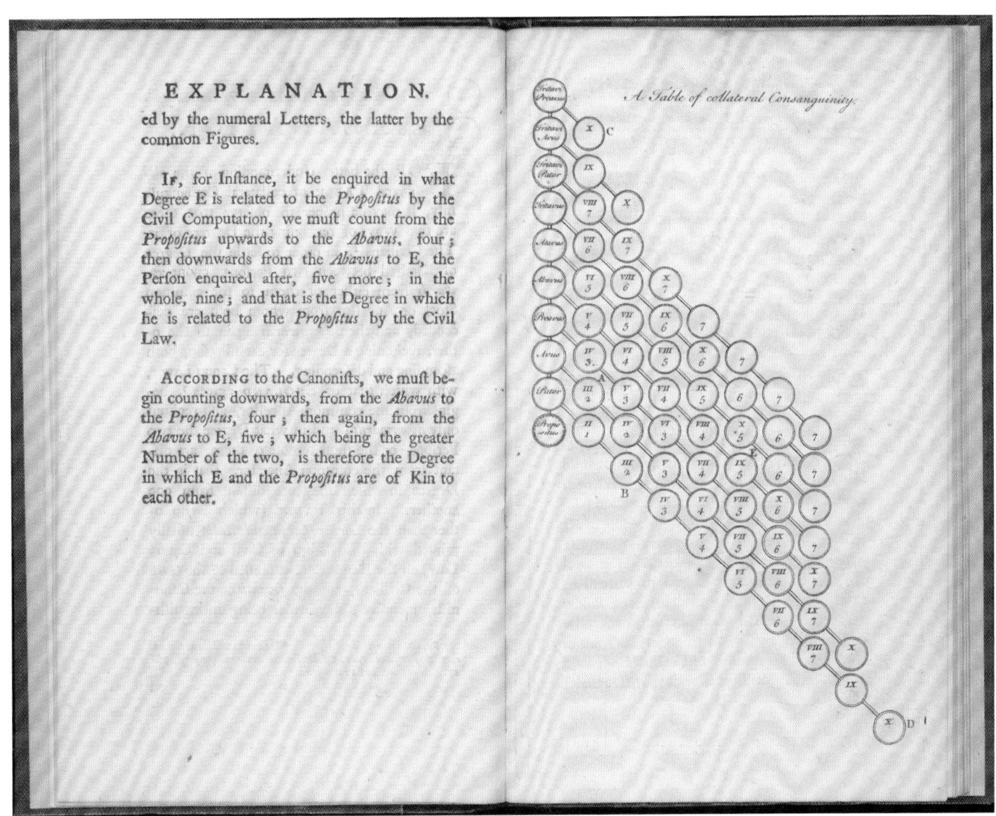

EXPLANATION.

ed by the numeral Letters, the latter by the common Figures.

If, for Inſtance, it be enquired in what Degree E is related to the *Propoſitus* by the Civil Computation, we muſt count from the *Propoſitus* upwards to the *Abavus*, four; then downwards from the *Abavus* to E, the Perſon enquired after, five more; in the whole, nine; and that is the Degree in which he is related to the *Propoſitus* by the Civil Law.

According to the Canoniſts, we muſt begin counting downwards, from the *Abavus* to the *Propoſitus*, four; then again, from the *Abavus* to E, five; which being the greater Number of the two, is therefore the Degree in which E and the *Propoſitus* are of Kin to each other.

In this seminal, first work of English jurist William Blackstone (1723-80), consanguinity is illustrated by a simple table. The essay concerns the issue of legacy admission to All Souls College, Oxford. In the words of legal historian S.F.C. Milsom, Blackstone's creative use of visual aids enabled him "to compress into a single chapter the mass of detailed rules which would in every possible case identify who a man's heir was."

The Law Tree, reproduced above, symbolizes in a concrete way the growth and development of the law. In many sciences classification is shown in some such manner. The idea of a tree is particularly apt in the case of the law, which is a living, growing organism, sending forth new shoots and branches as human activities increase and develop in extent and complexity.

This picture should not be regarded merely as a picture, it is also a working tool for law student and lawyer. The main limbs from the trunk, "Property," "Persons," "Contracts," "Torts," "Crimes," "Remedies," and "Government," represent the seven grand divisions of the Law as shown in The American Law Book Company's Law Chart. The branches from these main limbs represent the subdivisions of the seven grand divisions of the Law, and the smaller twigs from these branches are the standard titles of the law, used in the Corpus Juris-Cyc System and other modern search works.

HOW TO USE THE TREE

First: Select the main limb or grand division that covers your question.
Second: Select the pertinent branch or subhead.
Third: On the branch or subhead select the specific twig or title.

This tree and the Law Chart following can be used in finding the right title in the American Digest System and other compilations. See footnote on last page of chart.

Quick search manual: being a complete collection of the analyses and cross references in the Corpus Juris-Cyc system. 3.07

New York: American Law Book Co., 1926.

Over time, publishers put the tree to new uses, well beyond charting relationships of consanguinity – as in this chart, which "symbolizes in a concrete way the growth and development of the law." As a legal tradition based on the slow accretion of customary principles, the common law lends itself to being represented with organic metaphors drawn from nature.

3.08

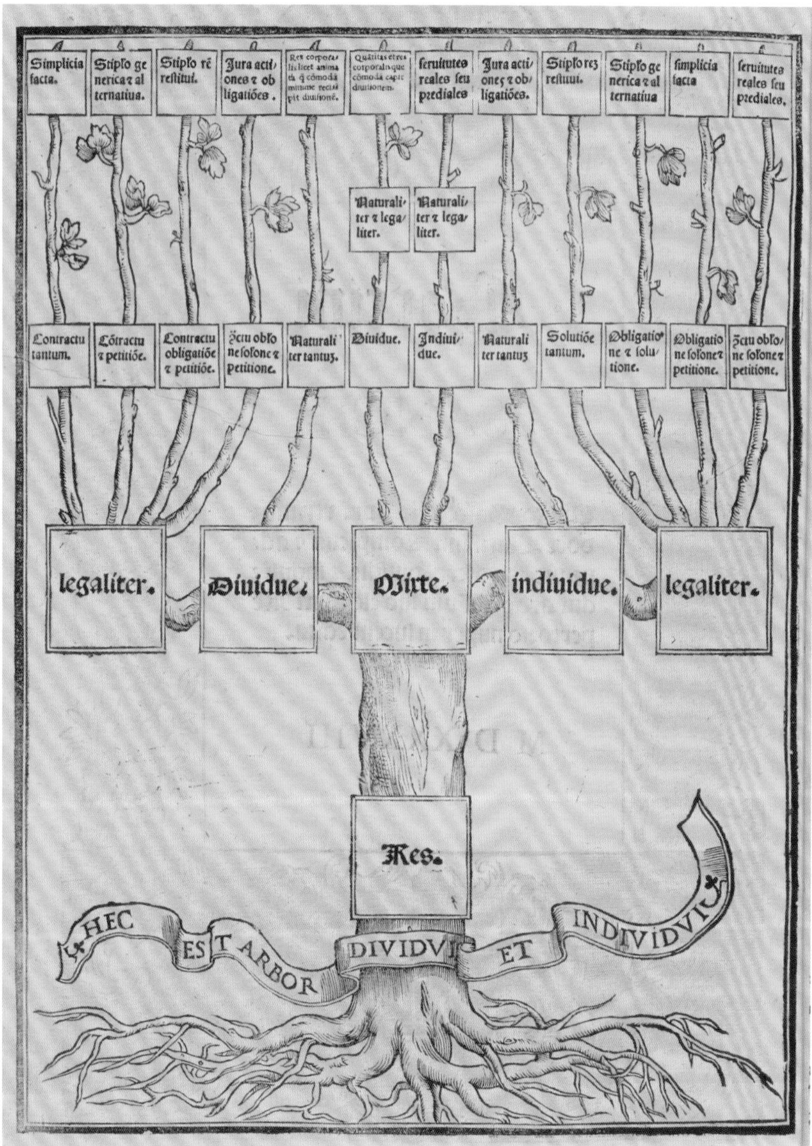

Martín Sánchez.
Conspicua et adprime frugifera dividui et individui arbor.

N.p., 1538. Roman-Canon Law Collection of the Association of the Bar of the City of New York.

This sixteenth-century volume uses the visual elements of a tree for purposes other than charting kinship. It outlines different types of legal actions concerning divisible and indivisible goods.

HUNGARY.

In causa Fisci Regii, contra Abbatem Josephum Ignatium Martinovits.

Pest: Michael Landerer de Füskút, 1795.

3.09

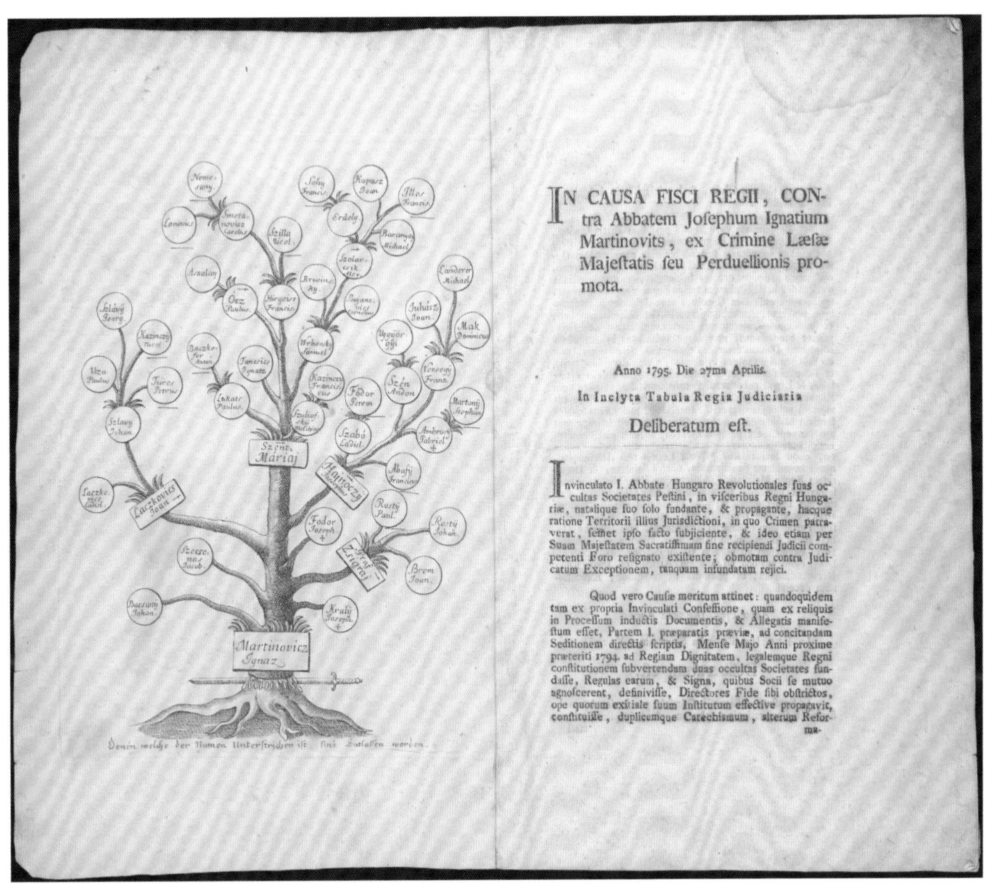

IN CAUSA FISCI REGII, CONTRA Abbatem Joſephum Ignatium Martinovits, ex Crimine Læſæ Majeſtatis ſeu Perduellionis promota.

Anno 1795. Die 27ma Aprilis.

In Inclyta Tabula Regia Judiciaria

Deliberatum eſt.

Invinculato I. Abbate Hungaro Revolutionales ſuas occultas Societates Peſtini, in viſceribus Regni Hungariæ, natalique ſuo ſolo fundante, & propagante, hacque ratione Territorii illius Juriſdictioni, in quo Crimen patraverat, ſemet ipſo facto ſubjiciente, & ideo etiam per Suam Majeſtatem Sacratiſſimam fine recipiendi Judicii competenti Foro reſignato exiſtente; obmotam contra Judicatum Exceptionem, tanquam infundatam rejici.

Quod vero Cauſæ meritum attinet: quandoquidem tam ex propria Invinculati Confeſſione, quam ex reliquis in Proceſſum inductis Documentis, & Allegatis manifeſtum eſſet, Partem I. præparatis præviæ, ad concitandam Seditionem directis ſcriptis, Menſe Majo Anni proxime præteriti 1794. ad Regiam Dignitatem, legalemque Regni conſtitutionem ſubvertendam duas occultas Societates fundaſſe, Regulas earum, & Signa, quibus Socii ſe mutuo agnoſcerent, definiviſſe, Directores Fide ſibi obſtrictos, ope quorum exitiale ſuum Inſtitutum effective propagavit, conſtituiſſe, duplicemque Catechiſmum, alterum Reforma-

A tree of conspiracy. This volume collects proceedings from forty-five treason cases against Hungarian Jacobins. Ignác Martinovics (1755-95) was a leader of the movement.

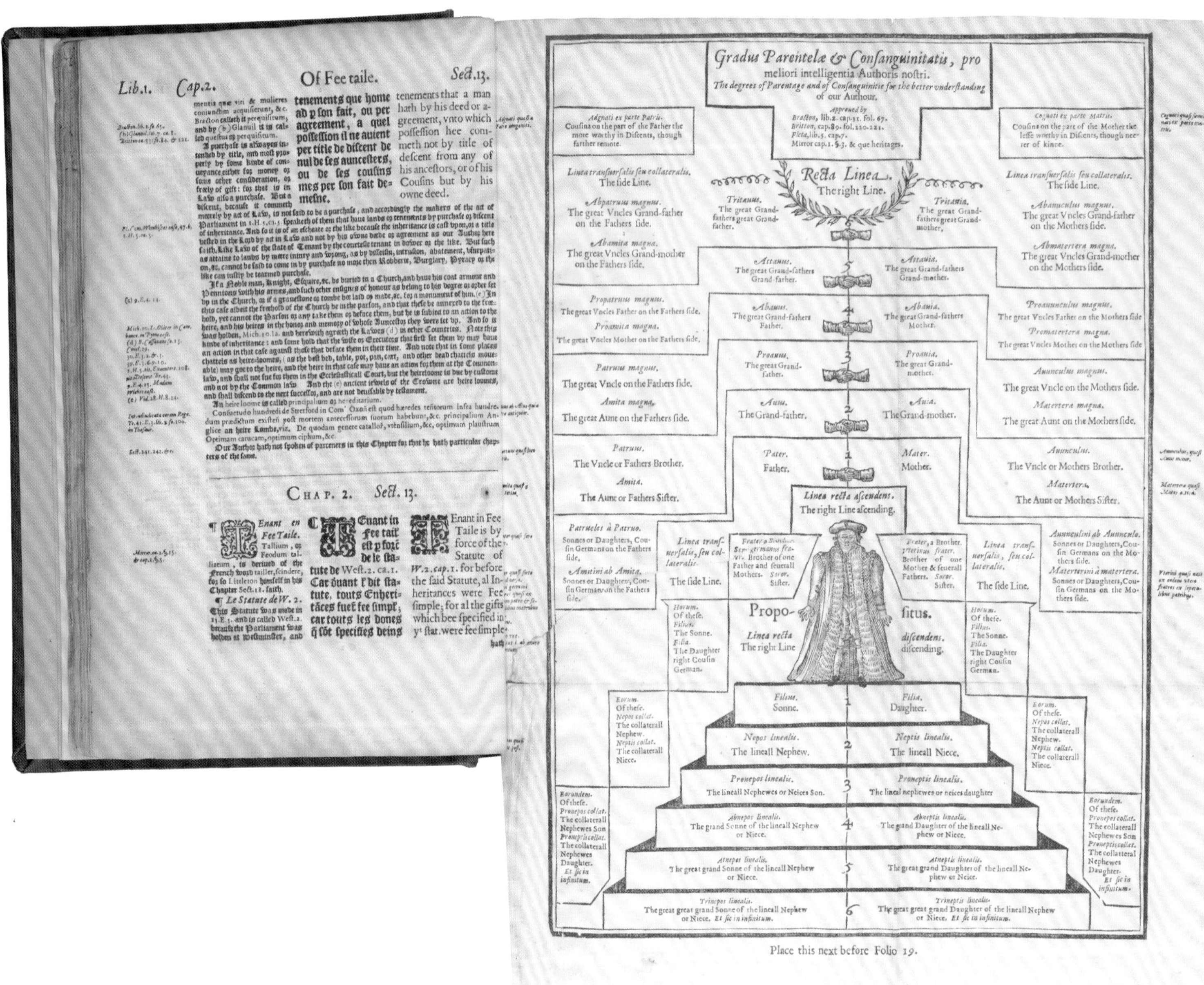

Lib. 1. Cap. 2. Of Fee taile. Sect. 13.

mentis quæ viri & mulieres coniunctim acquisierunt, &c. Bracton calleth it perquisitum, and by (b) Glanuil it is called questus or perquisitum.

A purchase is alwayes intended by title, and most properly by some kinde of conueyance either for money or some other consideration, or freely of gift: for that is in Law also a purchase. But a discent, because it commeth meerely by act of Law, is not said to be a purchase; and accordingly the makers of the act of Parliament in 1. H. 5. ca. 5. speaketh of them that haue lands or tenements by purchase or discent of inheritance. And so it is of an escheate or the like because the inheritance is cast vpon, or a title vested in the Lord by act in Law and not by his owne deede or agreement as our Author here saith. Like Law of the state of Tenant by the courtesie tenant in dower or the like. But such as attaine to lands by meere iniury and wrong, as by disseisin, intrusion, abatement, vsurpation, &c. cannot be said to come in by purchase no more then Robberie, Burglary, Pyracy or the like can iustly be tearmed purchase.

tenements que home ad p son fait, ou per agreement, a quel possession il ne auient per title de discent de nul de ses auncesters, ou de ses cousins mes per son fait demesne.

tenements that a man hath by his deed or agreement, vnto which possession hee commeth not by title of descent from any of his ancestors, or of his Cousins but by his owne deed.

If a Noble man, Knight, Esquire, &c. be buried in a Church, and haue his coat armour and Pennons with his armes, and such other ensignes of honour as belong to his degree or order set vp in the Church, or if a grauestone or tombe bee laid or made, &c. for a monument of him. (c) In this case albeit the freehold of the Church be in the parson, and that these be annexed to the freehold, yet cannot the Parson or any take them or deface them, but he is subiect to an action to the heire, and his heires in the honor and memory of whose Auncestor they were set vp. And so it was holden, Mich. 10. Ia. and herewith agreeth the Lawes (d) in other Countries. Note this kinde of inheritance: and some hold that the wife or Executors that first set them vp may haue an action in that case against those that deface them in their time. And note that in some places chattels as heire-loomes, (as the best bed, table, pot, pan, cart, and other dead chattels moueable) may goe to the heire, and the heire in that case may haue an action for them at the Common law, and shall not sue for them in the Ecclesiasticall Court, but the heireloome is due by custome and not by the Common law. And the (e) ancient iewels of the Crowne are heire loomes, and shall discend to the next successor, and are not deuisable by testament.

An heire loome is called principalium or hereditarium.

Consuetudo hundredi de Stretford in Com' Oxoñ est quod hæredes teñtorum Infra hundredum prædictum existeñ post mortem antecessorum suorum habebunt, &c. principalium Anglice an heire Lombe, viz. De quodam genere catallor, vtensilium, &c, optimum plaustrum Optimam carucam, optimum ciphum, &c.

Our Author hath not spoken of parceners in this Chapter for that he hath particular chapters of the same.

Bracton. lib. 2. fo. 65. (b) Glanuil. lib. 7. ca. 1. Britton ca. 33. fo. 84. & 121.

Pl. Com. Winbishes case, 47. b. 1. H. 5. ca. 5.

(c) 9. E. 4. 14.

Mich. 10. Ia. Obiter in Com. banco. in Tymes case. (d) B. Cassanus fo. 13. Concl. 29. 30. E. 3. 2. & 3. 39. E. 3. 6. 9. 10. 1. H. 5. tit. Executors. 108. tit. Discent. Br. 43. 9. E. 4. 15. Madam Wiches case. (e) Vid. 28. H. 8. 24.

Sect. 241. 242. &c.

Chap. 2. Sect. 13.

¶ Tenant en Fee Taile. Tallium, or Feodum talliatum, is deriued of the French word tailler, scindere, for so Littleton himselfe in his Chapter Sect. 18. saith.

¶ Le Statute de W. 2. This Statute was made in 13. E. 1. and is called West. 2. because the Parliament was holden at Westminster, and

C Tenant in Fee tail est p forc de le statute de West. 2. ca. 1. Car deuant l' dit statute, touts Enheritãces fuer fee simple; car touts les dones q̃ sont specifies deins

Tenant in Fee Taile is by force of the Statute of W. 2. cap. 1. for before the said Statute, al Inheritances were Fee simple; for al the gifts which bee specified in yᵗ stat. were fee simple

hath

Gradus Parentelæ & Consanguinitatis, pro meliori intelligentia Authoris nostri.

The degrees of Parentage and of Consanguinitie for the better vnderstanding of our Authour.

Approued by Bracton, lib. 2. cap. 31. fol. 67. Britton, cap. 89. fol. 220. 221. Fleta, lib. 5. cap. 7. Mirror cap. 1. §. 3. & que heritages.

Adgnati ex parte Patris. Cousins on the part of the Father the more worthy in Discents, though farther remote.

Cognati ex parte Matris. Cousins on the part of the Mother the lesse worthy in Discents, though neerer of kinne.

Linea transuersalis seu collateralis. The side Line.	*Recta Linea.* The right Line.		*Linea transuersalis seu collateralis.* The side Line.
Abpatruus magnus. The great Vncles Grand-father on the Fathers side. *Abamita magna.* The great Vncles Grand-mother on the Fathers side.	*Tritauus.* The great Grand-fathers great Grand-father.	*Tritauia.* The great Grand-fathers great Grand-mother.	*Abauunculus magnus.* The great Vncles Grand-father on the Mothers side. *Abmatertera magna.* The great Vncles Grand-mother on the Mothers side.
Propatruus magnus. The great Vncles Father on the Fathers side. *Proamita magna.* The great Vncles Mother on the Fathers side.	5 *Attauus.* The great Grand-fathers Grand-father.	*Attauia.* The great Grand-fathers Grand-mother.	*Proauunculus magnus.* The great Vncles Father on the Mothers side. *Promatertera magna.* The great Vncles Mother on the Mothers side.
Patruus magnus. The great Vncle on the Fathers side. *Amita magna.* The great Aunt on the Fathers side.	4 *Abauus.* The great Grand-fathers Father.	*Abauia.* The great Grand-fathers Mother.	*Auunculus magnus.* The great Vncle on the Mothers side. *Matertera magna.* The great Aunt on the Mothers side.
	3 *Proauus.* The great Grand-father.	*Proauia.* The great Grand-mother.	
Patruus. The Vncle or Fathers Brother. *Amita.* The Aunt or Fathers Sister.	2 *Auus.* The Grand-father.	*Auia.* The Grand-mother.	*Auunculus.* The Vncle or Mothers Brother. *Matertera.* The Aunt or Mothers Sister.
	1 *Pater.* Father.	*Mater.* Mother.	

Linea recta ascendens. The right Line ascending.

Patrueles à Patruo. Sonnes or Daughters, Cousin Germans on the Fathers side. *Amitini ab Amita.* Sonnes or Daughters, Cousin Germans on the Fathers side.

Linea transuersalis, seu collateralis. The side Line.

Frater, a Brother. Soror germanus frater. Brother of one Father and seuerall Mothers. *Soror.* Sister.

Frater, a Brother. Vterinus frater. Brother of one Mother & seuerall Fathers. *Soror.* Sister.

Linea transuersalis, seu collateralis. The side Line.

Auunculini ab Auunculo. Sonnes or Daughters, Cousin Germans on the Mothers side. *Materterini à matertera.* Sonnes or Daughters, Cousin Germans on the Mothers side.

Horum. Of these. *Filius.* The Sonne. *Filia.* The Daughter right Cousin German.

Propositus. *Linea recta* The right Line *discendens.* discending.

Horum. Of these. *Filius.* The Sonne. *Filia.* The Daughter right Cousin German.

Eorum. Of these. *Nepos collat.* The collaterall Nephew. *Neptis collat.* The collaterall Niece.

	Linea recta discendens	
1	*Filius.* Sonne.	*Filia.* Daughter.
2	*Nepos linealis.* The lineall Nephew.	*Neptis linealis.* The lineall Niece.
3	*Pronepos linealis.* The lineall Nephewes or Neices Son.	*Proneptis linealis.* The lineal nephewes or neices daughter
4	*Abnepos linealis.* The grand Sonne of the lineall Nephew or Niece.	*Abneptis linealis.* The grand Daughter of the lineall Nephew or Niece.
5	*Atnepos linealis.* The great grand Sonne of the lineall Nephew or Niece.	*Atneptis linealis.* The great grand Daughter of the lineall Nephew or Neice.
6	*Trinepos linealis.* The great great grand Sonne of the lineall Nephew or Niece. *Et sic in infinitum.*	*Trineptis linealis.* The great great grand Daughter of the lineall Nephew or Niece. *Et sic in infinitum.*

Eorundem. Of these. *Pronepos collat.* The collaterall Nephewes Son. *Proneptis collat.* The collaterall Nephewes Daughter. *Et sic in infinitum.*

Place this next before Folio 19.

Sir Edward Coke.

3.10

The first part of the Institutes of the lawes of England: or, A commentarie upon Littleton.

London: Societie of Stationers, 1628.

The *Institutes* are a series of learned treatises by Edward Coke (1552-1634) that lay the conceptual basis of the modern common law. The first volume was written as a commentary on the work of fifteenth-century jurist Thomas Littleton. Legal scholar Peter Goodrich writes that "it is no accident that the most emblematic and significant visual illustration in the foundational work of English common law ... is precisely of genealogical origin, a tree of consanguinity."

3.11

Vicente José Ferreira Cardoso da Costa.

Explicação da arvore que representa o prospecto do Codigo Civil Portuguez.

Lisbon: Antonio Rodrigues Galhardo, 1822.

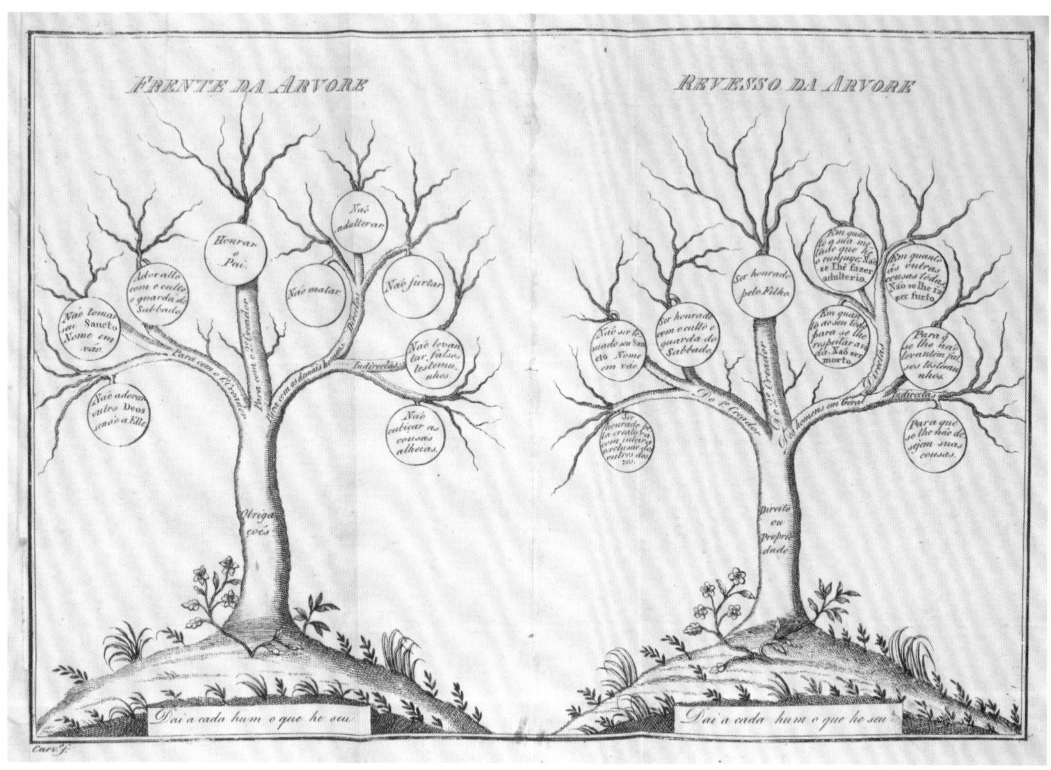

Following the liberal revolution of 1820, the Portuguese assembly offered a prize to the best prospectus for a civil code. A learned law professor offered this proposal, diagramming his conception of justice in the shape of a tree. The front of the tree, at left, illustrates "obligations," and features the Ten Commandments hanging from its branches. The back of the tree illustrates the civil rights that correspond to these obligations.

[A. Norton Fitch.]

3.12

A treatise on commercial law: with forms of ordinary legal and business documents, and copious questions with references.

Rochester, N.Y.: E.R. Andrews, 1889.

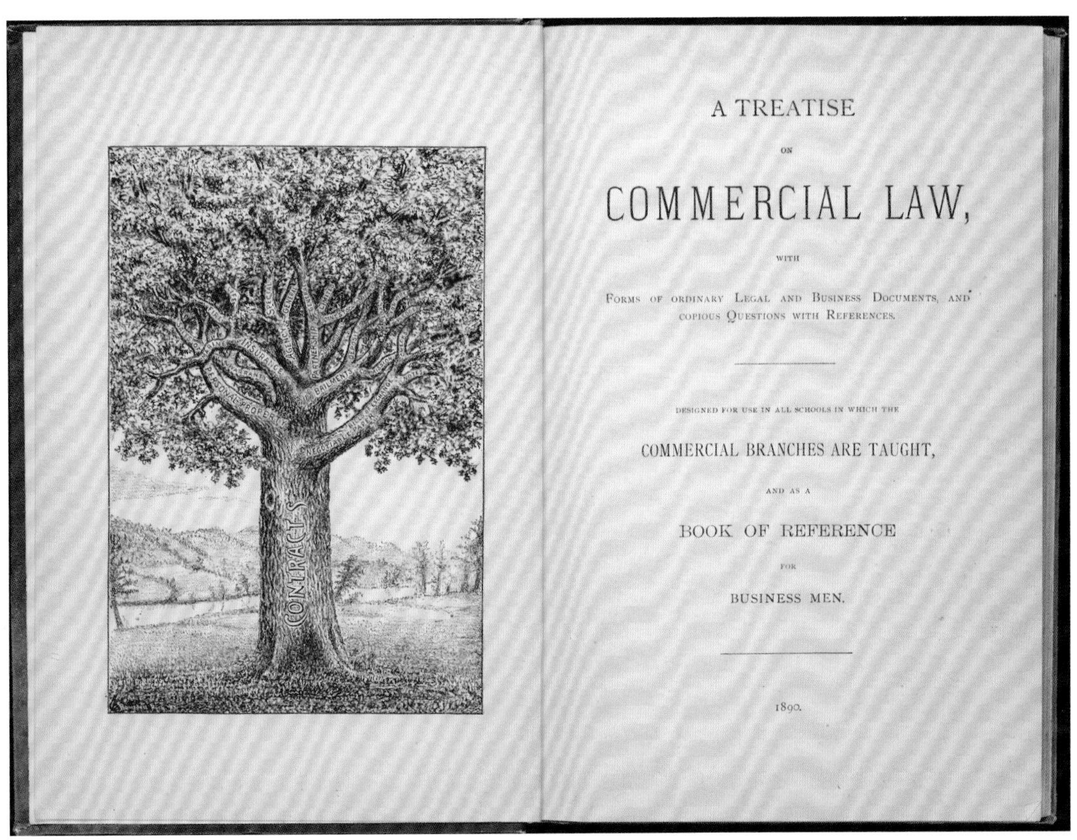

A TREATISE

ON

COMMERCIAL LAW,

WITH

Forms of ordinary Legal and Business Documents, and copious Questions with References.

DESIGNED FOR USE IN ALL SCHOOLS IN WHICH THE

COMMERCIAL BRANCHES ARE TAUGHT,

AND AS A

BOOK OF REFERENCE

FOR

BUSINESS MEN.

1890.

The frontispiece of this treatise for businessmen charts the growth of a central doctrinal field of common law: contracts. Yet compared with item 3.07, the conceptual framework here is weak. The success of the tree metaphor over time gave bud to new, more powerful ways to depict legal and conceptual relationships.

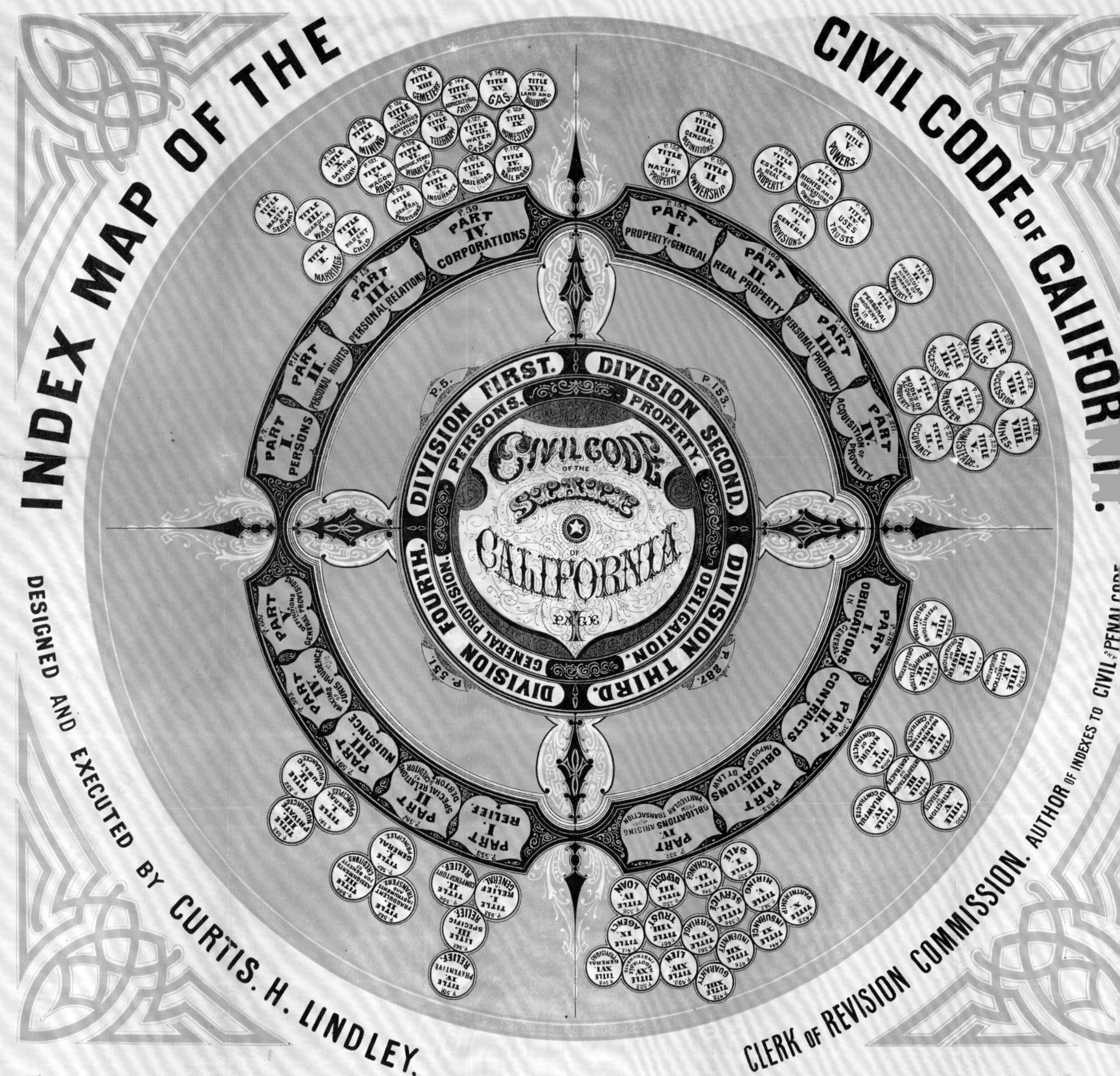
INDEX MAP OF THE
CIVIL CODE OF CALIFOR
DESIGNED AND EXECUTED BY CURTIS. H. LINDLEY,
CLERK OF REVISION COMMISSION. AUTHOR OF INDEXES TO CIVIL & PENAL CODE
CIVIL CODE OF THE STATE OF CALIFORNIA
PAGE 1
P. 5 DIVISION FIRST. PERSONS.
P. 153 DIVISION SECOND. PROPERTY.
P. 287 DIVISION THIRD. OBLIGATION.
P. 551 DIVISION FOURTH. GENERAL PROVISION.
P. 7 PART I. PERSONS
P. 11 PART II. PERSONAL RIGHTS
P. 15 PART III. PERSONAL RELATIONS
P. 59 PART IV. CORPORATIONS
P. 154 PART I. PROPERTY IN GENERAL
P. 160 PART II. REAL PROPERTY
P. 193 PART III. PERSONAL PROPERTY
P. 211 PART IV. ACQUISITION OF PROPERTY
P. 288 PART I. OBLIGATIONS IN GENERAL
P. 300 PART II. CONTRACTS
P. 325 PART III. OBLIGATIONS IMPOSED BY LAW
P. 331 PART IV. OBLIGATIONS ARISING FROM PARTICULAR TRANSACTIONS
P. 533 PART I. RELIEF.
P. 534 PART II. SPECIAL RELATIONS OF DEBTOR & CREDITOR
P. 581 PART III. NUISANCE
P. 593 PART IV. MAXIMS OF JURISPRUDENCE
P. 597 PART V. GENERAL DEFINITIONS PROVISIONS
TITLE I. MARRIAGE
TITLE II. PARENT & CHILD
TITLE III. GUARDIAN & WARD
TITLE IV. MASTER & SERVANT
TITLE I. GENERAL PROVISIONS
TITLE II. INSURANCE
TITLE III. RAILROAD
TITLE IV. STREET RAILROAD
TITLE V. WAGON ROAD
TITLE VI. BRIDGE, FERRY WHARF &C.
TITLE VII. TELEGRAPH
TITLE VIII. WATER & CANAL
TITLE IX. HOMESTEAD
TITLE X. SAVINGS & LOAN
TITLE XI. MINING
TITLE XII. RELIGIOUS BENEVOLENT ETC.
TITLE XIII. CEMETERY
TITLE XIV. AGRICULTURAL FAIR
TITLE XV. GAS
TITLE XVI. LAND AND BUILDING
TITLE I. NATURE OF PROPERTY
TITLE II. OWNERSHIP
TITLE III. GENERAL DEFINITIONS
TITLE I. GENERAL PROVISIONS
TITLE II. ESTATES IN REAL PROPERTY
TITLE III. RIGHTS AND OBLIGATIONS OF OWNERS
TITLE IV. USES & TRUSTS
TITLE V. POWERS
TITLE I. PERSONAL PROPERTY IN GENERAL
TITLE II. PARTICULAR KINDS OF PERSONAL PROPERTY
TITLE I. OCCUPANCY
TITLE II. ACCESSION
TITLE IV. TRANSFER
TITLE V. HOMESTEADS
TITLE VI. WILLS
TITLE VII. SUCCESSION
TITLE VIII. MINES
TITLE I. DEFINITIONS OF OBLIGATIONS
TITLE II. INTERPRETATION OF OBLIGATIONS
TITLE III. TRANSFER OF OBLIGATIONS
TITLE IV. EXTINCTION OF OBLIGATIONS
TITLE I. NATURE OF CONTRACT
TITLE II. MANNER OF CREATING CONTRACTS
TITLE III. INTERPRETATION OF CONTRACTS
TITLE IV. UNLAWFUL CONTRACTS
TITLE V. EXTINCTION OF CONTRACTS
TITLE I. SALE
TITLE II. EXCHANGE
TITLE III. DEPOSIT
TITLE IV. LOAN
TITLE V. HIRING
TITLE VI. SERVICE
TITLE VII. CARRIAGE
TITLE VIII. AGENCY
TITLE IX. TRUST
TITLE X. PARTNERSHIP
TITLE XI. INSURANCE
TITLE XII. INDEMNITY
TITLE XIII. GUARANTY
TITLE XIV. LIEN
TITLE XV. NEGOTIABLE INSTRUMENTS
TITLE XVI. GENERAL PROVISIONS
TITLE I. GENERAL PRINCIPLES
TITLE II. COMPENSATORY RELIEF
TITLE III. SPECIFIC RELIEF
TITLE IV. PREVENTIVE RELIEF
TITLE I. GENERAL PRINCIPLES
TITLE II. FRAUDULENT INSTRUMENTS & TRANSFERS
TITLE III. ASSIGNMENTS FOR BENEFIT OF CREDITORS
TITLE I. GENERAL PRINCIPLES
TITLE II. PUBLIC NUISANCES
TITLE III. PRIVATE NUISANCES

California. Commission to Revise the Laws of California.

3.13

Revised laws of the State of California, in four codes ...
[Volume 2] Civil Code.

Sacramento: D.W. Gelwicks, State Printer, 1871.

The State of California, innovative as ever, presented its revised laws in a circular chart. How might a diagram's *form* shape a reader's *substantive* understanding of its accompanying text? How might a tradition of graphic design, such as the tree of consanguinity, structure the development of legal ideas? How might new designs alter the legal imagination?

3.14

Castile (Kingdom).

Las siete partidas del sabio rey D. Alfonso el Nono.

Valencia: J.T. Lucas, 1758. Volume 4 of 7.

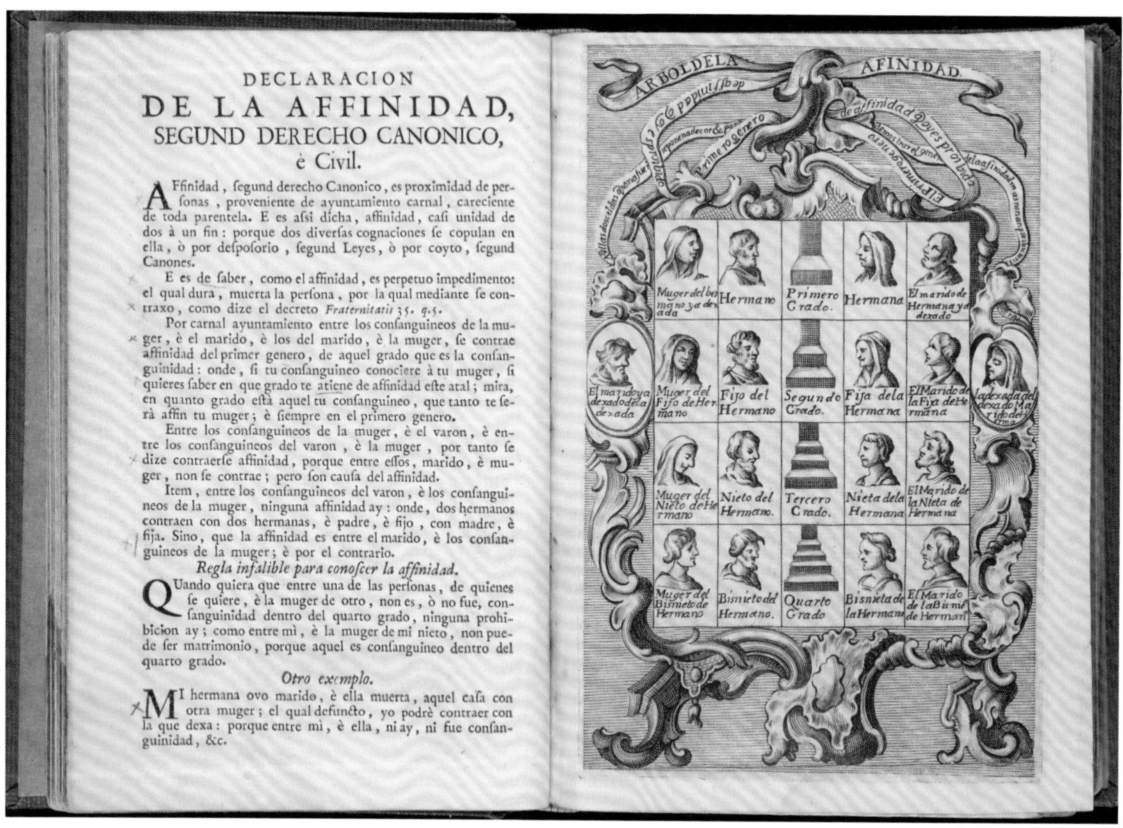

DECLARACION

DE LA AFFINIDAD,

SEGUND DERECHO CANONICO,

è Civil.

AFfinidad, ſegund derecho Canonico, es proximidad de perſonas, proveniente de ayuntamiento carnal, careciente de toda parentela. E es aſsi dicha, affinidad, caſi unidad de dos à un fin: porque dos diverſas cognaciones ſe copulan en ella, ò por deſpoſorio, ſegund Leyes, ò por coyto, ſegund Canones.

E es de ſaber, como el affinidad, es perpetuo impedimento: el qual dura, muerta la perſona, por la qual mediante ſe contraxo, como dize el decreto *Fraternitatis* 35. q.5.

Por carnal ayuntamiento entre los conſanguineos de la muger, è el marido, è los del marido, è la muger, ſe contrae affinidad del primer genero, de aquel grado que es la conſanguinidad: onde, ſi tu conſanguineo conociere à tu muger, ſi quieres ſaber en que grado te atiene de affinidad eſte atal; mira, en quanto grado eſtà aquel tu conſanguineo, que tanto te ſerà affin tu muger; è ſiempre en el primero genero.

Entre los conſanguineos de la muger, è el varon, è entre los conſanguineos del varon, è la muger, por tanto ſe dize contraerſe affinidad, porque entre eſſos, marido, è muger, non ſe contrae; pero ſon cauſa del affinidad.

Item, entre los conſanguineos del varon, è los conſanguineos de la muger, ninguna affinidad ay: onde, dos hermanos contraen con dos hermanas, è padre, è fijo, con madre, è fija. Sino, que la affinidad es entre el marido, è los conſanguineos de la muger; è por el contrario.

Regla infalible para conoſcer la affinidad.

QUando quiera que entre una de las perſonas, de quienes ſe quiere, è la muger de otro, non es, ò no fue, conſanguinidad dentro del quarto grado, ninguna prohibicion ay; como entre mì, è la muger de mi nieto, non puede ſer matrimonio, porque aquel es conſanguineo dentro del quarto grado.

Otro exemplo.

MI hermana ovo marido, è ella muerta, aquel caſa con otra muger; el qual defunčto, yo podrè contraer con la que dexa: porque entre mì, è ella, ni ay, ni fue conſanguinidad, &c.

In this eighteenth-century edition of a renowned legal code from the Middle Ages, the "tree" of the *arbol de la afinidad* ("tree of affinity") exists only as a memory within a decorative motif.

Eric Hilgendorf.

Dtv-Atlas Recht.

3.15

Munich: Deutscher Taschenbuch Verlag, 2003-2008.
Volume 1 of 2. Illustrations by Susanne Jünger.

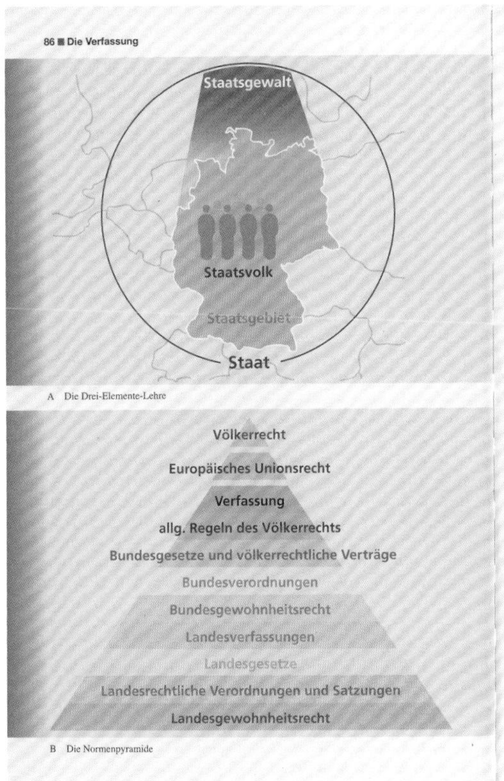

Staat und Verfassung I ■ 87

Der Begriff **Staat** setzt nach der »Drei-Elemente-Lehre« (A) Folgendes voraus: Ein bestimmtes, zumindest grundsätzl. umgrenztes Gebiet *(Staatsgebiet)*, auf diesem Gebiet wohnende Menschen *(Staatsvolk)* und eine Regierung, die auf dem Staatsgebiet die Ordnung wahrt *(Staatsgewalt)*.

Andere Aspekte des Staatswesens betonen die »Integrationslehre« Rudolf Smends (1882–1975), der den Staat als geistige Einheit der sich verbunden fühlenden Bürger verstand, und die von Hermann Heller (1891–1933) entwickelte »Lehre von der Wirkungseinheit«, nach der der Staat als fakt. Wirkungszusammenhang einer souveränen Gebietsherrschaft gesehen wird.

Die **Verfassung** eines Staates ist die Summe der geschriebenen oder ungeschriebenen Rechtsnormen, die die staatl. Grundordnung, also die Staats- und Gesellschaftsform mitsamt ihren wesentl. Organisationsprinzipien, festlegen.

Im engeren, formellen Sinn meint »Verfassung« nur das geschriebene Gesetz, das die Staatsgewalt **legitimiert, organisiert** und **bindet.**

Dtl. wurde, anders als etwa die USA oder Frankreich, erst spät zum Verfassungsstaat. Die dt. Geschichte der letzten 200 Jahre ist durch einen raschen Wechsel der Staats- und Verfassungsformen gekennzeichnet:

- 17. und 18. Jh.: In der **absoluten Monarchie** (Absolutismus) existiert keine Verfassung im heutigen Sinn. Die Staatsgewalt wurde von einer einzigen Person ausgeübt, die rechtl. nicht gebunden war *(princeps legibus solutus)*. Herrschaft legitimierte sich durch die Herkunft des Monarchen aus dem Hochadel.
- 18. Jh.: Der **aufgeklärte Absolutismus** stellt eine abgeschwächte Form der absoluten Monarchie dar. Der Herrscher wurde als zwar nicht rechtl., aber doch moral. gebunden betrachtet *(Monarch als erster Diener des Staates)*.
- 19. Jh.: In der **konstitutionellen Monarchie** ist der Herrscher an eine Verfassung gebunden. 1815 wurde in der *Bundesakte des Dt. Bundes* allen Bundesstaaten eine Verfassung versprochen. Die erste dt. Reichsverfassung entstand 1871, wobei auch das *Dt. Reich* eine konstitutionelle Monarchie war.
- 1918 wechselte die Staatsform erneut: Dtl. wurde eine **Republik.** Die neue Weimarer Reichsverfassung (WRV) wurde 1919 von der Nationalversammlung verabschiedet. Dtl. war nun ein demokrat. Verfassungsstaat.
- 1933: Mit der Machtübernahme durch die Nationalsozialisten wurde die WRV durch das Ermächtigungsgesetz vom 24. 3. 1933 in wesentl. Teilen außer Kraft gesetzt. Unter Hitlers **Diktatur** war der »Wille des Führers« oberste Rechtsquelle.
- 1945: Nach dem Zusammenbruch der nationalsozialist. Herrschaft wurde Dtl. geteilt. Mit dem Inkrafttreten des GG 1949 wurde West-Dtl. wieder ein **demokratischer Verfassungsstaat** (Bundesrepublik Deutschland).
  In Ost-Dtl. herrschte die Sozialist. Einheitspartei (SED), die nur auf dem Papier an die Verfassung gebunden war (Deutsche Demokratische Republik), bis zur Wende 1989. Durch den Einigungsvertrag vom 31. 8. 1990 traten die fünf neugegründeten ostdt. Bundesländer der BRD bei.

Grundlegend für das moderne Verfassungsdenken ist die von Sieyès (1748–1836) z. Zt. der Französ. Revolution entwickelte Unterscheidung zwischen der verfassunggebenden Gewalt (**pouvoir constituant**) und der durch die Verfassung eingesetzten und gebundenen Staatsgewalt (**pouvoir constitué**). Inhaber der verfassunggebenden Gewalt ist das Staatsvolk. Die Staatsgewalt ist nur durch die Verfassung legitimiert.

Zu unterscheiden sind das materielle und das formelle Verfassungsrecht.

Das **materielle Verfassungsrecht (Staatsrecht)** umfasst die grundlegenden Regeln über die Legitimation, Organisation und Bindung der Staatsgewalt (bes. Staatsorganisationsrecht und Grundrechte).

Teile davon sind auch außerhalb des GG geregelt.

Dagegen besteht das **formelle Verfassungsrecht** aus allen im GG enthaltenen Normen, einschl. solcher Regelungen, die sich auf spezielle Rechtsgebiete wie das Strafrecht (z. B. Art. 102 GG: Abschaffung der Todesstrafe) oder das Verwaltungsrecht (z. B. Art. 34 GG: Amtshaftung) beziehen.

Das GG nennt folgende **grundlegenden Verfassungsprinzipien (Verfassungsgrundsätze):** *Republik, Demokratie, Gewaltenteilung, Rechtsstaat, Bundesstaat, Sozialstaat* (Art. 20, 28 GG).

Die *Grundrechte* gewährleisten dem Einzelnen eine eigenständige und in ihrem Kern unantastbare Rechtsposition gegenüber der Staatsgewalt.

Die in der Verfassung vorgesehenen obersten Staatsorgane heißen **Verfassungsorgane.**

Nach dem GG sind dies der Bundestag (Parlament), der Bundesrat, der Gemeinsame

The normative hierarchy of German law is represented as a pyramid, at lower-left. A prominent specialist in criminal law, the author of this "legal atlas" is also a scholar of law and visual studies.

Law divides the waters. This comprehensive work on the law governing rivers – a body of jurisprudence dating back to the Roman republic – provides a letter designation for individual subjects treated in the text. The book also considers aqueducts, canals, and hydro-engineering. The difference between the points in the river labeled A, B, and C have legal significance.

Francesco Maria Pecchio.
Tractatus de aquaeductu.
Pavia: Giovanni Andrea Magri, [1673?]. Volume 2 of 4.

Caput Decimum, Quæst. II. Lib. II. 341

Pecchij de Aquæduct. Lib. II. Vu Aliud

Calculating the Law 4

One aspect of law which makes it so compelling as a profession, as a field of study, and as a subject for book collecting, is that it is a tool for solving real human problems. The peculiar beauty of law books derives in part from this usefulness. They were made to be touched, handled, and put to work. Many law book illustrations thus aid readers – users – in actively applying the law to human affairs.

The books here help practitioners solve legal problems through a tool of great importance to the law – mathematics – and they focus on legal problems involving water and land. Overflowing with formal beauty, these illustrations invite readers to shift their attention from their book onto a specific problem in the world – and back again.

4.01

Bartolo of Sassoferrato.

Consilia cum summariis, quaestiones & tractatus.

Lyon: Jacques Sacon, 1518.

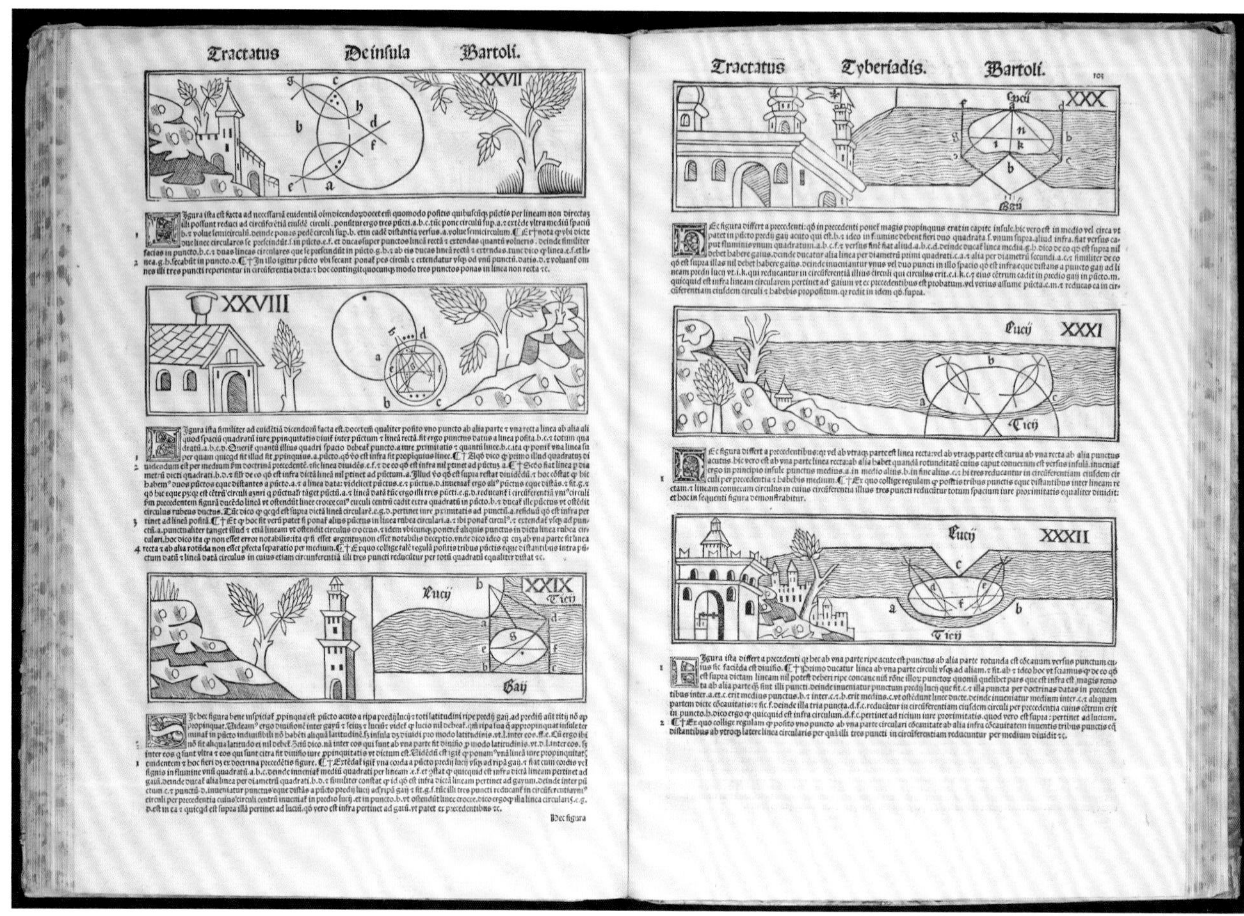

A particular favorite of the exhibit curators, this treatise on watercourses and riparian rights is filled with enchanting woodcuts of riverside life, especially along the river Tiber. Waterways, mills, farms, villages – all are used to illustrate mathematical principles of surveying, which made great strides during the renaissance. The book builds on the work of the great medieval jurist Bartolus (1313-57).

Giuseppe Carmagnola. 4.02

Trattato delle alluvioni: diviso in ragionamenti teorico-pratici sopra l'origine, il diritto, e la divisione degli incrementi fluviali.

Torino: Nella Stamperia Soffietti, 1793.

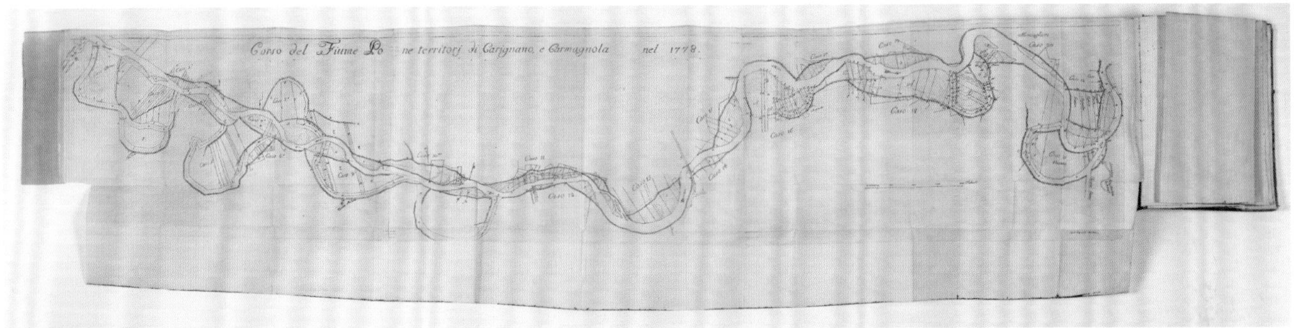

The longest river in Italy, the Po, is notorious for its floods – and for the legal problems those floods create. This treatise on water law charts the river's course while referencing legal case studies discussed in the text. The plate shown here, measuring five feet when folded out, illustrates the course of the river in Piedmont, indexed to the case studies.

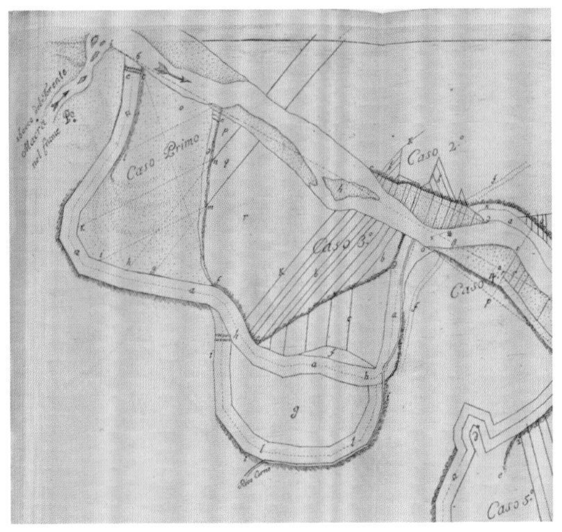

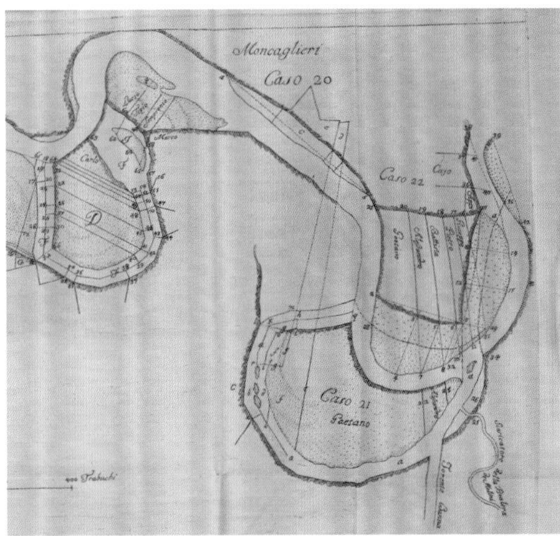

4.03

Battista Aimo.

De alluvionum iure universo.

Bologna: Giovanni de' Rossi, 1580. Roman-Canon Law Collection of the Association of the Bar of the City of New York.

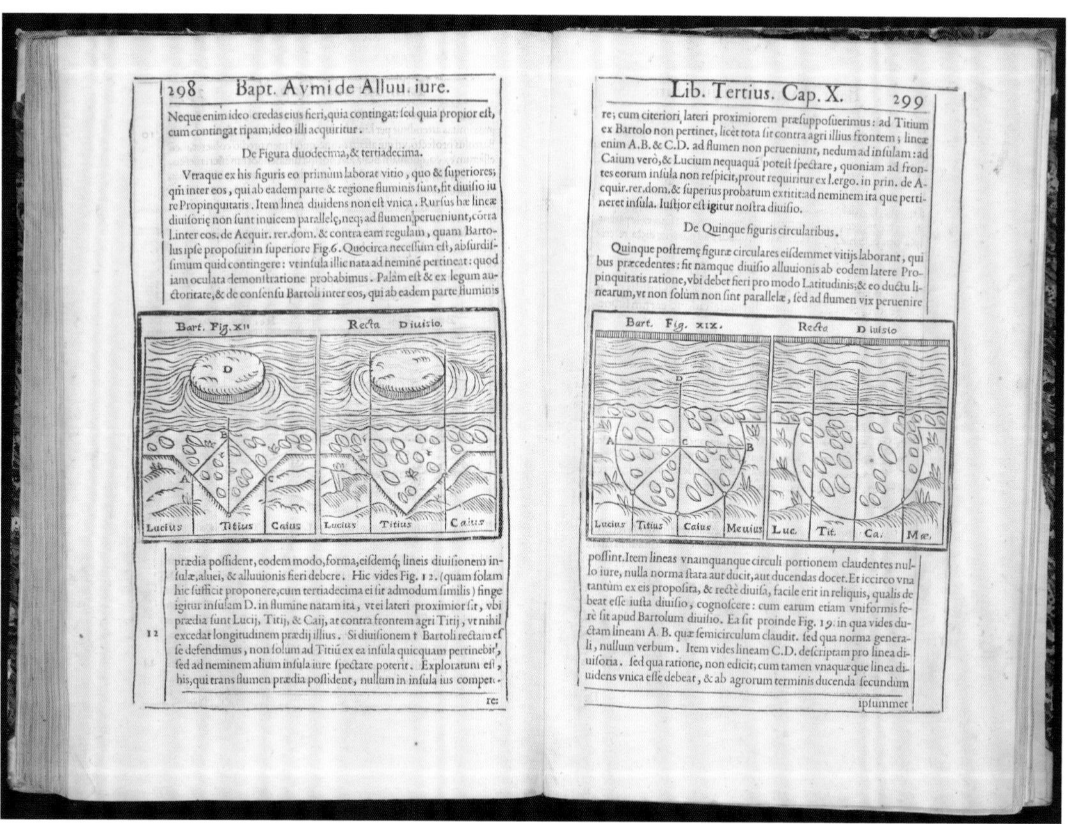

This is the book that inspired Mike Widener to develop the Yale Law Library's illustrated law book collection. It is the first edition of an influential treatise on alluvium and riparian rights by Battista Aimo (1550-89). Alluvium is soil deposited on a shore by a river, which may change the size and shape of a parcel of land.

Francisco Javier de Gamboa.

Comentarios a las ordenanzas de minas.

4.04

Madrid: Joaquín Ibarra, 1761. Engravings by Joan Minguet.
Acquired with the Energy Law Collection Fund.

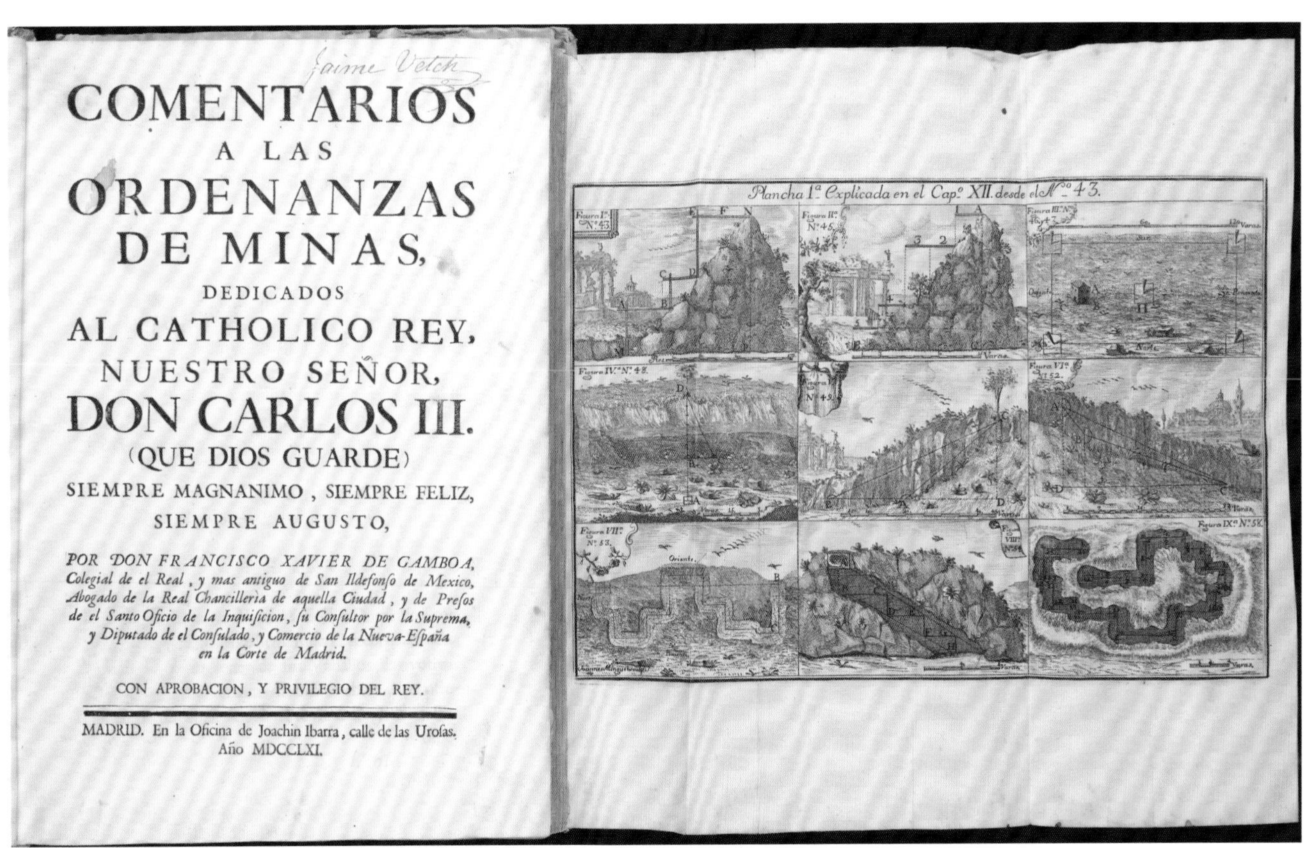

COMENTARIOS
A LAS
ORDENANZAS
DE MINAS,
DEDICADOS
AL CATHOLICO REY,
NUESTRO SEÑOR,
DON CARLOS III.
(QUE DIOS GUARDE)
SIEMPRE MAGNANIMO, SIEMPRE FELIZ,
SIEMPRE AUGUSTO,

POR DON FRANCISCO XAVIER DE GAMBOA, Colegial de el Real, y mas antiguo de San Ildefonso de Mexico, Abogado de la Real Chancilleria de aquella Ciudad, y de Presos de el Santo Oficio de la Inquisicion, su Consultor por la Suprema, y Diputado de el Consulado, y Comercio de la Nueva-España en la Corte de Madrid.

CON APROBACION, Y PRIVILEGIO DEL REY.

MADRID. En la Oficina de Joachin Ibarra, calle de las Urosas. Año MDCCLXI.

One of the premiere lawyers of New Spain, Francisco Javier de Gamboa (1717-1794) illustrated this exhaustive treatise on mining law with three copperplate engravings. Indexed to paragraph numbers in the text, the illustrations highlight Gamboa's celebrated passion for precision.

4.05

Gelderland (Netherlands).

Water-recht waar nae een yder in het Furstendom Gelre en Graafschap Zutphen.

Arnhem: Wed. de Haas, 1715.

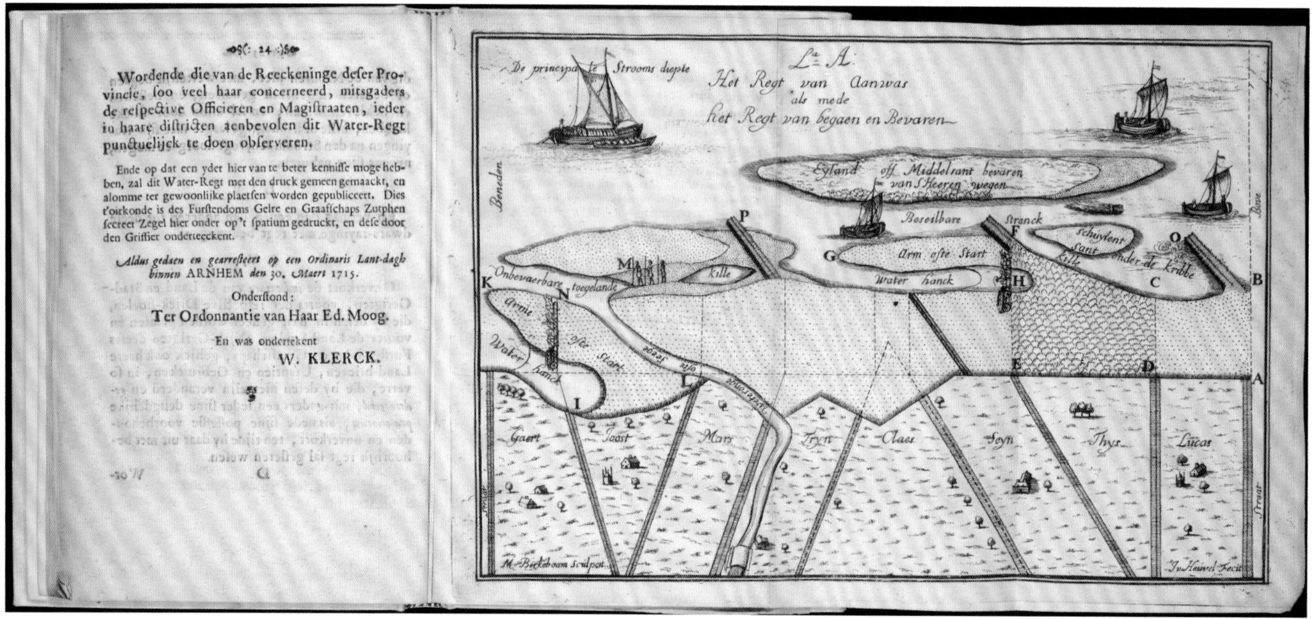

Unsurprisingly, many excellent works about water law were published in the Netherlands. This book standardized water rights in the province of Gelderland, and it includes eight folding riverbank maps, with features of special significance marked with letters. Note how the image illustrates the varying rights of owners Gaert, Joost, Mars, Tryn, Claes, Seyn, Thys, and Lucas, and the detailed individual illustrations of churches, houses, trees, soldiers, horse-drawn wagons, and ships.

Jean Borrel.

Opera geometrica.

Lyon: Thomas Bertheau, 1554.

4.06

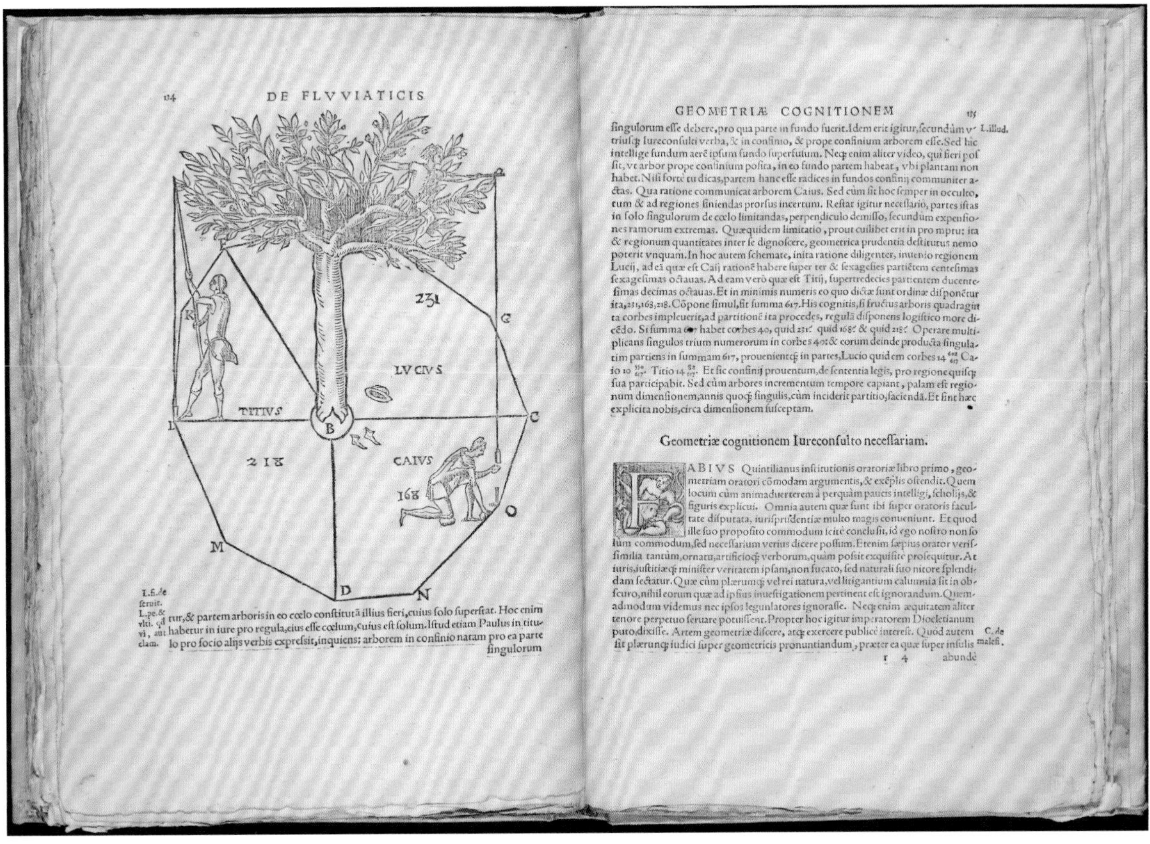

This work is the first book of geometry for lawyers. The problem illustrated at left concerns the ownership of fruit produced by a tree that grows at the junction of several property lines. In the illustration, the man perched precariously in the branches of the tree appears to have left his shoes and hat beside its trunk. The author took pains to correct some mathematical errors promulgated by Bartolus (see item 4.01).

4.07

Christian Gottfried Leiser.

Jus georgicum, sive, Tractatus de praediis.

Leipzig: heirs of Friedrich Lanckisch, 1698.

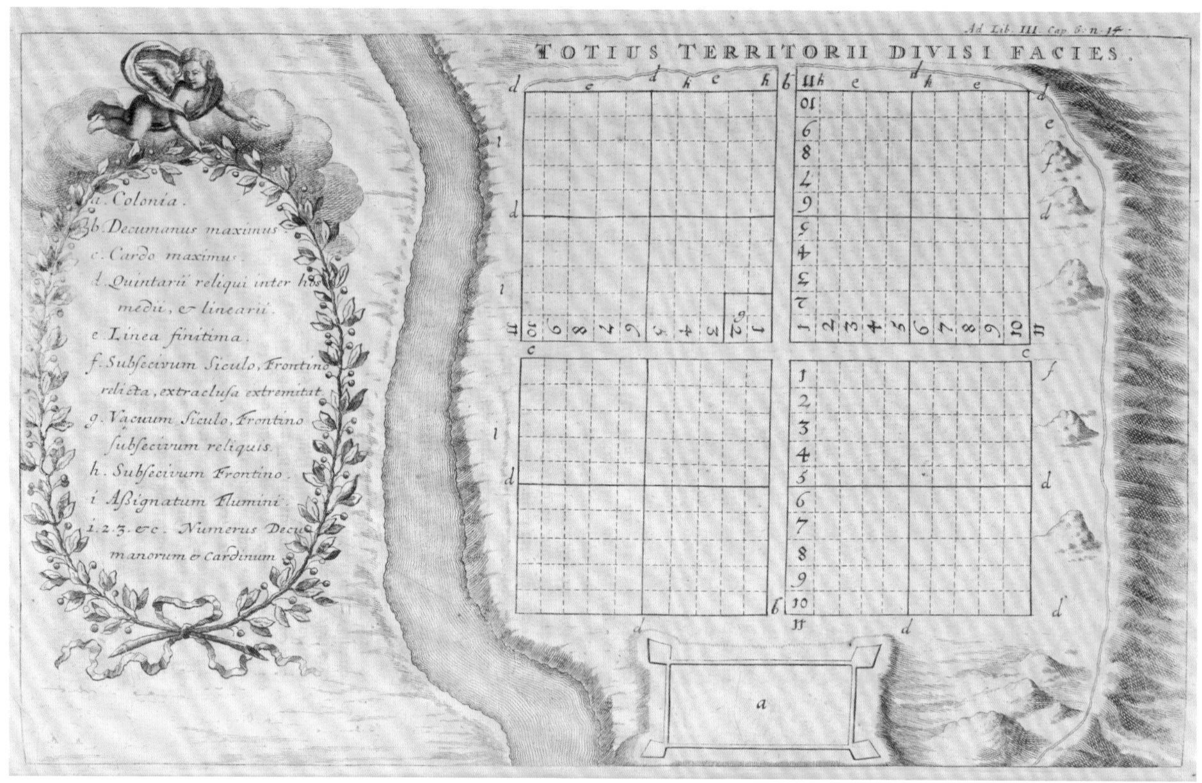

A treatise on agricultural law and estates, this volume features a grid for understanding the parceling of land. Charts like these not only diagram law, but also help practitioners apply it.

Luigi Piccoli.

Le servitù prediali sanzionate dal Codice Napoleone.

4.08

Brescia: Nicolò Bettoni, 1808.
Engravings by Carlo Donegani.

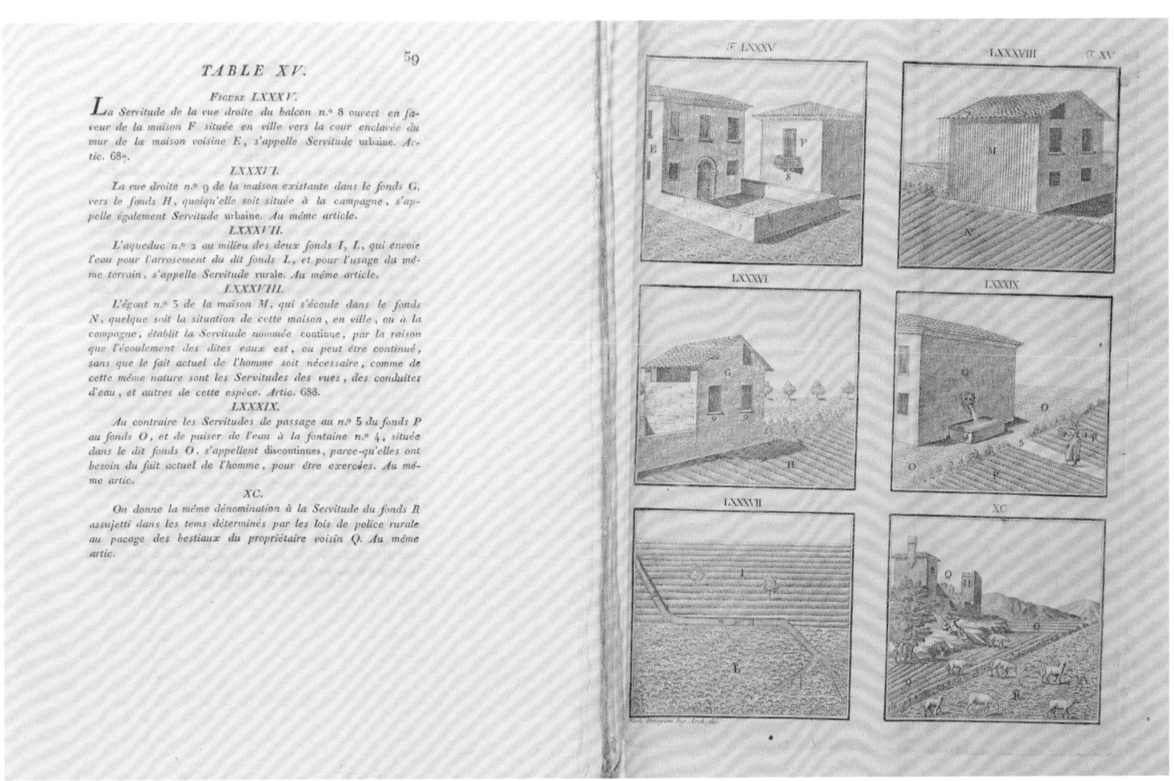

59

TABLE XV.

Figure LXXXV.

La Servitude de la vue droite du balcon n.° 8 ouvert en faveur de la maison F située en ville vers la cour enclavée du mur de la maison voisine E, s'appelle Servitude urbaine. *Artic.* 687.

LXXXVI.

La vue droite n.° 9 de la maison existante dans le fonds G, vers le fonds H, quoiqu'elle soit située à la campagne, s'appelle également Servitude urbaine. *Au même article.*

LXXXVII.

L'aqueduc n.° 2 au milieu des deux fonds I, L, qui envoie l'eau pour l'arrosement du dit fonds L, et pour l'usage du même terrain, s'appelle Servitude rurale. *Au même article.*

LXXXVIII.

L'égout n.° 3 de la maison M, qui s'écoule dans le fonds N, quelque soit la situation de cette maison, en ville, ou à la compagne, établit la Servitude nommée continue, *par la raison que l'écoulement des dites eaux est, ou peut être continué, sans que le fait actuel de l'homme soit nécessaire, comme de cette même nature sont les Servitudes des vues, des conduites d'eau, et autres de cette espèce. Artic.* 688.

LXXXIX.

Au contraire les Servitudes de passage au n.° 5 du fonds P au fonds O, et de puiser de l'eau à la fontaine n.° 4, située dans le dit fonds O, s'appellent discontinues, *parce-qu'elles ont besoin du fait actuel de l'homme, pour être exercées. Au même artic.*

XC.

On donne la même dénomination à la Servitude du fonds R assujetti dans les tems déterminés par les lois de police rurale au pacage des bestiaux du propriétaire voisin Q. Au même artic.

This Italian treatise is based on the Napoleonic Code (1804), which was introduced into northern Italy in the wake of Bonaparte's conquering revolutionary army. The book concerns servitudes, a civil law subject about nonposessory interests in land comparable to common law easements, about which the author published numerous illustrated volumes. Reference numbers bind the book's images and text closely together. This edition includes 144 copperplates.

In real life, the authority of law is displayed through spatial relationships between people. Books translate those relationships into lines and shapes. They offer a message about what law is through the depiction of the actual. Joost de Damhoudere (1507–1581) took a special interest in issues of guardianship, illustrated here in a composition featuring legal actors arranged on five different horizontal planes.

Joost de Damhoudere.
Pupillorum patrocinium.
Antwerp: Jean Beller, 1564.
Acquired with the John A. Hoober Fund.

Staging the Law

5

All the law's a stage, and law books often raise the curtain to reveal its players carefully arranged on a complex set. They depict judges, lawyers, and litigants in the formal spaces where law takes place, especially courtrooms, law offices, and law libraries.

These illustrations have many purposes, including public education, political critique, and the promotion of commercial sales. Yet whatever their purpose, by depicting law's stage, the books also portray law's character as a public ritual – as a theater of social meaning. They are the most concrete form of symbolic representation in the tradition of law book illustration.

5.01

Ceremonial for the trial of a peer.

London: T. Payne, 1776.

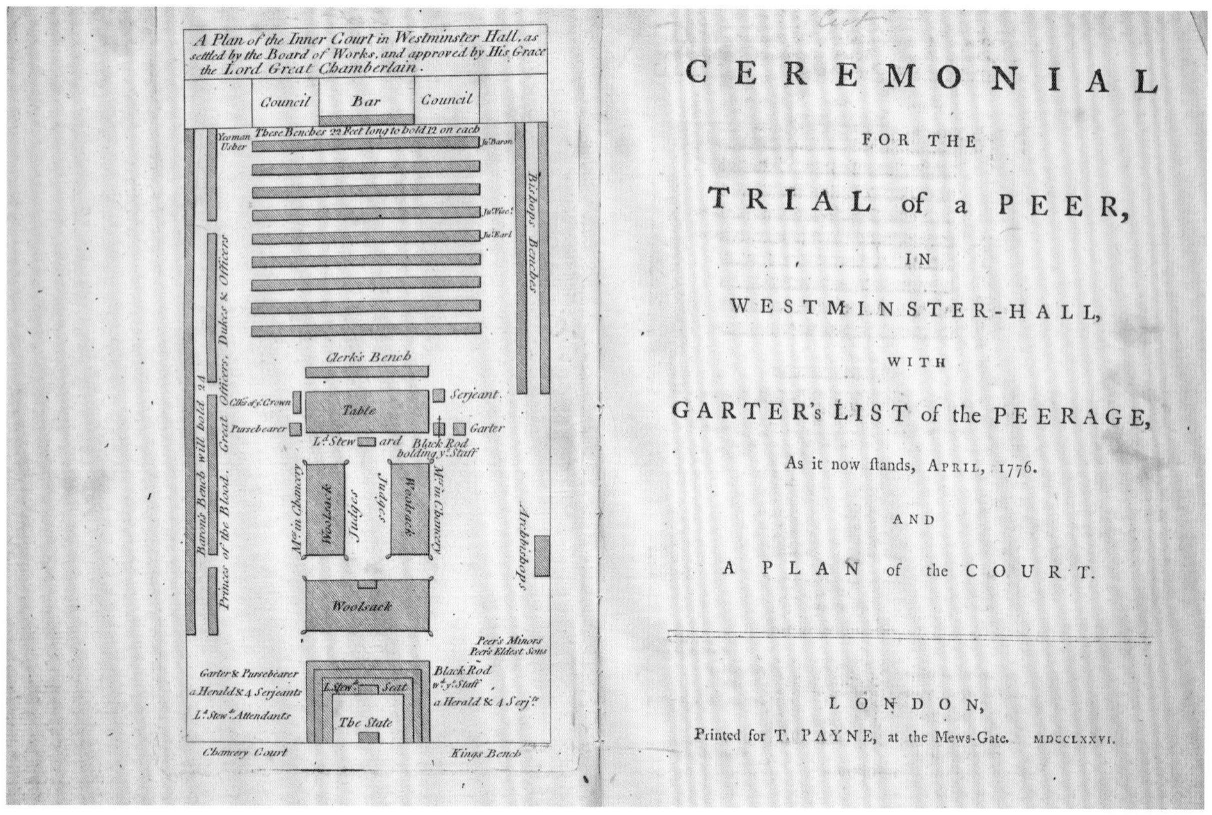

CEREMONIAL

FOR THE

TRIAL of a PEER,

IN

WESTMINSTER-HALL,

WITH

GARTER's LIST of the PEERAGE,

As it now ſtands, April, 1776.

AND

A PLAN of the COURT.

LONDON,

Printed for T. PAYNE, at the Mews-Gate. MDCCLXXVI.

These are stage directions for a trial. This pamphlet was likely issued as a handy reference for the bigamy prosecution of the scandal-ridden Elizabeth Pierrepont, Duchess of Kingston-on-Hull (1721-88). She was found guilty and fled to the continent. The engraved schematic floor plan is detailed down to the length of the benches (22 feet long, each to hold 12 peers).

GERARD VAN WASSENAER.

Practyk judicieel, ofte, Instructie op de forme en manier van procederen voor hoven en recht-banken.

Utrecht: Jacob van Poolsum, 1746.

5.02

Every dog has its day. A surprising number of law office and courtroom illustrations in the Yale Law Library collection contain images of dogs in the foreground. Dogs are especially numerous in books from the Netherlands in the seventeenth and eighteenth centuries. Why? The phenomenon certainly should give us paws – and excite the interest of researchers. See also item 5.0.

Representation of the House of Lords during the Trial of her Majesty Queen Caroline

The life, trial & defence, of Her Most Gracious Majesty, Caroline, Queen of Great-Britain.

5.03

London: Dean & Munday, 1820. Acquired with the Charles J. Tanenbaum Fund.

Gates and walls and curtains. Parallel and intersecting architectural lines. Legal players aligned on different horizontal and vertical planes. In their realism, pictorial elements such as these depict law as a theater of social meaning. The scandalous trial of Queen Caroline for adultery – initiated by George IV, who sought a divorce – was one of the most notorious legal and political events of its day, and served as a vehicle for popular criticism of government.

5.04

Karl Ferdinand Hommel.

Iurisprudentia numismatibus illustrata.

Leipzig: Johann Wendler, 1763.

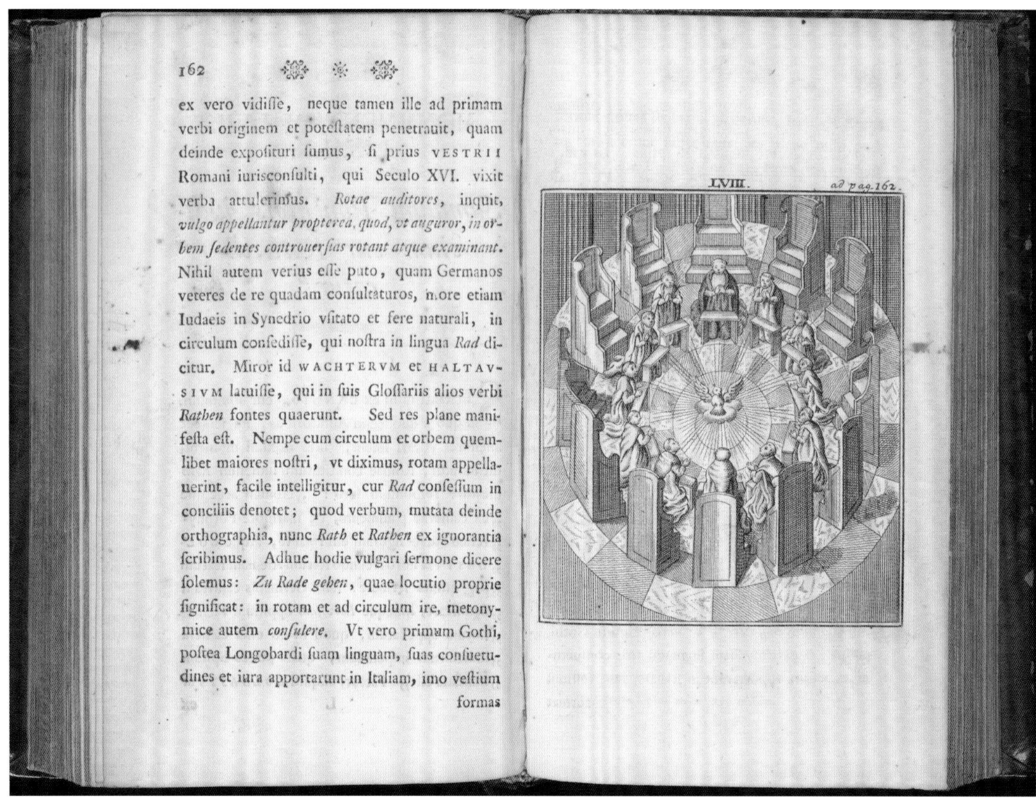

162

ex vero vidiſſe, neque tamen ille ad primam verbi originem et poteſtatem penetrauit, quam deinde expoſituri ſumus, ſi prius VESTRII Romani iurisconſulti, qui Seculo XVI. vixit verba attulerimus. *Rotae auditores*, inquit, *vulgo appellantur propterea, quod, vt auguror, in orbem ſedentes controuerſias rotant atque examinant.* Nihil autem verius eſſe puto, quam Germanos veteres de re quadam conſultaturos, more etiam Iudaeis in Synedrio vſitato et fere naturali, in circulum conſediſſe, qui noſtra in lingua *Rad* dicitur. Miror id WACHTERVM et HALTAVSIVM latuiſſe, qui in ſuis Gloſſariis alios verbi *Rathen* fontes quaerunt. Sed res plane manifeſta eſt. Nempe cum circulum et orbem quemlibet maiores noſtri, vt diximus, rotam appellauerint, facile intelligitur, cur *Rad* conſeſſum in conciliis denotet; quod verbum, mutata deinde orthographia, nunc *Rath* et *Rathen* ex ignorantia ſcribimus. Adhuc hodie vulgari ſermone dicere ſolemus: *Zu Rade gehen*, quae locutio proprie ſignificat: in rotam et ad circulum ire, metonymice autem *conſulere*. Vt vero primum Gothi, poſtea Longobardi ſuam linguam, ſuas conſuetudines et iura apportarunt in Italiam, imo veſtium formas

The Roman Rota is the highest appellate court of the Catholic Church – a tribunal whose name, "wheel," derives from the shape of the room in which it originally met. This curious volume examines a wide range of legal issues through the use of illustrations, especially of coins, medals, and gems. Indeed, the legal topics were chosen precisely because they could be illustrated.

Bernard Rosenfield.

Let's go to the Supreme Court.

New York: Putnam, 1960. Illustrated by Gustav Schrotter.
Gift of Gloria Cohen, from the library of Morris L. Cohen, 2014.

5.05

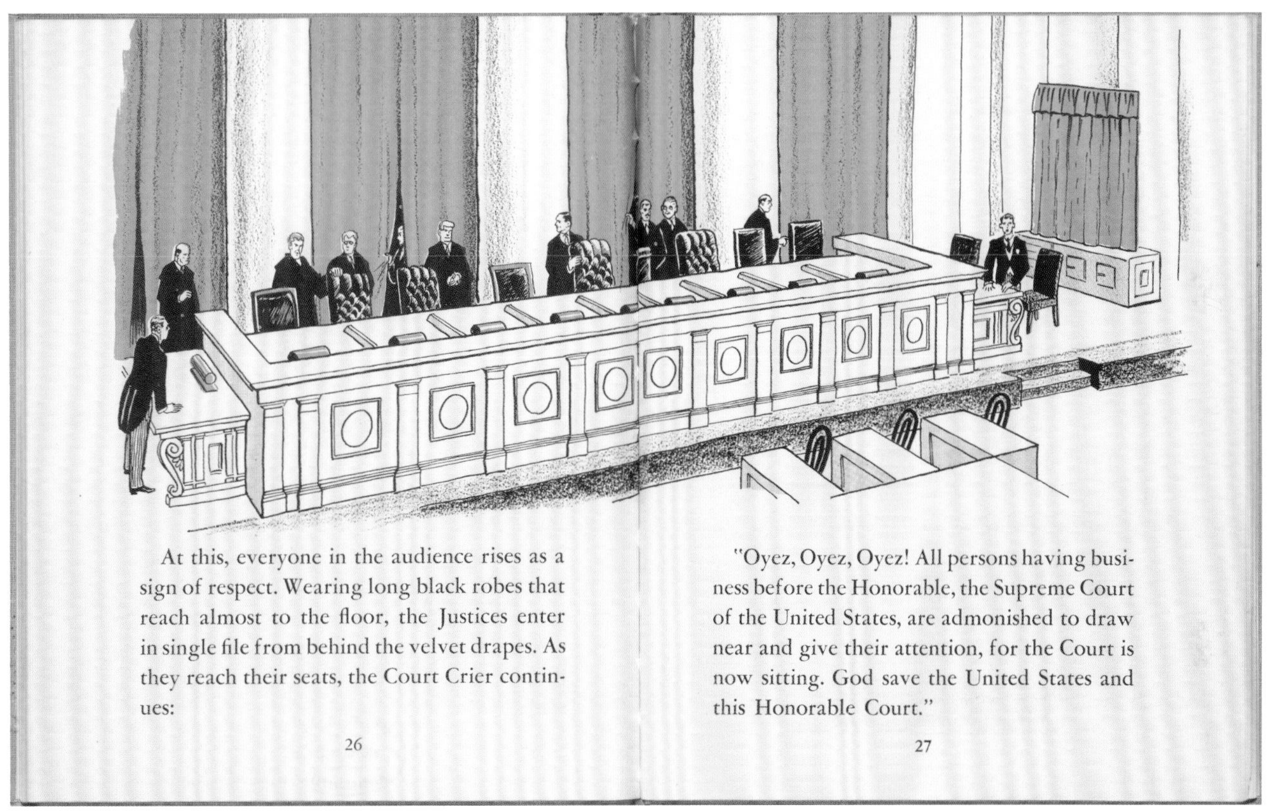

At this, everyone in the audience rises as a sign of respect. Wearing long black robes that reach almost to the floor, the Justices enter in single file from behind the velvet drapes. As they reach their seats, the Court Crier continues:
26
"Oyez, Oyez, Oyez! All persons having business before the Honorable, the Supreme Court of the United States, are admonished to draw near and give their attention, for the Court is now sitting. God save the United States and this Honorable Court."
27

Stay behind the railing – but read on! This book for young people about the U.S. Supreme Court contains surprisingly detailed descriptions, and illustrations, of mundane courtroom architecture. "At the end of the Justices' bench is a desk that is raised, but not quite so high as the Justices'."

5.06

Consultatien, advysen en advertissementen, gegeven ende geschreven by verscheyden treffeljcke rechts-geleerden in Hollandt.

Rotterdam: J. Naeranus, 1648-1666. Volume 1 of 7. Acquired with the John A. Hoober Fund.

The majority of legal work takes place in law offices, not in courtrooms. And the law office is a stage set with books, as illustrated in each of the three panels here. The text at the bottom of the image exhorts: "live well – and to each his due."

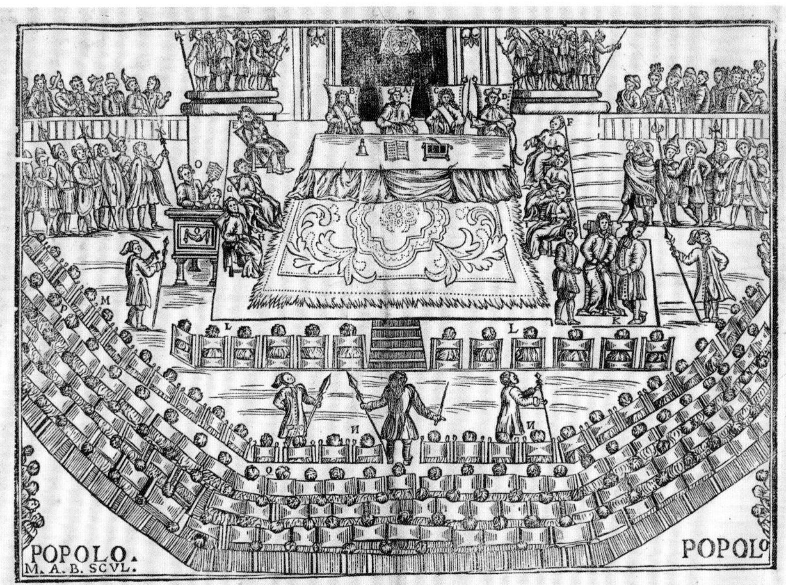

A L'Eminentissimo, e Reverendissimo Sig. Cardinal Gio: Badoaro Vescovo.
B L'Illustrissimo, ed Eccellentissimo Sig. Renier Zen Podestà.) Rettori.
C L'Illustrissimo, ed Eccellentissimo Sig. Ferigo Barbarigo Capitanio)
D Reverendissimo P: Maestro Tomaso Manganoni da Bergamo Inquisitore.
E Illustrissimo Sig. Co: Ottavio Fenicio Governator dell' Armi.
F Padre Maestro Vicenzo Sala Vicario del Sant' Officio.
G Illustris., e Reverendiss. Sig. Co: Alessandro Prior Canonico Durante) Testi-
H Illustris., e Reverendiss. Sig. Scipion Canonico Abb. Luzzago.) monj.
K Il Beccarello, con due Sbirri, che lo tengon legato.
L Dodeci Consultori del Sant' Officio.
M Illustrissimi, e Reverendissimi Signori Canonici della Cattedrale.
N Illustrissimi Sig. Publici della Città, ed Illustrissimi Sig. Curiali.
O Pulpito con due Lettori, che leggono le Colpe.
P Rever. Clero della Cattedrale.
Q Religiosi, e Nobiltà in gran numero.

Veridica Descrizione, e Ragguaglio distinto della Promulgazione delle Colpe, dell'Abjura solenne, e della Condanna di Galera fulminata dal Santo Tribunale dell' Inquisizione di Brescia, contro GIUSEPPE BECCARELLI da Vrago d'Olio, li 13. Settembre 1710.

'Idra contumace dell' Eresia, benche vedasi tante volte reciso il capo rubelle da Santissimi Tribunali della Fede, tuttavia và di quando in quando fecondando nuove Teste, che spargono aliti funesti, ed avvelenano la purità della Religione Cattolica. Brescia lo sà pur troppo, quale benche porti in fronte il titolo luminoso di fedele non meno al suo Principe, che à Dio, nata con le Città primogenite della Fede, allattata col Sangue d' innumerabili Martiri suoi Figli, ed allevata sotto le leggi de' suoi Santissimi Vescovi; pure hà qualche volta risentiti sintomi mortali, massime da Novatori, che allontanati dal Santuario, si sono fatti inventori di novi Demonj.

Sacrilego, e convinto Tralignante dalle Massime Evangeliche, fù Giuseppe Beccarelli, che sparse ne' seminati della Chiesa, zizanie di nefandissimi errori. Nacque costui di sangue oscuro, e villano nella Terra di Urago d'Olio; e portatosi da' suoi primi Anni, per Causa de' studj in Brescia, sortì in essi talento rozzo, ed eguale alla nascita. Mà perche il Demonio con parziali influenze assiste sempre à coloro, benche idioti, che prevede fazionarj, e propagatori della sua infernal giurisdizione, toccò à costui in poco tempo, d'essere Direttore, non solo d'un Collegio numeroso di Giovani, ma d' altre persone ancora, massime del Sesso più facile, ed inclinato à novità: ed accioche la infezzione pigliasse più piede, condiva i suoi Dogmi attossicati con balsamo di titoli speciosi di perfezione Cristiana, e con affettazione di sacrilega, empia Santità.

Mà Iddio, che hà sempre mirata questa sua fedele Provincia con occhio di parzialissima predilezzione, non volle permettere, che questa peste caminasse così lungamente baldanzosa, con la fronte levata, facendo misera stragge d'Anime ingannate, e sedotte. Che perciò la Divina Misericordia riguardò dal Cielo, prendendosi essa l'impegno di provedere questa Chiesa del Zelo Vigilantissimo dell' Eminentissimo, e Reverendissimo Signor Giovanni Badovaro Cardinale, e Vescovo, e della sperimentata destrità, e matura Prudenza del Reverendissimo Padre Maestro Tomaso Antonio Manganoni da Bergamo Inquisitor Generale, a' quali erasi riserbata la gloria di scoprire, e strozzar questo Serpe, che cò suoi giri tortuosi si nascondeva astutamente trà fiori, e si rannicchiava in se stesso. Intanto dalla Pietà dell' Eminentissimo Pastore tentati indarno con quest' animo indomabile, tutti i lenitivi della Clemenza, per indurlo à un pentimento volontario; seguì poi per comando Publico nel dì 4. Giugno 1708. l'arresto del Beccarelli, con universale applauso della Città, che lo vidde condotto cautamente in un Torrione del Castello, dove poscia à richiesta ancora del Santo Tribunale fù custodito priggione.

Dopo lunghi esami restò il Reo confesso, convinto, e condannato, dichiarate le sue Proposizioni eretiche, spergiure, e perversive dalla Catolica Fede, decretatosi inoltre, che nella Piazza grande della Città, dovesse in presenza del Santo Officio, e di tutta la Republica Cristiana, abjurare le Massime sudette, ed udire la Sentenza della sua condanna, che seguì li 13. Settembre 1710.

Tutta la notte antecedente, dalle cinque ore di notte, sin verso le dodici, affollavasi il Popolo d'ogni sesso, e d'ogni grado per prevenire, ed occupare i primi posti. Non mirò mai la Religione Bresciana Scena più gioconda, ne spettacolo più sospirato di questo. Ergevasi rimpetto la Porta sinistra della facciata del Duomo Nuovo, un Palco grande, con quattro Sedie, ed una Tavola, il tutto coperto di Veluto Cremese maestosamente disposto per servizio del Santo Tribunale, ed Assistenza, oltre altri minori Sedili. Dal lato destro vedeasi inalzata una Catedra, ed al sinistro giacere un piccolo Palco nudo, con una Sedietta lavorata dal ludibrio, e dallo scherno. Avanti il Palco maggiore, sul piano, piegavasi in arco uno steccato, ov' erano distribuite tredici sedie, e dopo questo un' altro Steccato spaziosissimo destinato per i Religiosi, e Nobiltà.

Gionta la mattina del Sabbato, che fù li 13. Settembre 1710. verso le ore 12. per una Scala segreta comparve distinto ne' suoi luoghi sul Palco maggiore il Santo Tribunale, con l'Assistenza degl' Illustrissimi, ed Eccellentissimi Signori Rettori, imprimendo in tutti gli Astanti, con ribrezzo un sagro orrore di Maestà sovraumana. Discesero dopo nel primo Steccato gl' Illustrissimi Signori Fiscale, e Consultori, essendo già avanzati nello Steccato maggiore gl' Illustrissimi Signori Publici, e Curiali: Viddesi poi sul Palco sinistro il Beccarelli in mezzo à due Sbirri, con le manette a' polsi, qual Vittima rea della Divina vendetta, e della publica quiete.

Ascesero intanto il Pulpito i due Promulgatori della Sentenza, che subintravano à vicenda alla lunga lettura quale durò due ore, e mezza con fremito, e mormorio del Popolo, alla publicazione de i dogmi ereticali, e delle massime così sozze, ed immonde, che contaminavano il core, di chi con odio le udiva.

Compita la promulgazione delle colpe, insorse contro il Reo, con invettiva Evangelica il Reverendiss. P. Inquisitore acceso di tanto zelo, che ben parve, che sopra la sua lingua, si unissero tutte le lingue infocate, e i tuoni veheměti dello Spirito Santo, per infiammare i Fedeli, e fulminare i ribelli della Verità increata. Pianse con lagrime di zelo Apostolico il Nostro Clementissimo Pastore, che commossero tutto il Popolo, toltone il Beccarelli, che stette sempre con occhi asciutti.

Dopo il sudetto Raggionamento, fù letta la Sentenza definitiva, per la quale fù dichiarato detto Beccarello sospetto vehementemente d'Eresia, cioè di aver tenute, e credute Proposizioni Ereticali, erronee &c. Fù da poi obligato all' Abjura delle medesime, con la condanna di sette Anni di Gallera, ed ingionte altre Penitenze salutari. Finita la lettura, si prostese ginocchione il Beccarelli a' piedi del Santo Magistrato, facendo con i soliti Riti di Chiesa Santa, l'Abjura, che sottoscrisse di proprio pugno, con l'intervento di due Illustrissimi Signori Canonici della Catedrale Testimonj rogati; dopo il che ottenne dal Reverendissimo P. Inquisitor Generale l'assoluzione dalle Censure.

IN BRESCIA, Per Gio: Maria Rizzardi, Con Licenza de' Superiori. 1710.

5.07

Veridica descrizione ... della condanna di galera fulminata dal Santo Tribunale dell' Inquisizione di Brescia, contro Giuseppe Beccarelli.

Brescia: Gio. Maria Rizzardi, 1710.
Acquired with the John A. Hoober Fund.

An alphabetic key identifies the participants in this Italian trial, including the accused ("Il Beccarello"), the presiding officer, Cardinal Gianalberto Badoaro, the inquisitors, clergy, and the public ("Popolo"). The defendant, Giuseppe Beccarelli, was a priest accused of promoting the heresy of Quietism. He spent the last years of his life in prison. This is the only known library copy.

5.08

Prieur de Saint Pierre.

L'arbitre charitable: pour eviter les procez et les querelles.

Paris: Laurens Raueneau, 1668. Acquired with the Albert S. Wheeler Fund.

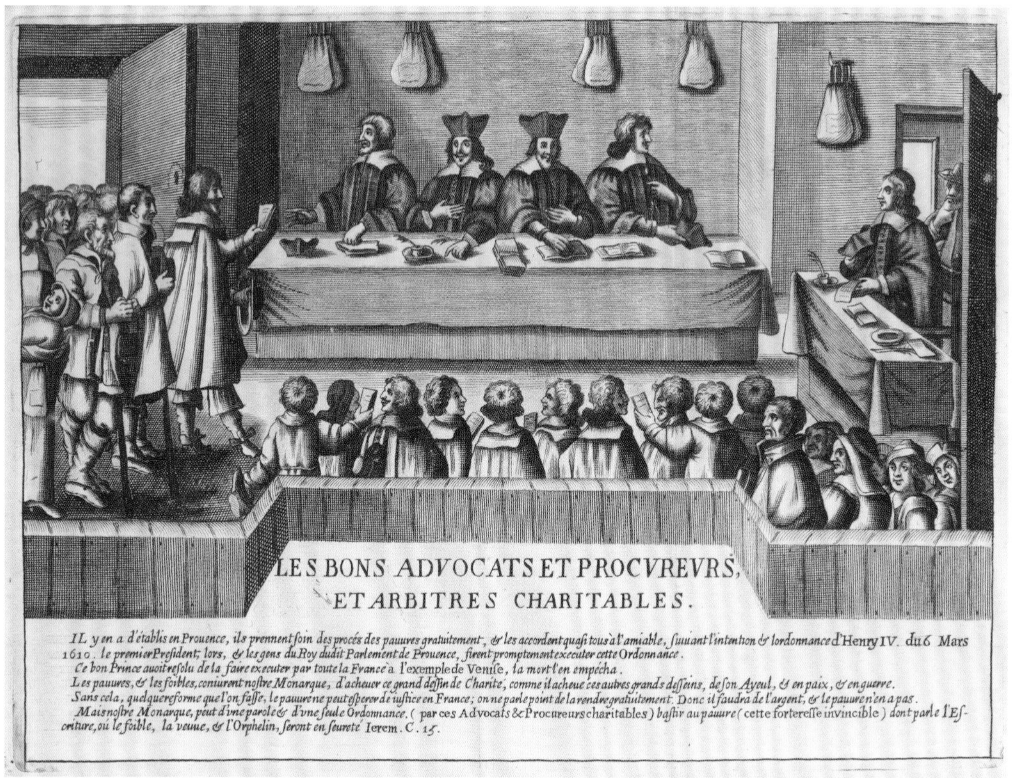

In this treatise on legal aid for the poor, law is given meaning through a composition divided into four distinct spaces. The bags hanging on the wall contain legal papers – they are the equivalent of modern-day filing cabinets.

H. G. Hayes.

A complete history of the trial of Guiteau, assassin of President Garfield.

Philadelphia: Hubbard Bros.; San Francisco: A.L. Bancroft; St. Louis, Mo.: J. Burns, 1882.

5.09

The meaning of architecture and interior design can be shaded through the depiction of a telling gesture. With the proper tilt of a hand, illustrations of a courtroom can cast the legitimacy of a legal process into doubt.

SCENE IN COURT—GUITEAU INTERRUPTING PROCEEDINGS.

98 TRIAL OF CHARLES J. GUITEAU.

The applause that greeted this declaration was so impetuous, so spontaneous and so unexpected that the District-Attorney and counsel for the government looked amazed, for they seemed to interpret it as the first triumph won by the defense. The District-Attorney could hardly believe his own ears as he stood there in anything but a pleasing mood. His associate counsel could conceal neither their vexation nor surprise. Mr. Davidge frowned; Mr. Smith looked a little startled; Judge Porter, of New York, grew more thoughtful in look. Every eye was directed to the government counsel. Judge Cox, unmoved, awaited further remarks, while the bailiff ordered silence.

I had considered (continued Mr. Scoville), that this evidence was competent.

Prisoner: You will not have any success from the Lord by lying. You lie. I've found you out. When a man lies to me once I never believe him again. You have lied to me once, and that is played out.

The prisoner in making this speech seemed to be convulsed with passion, and it was in vain that his brother and sister attempted to quiet him.

Mr. Scoville: All I want in this case is that the truth shall prevail.

Prisoner: That is what I want, and I am going to have it, too.

Mr. Scoville, to the jury: All I want is that the truth shall prevail. If there is any evidence

5.10

Adolf Glassbrenner.

Eine Volks-Jury in Berlin.

Leipzig: Verlag von Ignaz Jackowitz, 1848.
From the library of Harold D. Lasswell.

Eine Volks-Jury in Berlin.

Berlin
wie es ist und — trinkt.

Von
Ad. Brennglas.

Achtundzwanzigstes Heft:
„Eine Volks-Jury in Berlin."

Mit einem colorirten Titelkupfer.

Leipzig, 1848.
Verlag von Ignaz Jackowitz.

Members of a democratic political club in Berlin put their existing system of justice on trial. In the words of one scholar, "what is of interest is the manner in which the trial is conducted. Everyone is allowed to express his viewpoint, either for or against the accused. The entire trial is conducted in an absolutely democratic way." How does the composition of the illustration depict the club's democratic legal ideal?

Jean Baptiste Selves.

Au roi: La vérité sur l'administration de la justice.

5.11

Paris: Chez Le Normant, Libraire, rue de Seine, [ca. 1815].

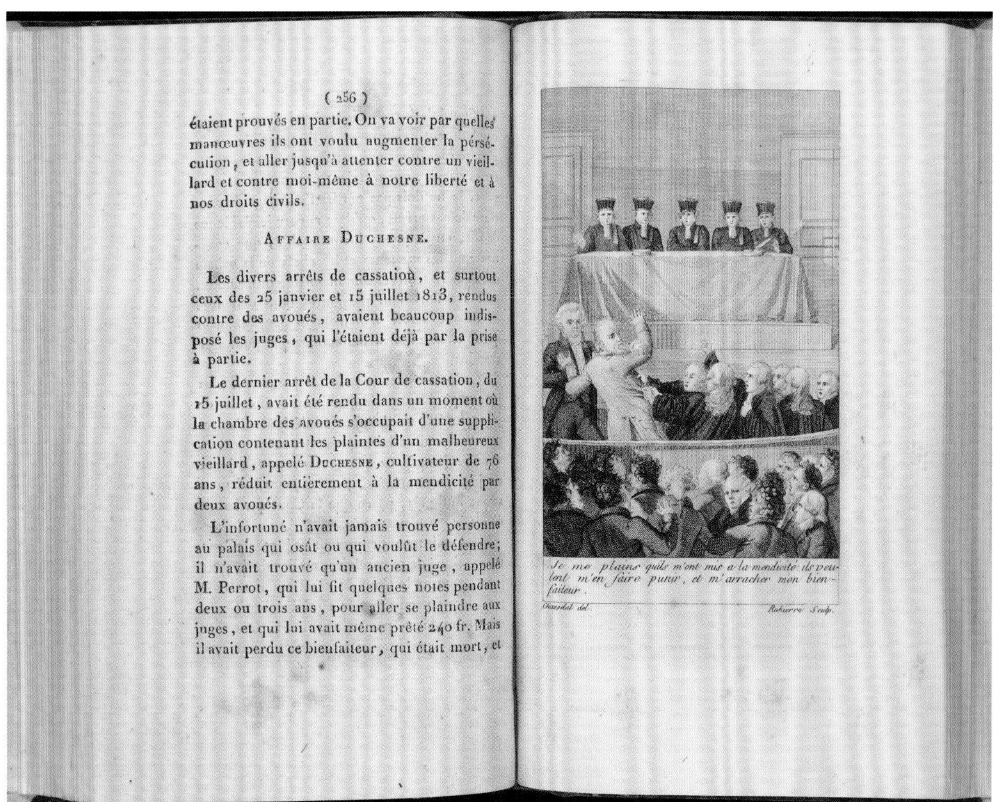

(256)

étaient prouvés en partie. On va voir par quelles manœuvres ils ont voulu augmenter la persécution, et aller jusqu'à attenter contre un vieillard et contre moi-même à notre liberté et à nos droits civils.

Affaire Duchesne.

Les divers arrêts de cassation, et surtout ceux des 25 janvier et 15 juillet 1813, rendus contre des avoués, avaient beaucoup indisposé les juges, qui l'étaient déjà par la prise à partie.

Le dernier arrêt de la Cour de cassation, du 15 juillet, avait été rendu dans un moment où la chambre des avoués s'occupait d'une supplication contenant les plaintes d'un malheureux vieillard, appelé Duchesne, cultivateur de 76 ans, réduit entièrement à la mendicité par deux avoués.

L'infortuné n'avait jamais trouvé personne au palais qui osât ou qui voulût le défendre; il n'avait trouvé qu'un ancien juge, appelé M. Perrot, qui lui fit quelques notes pendant deux ou trois ans, pour aller se plaindre aux juges, et qui lui avait même prêté 240 fr. Mais il avait perdu ce bienfaiteur, qui était mort, et

In a scathing critique of the French judicial system, three distinct planes powerfully divide an illustration of the "Affair Duchesne." Amable Duchesne, a seventy-six-year-old farmer, sued unsuccessfully for the return of his cattle in the Palais de Justice in Paris, and was left destitute. The author, Jean-Baptiste Selves (1757-1823), had been a judge of the Criminal Court of the Seine under Bonaparte. His attacks on the judicial system effectively ended his career.

5.12

Clark Stoeckley.

The United States vs. Pvt. Chelsea Manning.

New York: OR Books, 2014.

Private Chelsea Manning was prosecuted before a military court for leaking national defense information to WikiLeaks. The cover of this illustrated book about the court martial contains an implicit critique of the military justice system, and the legitimacy of its guilty verdict, by boxing Manning into the lower-right corner of a hierarchically arranged frame.

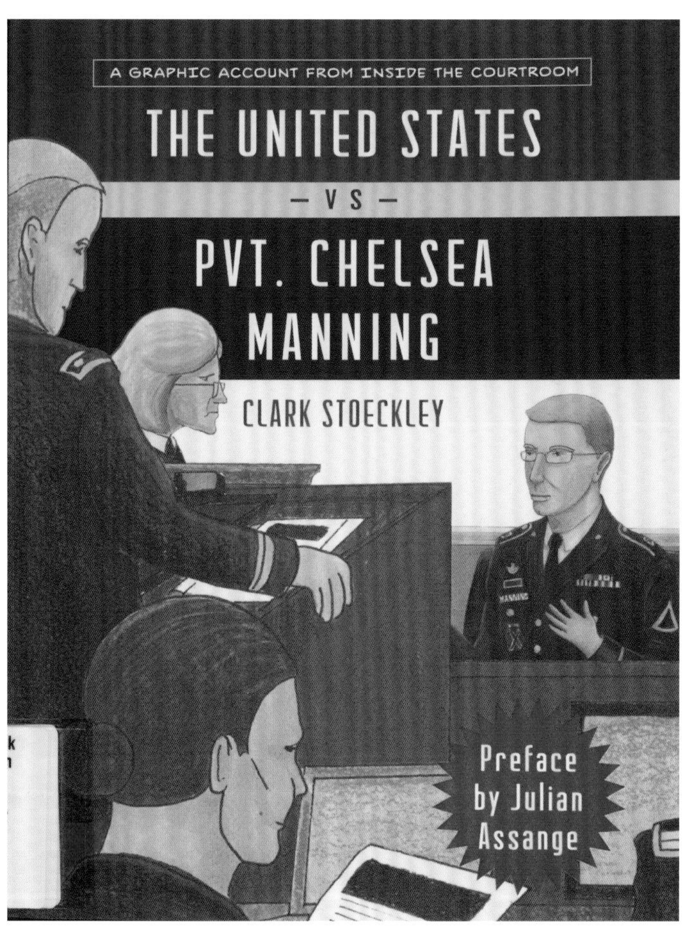

Noe Meurer.

Tractatus juridicus de successione ab intestato.

Nürnberg: In Verlegung Johann Albrecht, gedruct bey Johann Ernst Adelbulnern, 1730.
Acquired with the Arthur Hobson Dean Purchase Fund in International Law.

5.13

TRACTATUS JURIDICUS,
De
SUCCESSIONE AB INTESTATO
Oder
Vollkommener Unterricht
Von
Erbschafften/
Und
Erb-Gerechtigkeiten/
wann kein Testament, oder letzter Wille, vorhanden ist.
Darinnen umständlich, klärlich und deutlich gewiesen wird, wie
man sich bey Antrettung, oder auch Entschlagung der Erbschafften zu verhalten.
Ingleichen auch was die Wiedereinwerffung in die Erbschafft angehet; item von *Possession*
und *Immission* der Erbschafften, auch wie ein in Rechten beständiges *Inventarium* zu verfer-
gen, und aufzurichten, und was dabey zu *observiren*, und in acht zu nehmen. Ingleichen
wie man an Kayserlichen Cammer-Gericht von Erbschafften und derselben
Gerechtigkeit, handelt.
Ein Werck, dergleichen in Teutscher Sprach noch niemals
ausgegangen.
Deme ferner, wegen Gleichheit der Materie, beygefüget worden:
Sr. Chur-Fürstl. Durchl. zu Sachsen, &c. &c. Herzogs Augusti Constitution,
Distinction &c. von Erb-Fällen. Ferner was die Hochfürstl Würtenbergis. und
Fürstl. Jülich und Bergischen, ingleichen die Gräfl. Solmische Land-Rechte davon melden.
Item, was die, des H. Röm. Reichs freye Städte, Worms, Nürnberg und Franckfurt,
Reformationes, deswegen in sich halten.
Männiglichen / absonderlich denen, so bey Gerichten zu handlen haben, noth-
wendig, und nützlich, verfertiget.
Von Tit. Hn. Noa Meurern, J.U.D. und Jh. Churfl. Durchl. zu
Pfaltz Hof-Cammer-Rath, &c. &c.
Nürnberg / In Verlegung Johann Albrecht. Anno 1730.
Gedruckt bey Johann Ernst Adelbulnern.

Illustrations of legal interiors often promote the practice of law as a profession – and they flatter those who already practice it. In headpieces, vignettes, and printing devices, illustrations of law offices and courtrooms depict law's spaces for the purposes of ornament and advertising.

In a compilation of the customary laws of Artois, the right index finger of the executed man points downward, toward the text. The text explains the legal procedures applied to cases of murder.

ARTOIS (FRANCE).
Coutumes generales d'Artois.
Paris: Chez Le Clerc, à la Toison d'Or. ... [and 6 others], 1756.
Acquired with the Albert S. Wheeler Fund.

50 Anciens Usages d'Artois. Titre XLIX.

SEPTIE'ME PLANCHE.

EXECUTION D'UN JUGEMENT DE MORT, contre un Voleur.

A la page *65.* de l'Original, le fond de cette Miniature est bleu.

Quel chose Justice doit faire de l'Homme, qui li est accusé. XLIX.

1. SE aucun Hom est accusé de lait fait où il perde vie : s'il en estoit atains, & ne soit de Lieu prochain où il sera arriesté, où il ne soit de le Jurisdiction à le Justice qui l'aroit ariesté. La Justice li doit demander s'il nie ce qu'il li metera sus ; s'il se veut mettre en le verité de sen Païs.

2. Si dist oïl, il li doit demander s'il estoit si ignorant qu'il ne le seust requerre :

3. S'il ï a ame en sen Païs, de qui il soit haï. Et c'est de Droit escrit.

4. Car mes Anemi, ne Hom, auquel a esté fait afoleures par me Partie ne me puet, ne doit jugier, se pais n'en a esté faite : Et que teus Personnes sont à refuser, & li Tiesmoings qui amenès sont.

5. Et s'il estoit treuvé par l'Enqueste, qu'il soit Preu-d'Omme, li Justice le doit delivrer.

Inflicting the Law

6

In Franz Kafka's disturbing, enigmatic short story "In the Penal Colony," a prison camp officer proudly demonstrates an execution machine to a perplexed visitor – "the Traveler." The machine uses a collection of needles to inscribe the body of a condemned man with the text of the law he has violated. In the illustrations in this section, law likewise leaves its mark upon the human body: they depict acts of corporal and capital punishment, as well as torture used to extract evidence.

This is a gruesome subject, yet it is pervasive in the history of legal publishing, indeed in the history of law. From the perspective of today, such illustrations of lifelessness and pain may leave us silent. They even may cause modern Travelers to turn away our faces, just as the figure of Lady Justice does in the great eighteenth-century reform treatise by Cesare Beccaria.

6.01

Bambergische peinliche Halszgerichtszordnung.

Bamberg: Johann Wagner, 1580.

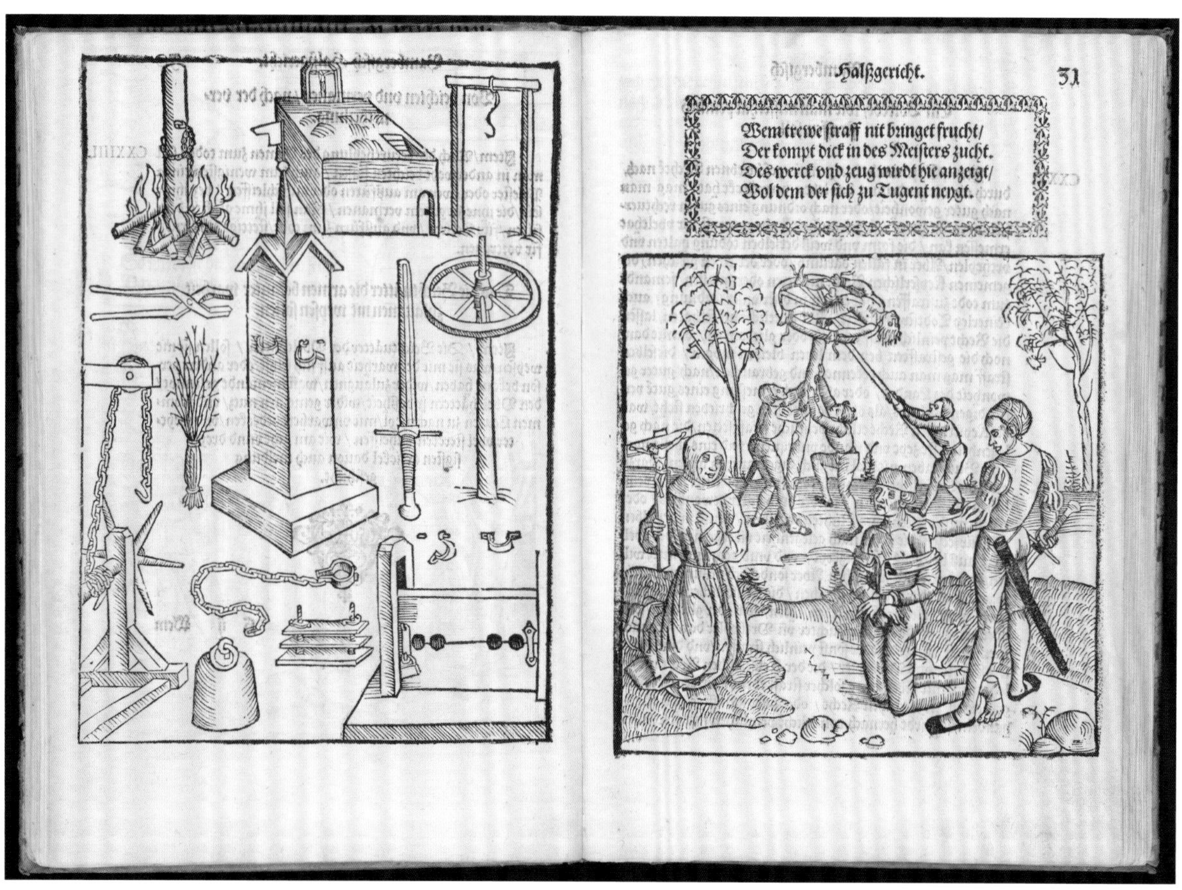

Exquisitely illustrated, the *Bambergensis* details the legal procedure used in cases of capital crime. Compiled in 1507 by Johann von Schwarzenberg (1463-1528), a reformist judge and official of the prince-bishopric of Bamberg, the book laid the foundation for the unification of criminal law in the Holy Roman Empire in 1530.

6.02

Agnello de Sarno.

Novissima praxis criminalis, et civilis.

Naples: Michael Monaco, 1687.

The book is open, the pen is poised, and the doctor is in. This comprehensive treatise on the civil and criminal law and procedure of the Kingdom of Naples contains a section on medical jurisprudence by Dr. Orazio Greco, shown here, which surveys methods of torture, forensic evidence, and tests to determine virginity and rape.

6.03

Joost de Damhoudere.
Praxis rerum criminalium.
Frankfurt: Johann Wolff, 1565.

Bodies in pain reveal their secrets, which are transcribed into text. The scene illustrated in this image was not a form of punishment, but rather was a method for extracting facts. As a method of proof, torture was long routine in Europe, in part because standards for conviction based on eyewitness evidence were especially high.

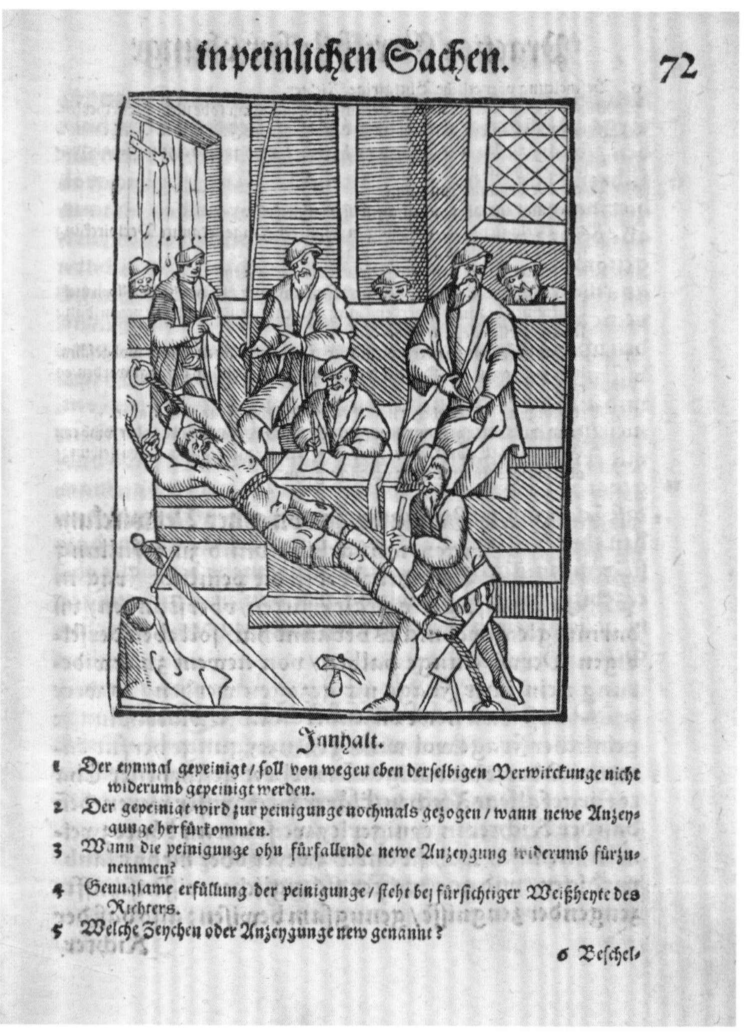

in peinlichen Sachen. 72

Innhalt.

1 Der eynmal gepeinigt / soll von wegen eben derselbigen Verwirckunge nicht widerumb gepeinigt werden.
2 Der gepeinigt wird zur peinigunge nochmals gezogen / wann newe Anzeygunge herfürkommen.
3 Wann die peinigunge ohn fürfallende newe Anzeygung widerumb fürzunemmen?
4 Genugsame erfüllung der peinigunge / steht bej fürsichtiger Weißheyte des Richters.
5 Welche Zeychen oder Anzeygunge new genannt?

6 Beschel-

Edme Théodore Bourg.

6.04

Dictionnaire de la pénalité dans toutes les parties du monde connu: tableau historique.

Paris: Rousselon, 1824-1828. Volume 4 of 5.

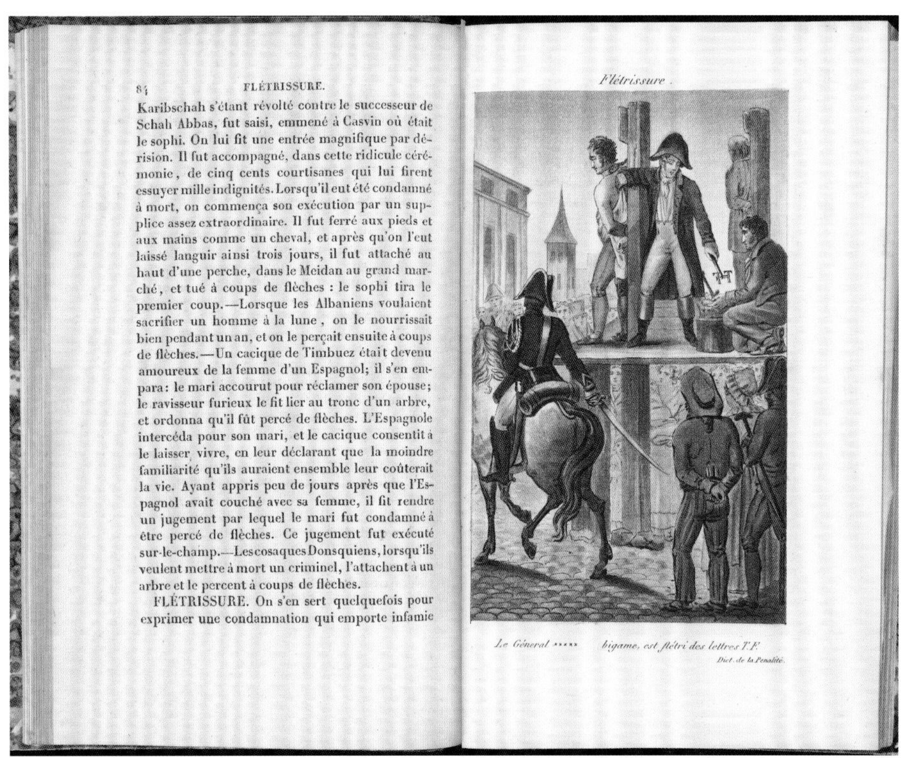

84 FLÉTRISSURE.

Karibschah s'étant révolté contre le successeur de Schah Abbas, fut saisi, emmené à Casvin où était le sophi. On lui fit une entrée magnifique par dérision. Il fut accompagné, dans cette ridicule cérémonie, de cinq cents courtisanes qui lui firent essuyer mille indignités. Lorsqu'il eut été condamné à mort, on commença son exécution par un supplice assez extraordinaire. Il fut ferré aux pieds et aux mains comme un cheval, et après qu'on l'eut laissé languir ainsi trois jours, il fut attaché au haut d'une perche, dans le Meidan au grand marché, et tué à coups de flèches : le sophi tira le premier coup.—Lorsque les Albaniens voulaient sacrifier un homme à la lune, on le nourrissait bien pendant un an, et on le perçait ensuite à coups de flèches.—Un cacique de Timbuez était devenu amoureux de la femme d'un Espagnol; il s'en empara: le mari accourut pour réclamer son épouse; le ravisseur furieux le fit lier au tronc d'un arbre, et ordonna qu'il fût percé de flèches. L'Espagnole intercéda pour son mari, et le cacique consentit à le laisser vivre, en leur déclarant que la moindre familiarité qu'ils auraient ensemble leur coûterait la vie. Ayant appris peu de jours après que l'Espagnol avait couché avec sa femme, il fit rendre un jugement par lequel le mari fut condamné à être percé de flèches. Ce jugement fut exécuté sur-le-champ.—Les cosaques Donsquiens, lorsqu'ils veulent mettre à mort un criminel, l'attachent à un arbre et le percent à coups de flèches.

FLÉTRISSURE. On s'en sert quelquefois pour exprimer une condamnation qui emporte infamie

Flétrissure.

*Le Général ***** bigame, est flétri des lettres T.F.*

Dict. de la Penalité.

A bigamist is branded with the letters TF – for *travaux forcés,* or forced labor – while a crowd watches. The branding of convicts in France was abolished by the French Assembly in 1832. Once common throughout Europe, the practice likely traces its ancient origins to markings of slave ownership. The same letters appear on the shoulder of Balzac's character Vautrin in his series *La Comédie humaine.*

6.05

Austria.

Constitutio criminalis Theresiana.

Vienna: J. T. Edlen von Trattnern, 1769. Acquired with the Yale Law Library Patrons Fund.

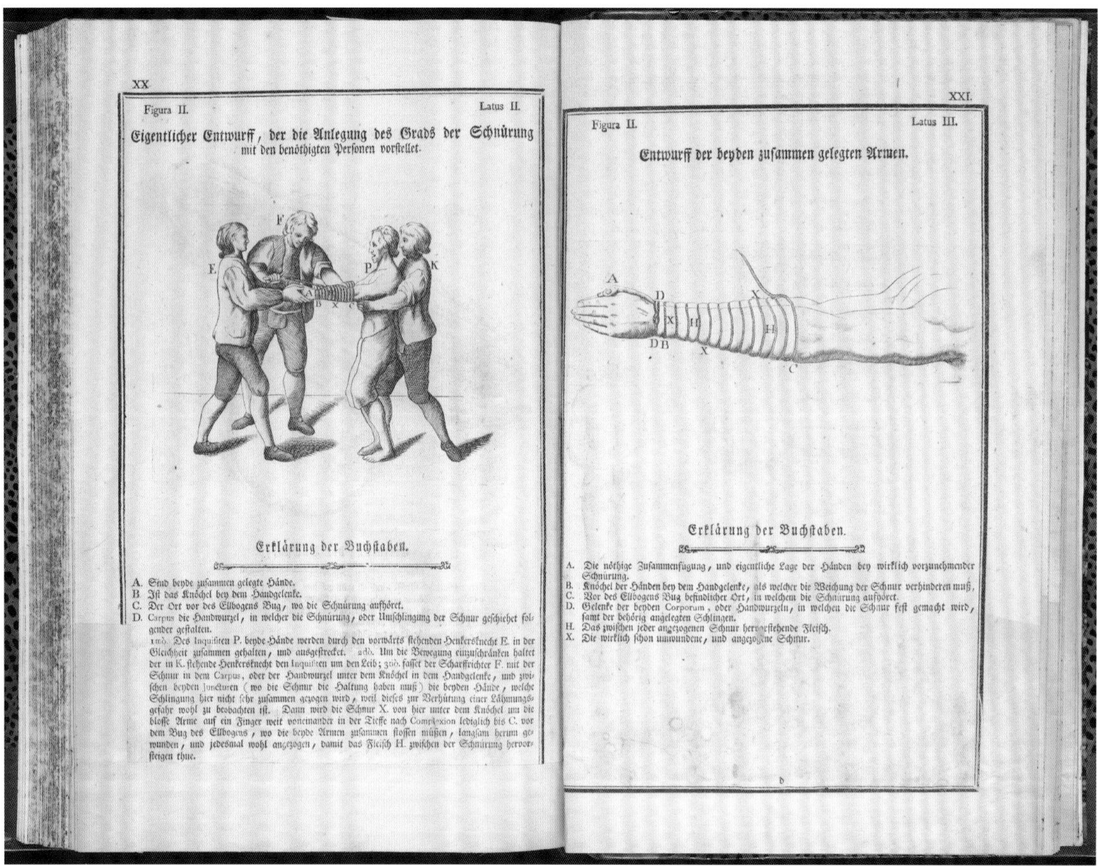

XX

Figura II. Latus II.

Eigentlicher Entwurff, der die Anlegung des Grads der Schnürung mit den benöthigten Personen vorstellet.

Erklärung der Buchstaben.

A. Sind beyde zusammen gelegte Hände.
B. Ist das Knöchel bey dem Handgelenke.
C. Der Ort vor des Ellbogens Bug, wo die Schnürung aufhöret.
D. Carpus die Handwurzel, in welcher die Schnürung, oder Umschlingung der Schnur geschiehet folgender gestalten.

1mò. Des Inquisiten P. beyde Hände werden durch den vorwärts stehenden Henkersknecht E. in der Gleichheit zusammen gehalten, und ausgestrecket. 2dò. Um die Bewegung einzuschränken haltet der in K. stehende Henkersknecht den Inquisiten um den Leib; 3tiò. fasset der Scharfrichter F. mit der Schnur in dem Carpus, oder der Handwurzel unter dem Knöchel in dem Handgelenke, und zwischen beyden Juncturen (wo die Schnur die Haltung haben muß) die beyden Hände, welche Schlingung hier nicht sehr zusammen gezogen wird, weil dieses zur Verhütung einer Lähmungsgefahr wohl zu beobachten ist. Dann wird die Schnur X. von hier unter dem Knöchel um die blosse Arme auf ein Finger weit voneinander in der Tieffe nach Complexion lediglich bis C. vor dem Bug des Ellbogens, wo die beyde Armen zusammen stossen müssen, langsam herum gewunden, und jedesmal wohl angezogen, damit das Fleisch H. zwischen der Schnürung hervorsteigen thue.

XXI.

Figura II. Latus III.

Entwurff der beyden zusammen gelegten Armen.

Erklärung der Buchstaben.

A. Die nöthige Zusammenfügung, und eigentliche Lage der Händen bey wirklich vorzunehmender Schnürung.
B. Knöchel der Händen bey dem Handgelenke, als welcher die Weichung der Schnur verhinderen muß,
C. Vor des Ellbogens Bug befindlicher Ort, in welchem die Schnürung aufhöret.
D. Gelenke der beyden Corporum, oder Handwurzeln, in welchen die Schnur fest gemacht wird, samt der behörig angelegten Schlingen.
H. Das zwischen jeder angezogenen Schnur hervorstehende Fleisch.
X. Die wirklich schon umwundene, und angezogene Schnur.

The body, labeled. The *Constitutio criminalis Theresiana* marked a major effort under Maria Theresa of Austria (r. 1740-80) to centralize law for the Austrian empire. It also provided detailed standards about when and *how* to torture. Torture was abolished in the Austrian Empire in 1777, due in part to the efforts of Joseph von Sonnenfels (1733-1817) (see his work *Ueber die Abschaffung der Tortur* [6.10]).

The trial of Lieutenant-Colonel Joseph Wall, late governor of Goree.

London : Sabine & Son, [1802?].

6.06

Lieutenant-Colonel Joseph Wall ordered slaves in Senegal to whip Sergeant Benjamin Armstrong with a one-inch cord. The case caused a sensation, and it rendered infamous not the victim but the perpetrator – and the law under which he acted. The marks left on the sergeant's back are carefully rendered here with thirteen parallel lines. Graphic illustrations in popular books threw the practice of torture into increasing doubt.

THE
TRIAL
OF
LIEUTENANT-COLONEL
JOSEPH WALL,
LATE
GOVERNOR OF GOREE,
AT THE
OLD BAILEY,
On WEDNESDAY, *January* 20, 1802;
FOR THE
WILFUL MURDER
OF
BENJAMIN ARMSTRONG,
A SERJEANT OF THE AFRICAN CORPS,
July 10, 1782.

London:
PRINTED AND SOLD BY
SABINE AND SON, 81, SHOE LANE, *Fleet Street.*
[*Price Sixpence.*]

6.07

Trial and imprisonment of Jonathan Walker, at Pensacola, Florida, for aiding slaves to escape from bondage.

Boston: Published at the Anti-Slavery Office, 1845.

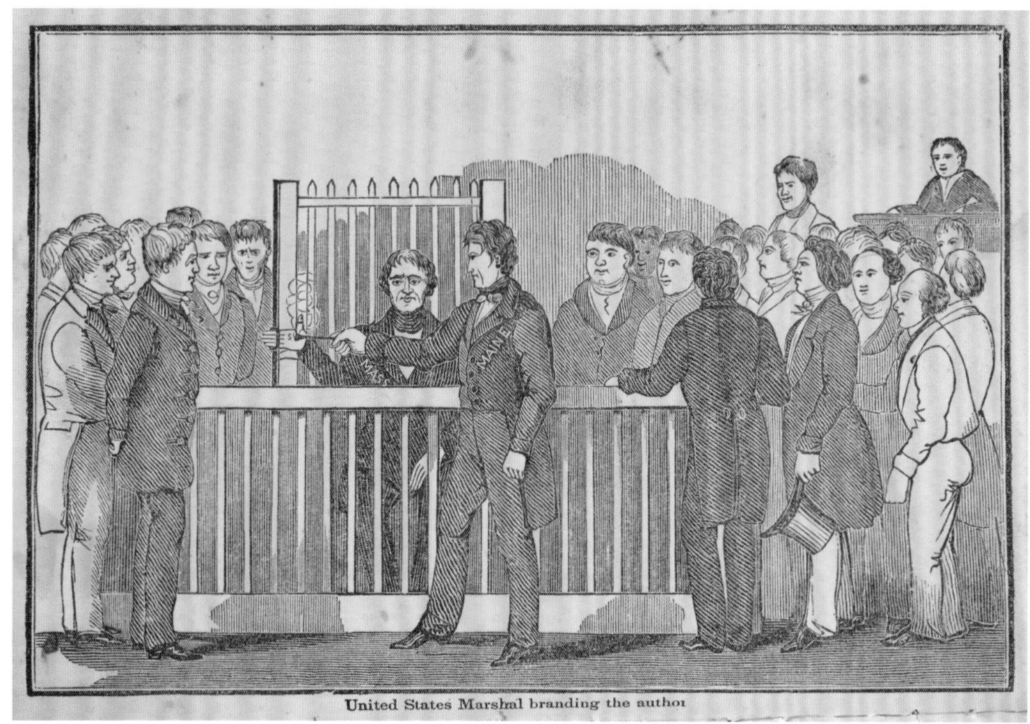

United States Marshal branding the author

The hand of Captain Jonathan Walker was branded by a federal marshal with the letters "S.S" – slave stealer. The incident inspired John Greenleaf Whittier's poem "The Man with the Branded Hand" (1846): "Then lift that manly right-hand, bold ploughman of the wave! / Its branded palm shall prophesy, 'Salvation to the Slave!' / Hold up its fire-wrought language, that whoso reads may feel / His heart swell strong within him, his sinews change to steel."

George Henry Mason.

6.08

The punishments of China: illustrated by twenty-two engravings, with explanations in English and French.

London: Printed for W. Miller by S. Gosnell, 1808.
Engravings by J. Dadley.

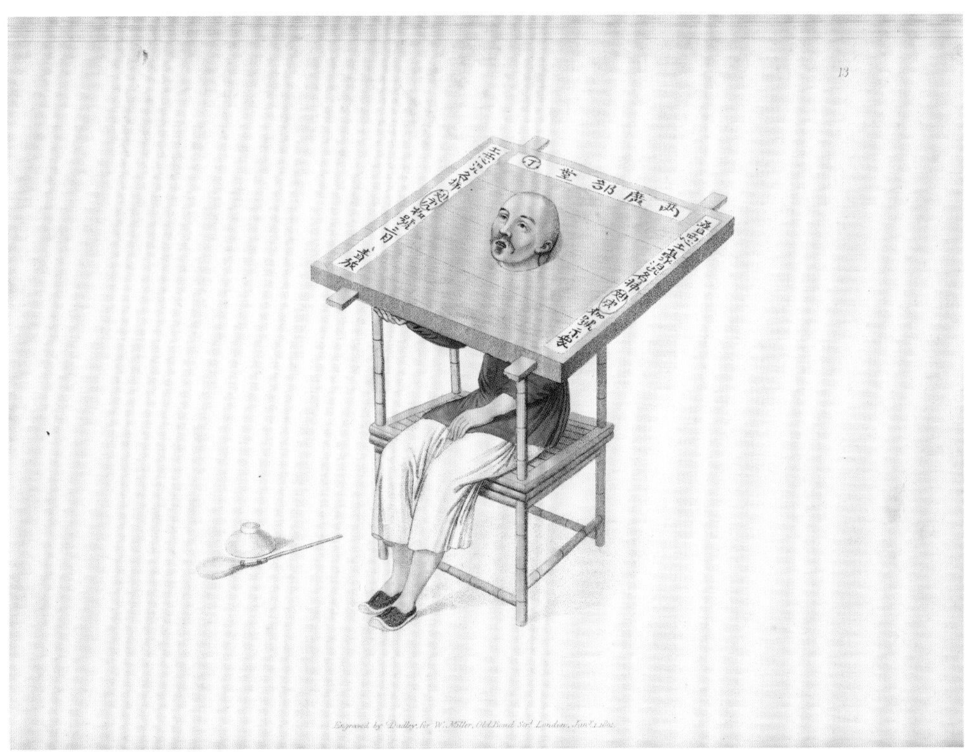

From the text: "When this ponderous incumberance is fixed upon an offender, it is always before the magistrate who has decreed it; and upon each side, over the places where the wood is joined, long slips of paper are pasted, upon which the name of the person, the crime he has committed, and the duration of his punishment are written in very distinct characters."

6.09

Cesare Beccaria.

Dei delitti e delle pene.

London: Società dei Filosofi, 1774.

Cesare Beccaria's seminal *On Crimes and Punishments* (1764) lay the foundation for modern penology and criminal justice. Beccaria (1738-94) argued strongly against torture and the death penalty. The frontispiece image at left was engraved on Beccaria's detailed instructions, and it was frequently reproduced and copied by eighteenth-century publishers. Lady Justice recoils from an executioner's offering of three decapitated heads and instead gazes approvingly at various instruments of labor, measurement, and detention.

Joseph von Sonnenfels.

Ueber die Abschaffung der Tortur.

Zürich: Orell, Gessner, Fuesslin, 1775.

6.10

Joseph von Sonnenfels's *Ueber die Abschaffung der Tortur* (*On the Abolition of Torture*) was instrumental in ending the practice of torture in Austria. For unknown reasons, Beethoven dedicated his Piano Sonata No. 15, Op. 28 (1801) to Sonnenfels. The image clearly declares the author's position on the subject.

Ueber die

Abschaffung

der

Tortur.

Von

J. v. Sonnenfels.

K. K. N. Oe. Regierungsrath und öffentlichen Lehrer der politischen Wissenschaften.

Zürich, bey Orell, Geßner, Füeßlin und Compagnie.

1775.

A
B
C
E
D

Giovanni Battista Marinoni.

La sferza de bruti e delle cose insensate.

Pavia: Giovanni Andrea Magri, 1636. Etchings by Giovanni Paolo Bianchi.

6.11

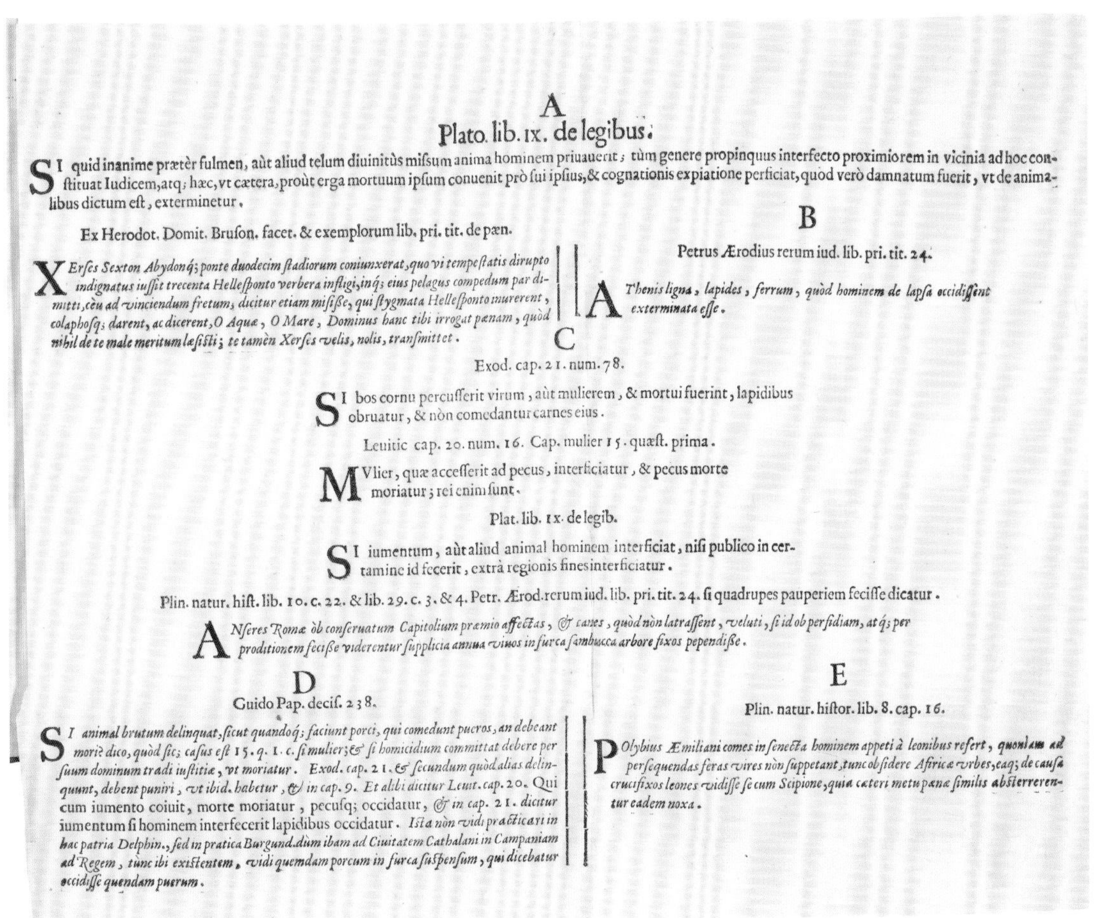

A

Plato. lib. IX. de legibus.

SI quid inanime prætèr fulmen, aùt aliud telum diuinitùs missum anima hominem priuauerit; tùm genere propinquus interfecto proximiorem in vicinia ad hoc constituat Iudicem, atq; hæc, vt cætera, proùt erga mortuum ipsum conuenit prò sui ipsius, & cognationis expiatione perficiat, quod verò damnatum fuerit, vt de animalibus dictum est, exterminetur.

Ex Herodot. Domit. Bruson. facet. & exemplorum lib. pri. tit. de pæn.

XErses Sexton Abydonq; ponte duodecim stadiorum coniunxerat, quo vi tempestatis dirupto indignatus iussit trecenta Hellesponto verbera infligi, inq; eius pelagus compedum par dimitti, cèu ad vinciendum fretum, dicitur etiam misisse, qui stygmata Hellesponto inurerent, colaphosq; darent, ac dicerent, O Aquæ, O Mare, Dominus hanc tibi irrogat pænam, quòd nihil de te male meritum læsisti; te tamèn Xerses velis, nolis, transmittet.

B

Petrus Ærodius rerum iud. lib. pri. tit. 24.

AThenis ligna, lapides, ferrum, quòd hominem de lapsa occidissent exterminata esse.

C

Exod. cap. 21. num. 78.

SI bos cornu percufferit virum, aùt mulierem, & mortui fuerint, lapidibus obruatur, & nòn comedantur carnes eius.

Leuitic cap. 20. num. 16. Cap. mulier 15. quæst. prima.

MVlier, quæ accesserit ad pecus, interficiatur, & pecus morte moriatur; rei enim sunt.

Plat. lib. IX. de legib.

SI iumentum, aùt aliud animal hominem interficiat, nisi publico in certamine id fecerit, extrà regionis fines interficiatur.

Plin. natur. hist. lib. 10. c. 22. & lib. 29. c. 3. & 4. Petr. Ærod. rerum iud. lib. pri. tit. 24. si quadrupes pauperiem fecisse dicatur.

ANseres Romæ òb conseruatum Capitolium præmio affectas, & canes, quòd nòn latrassent, veluti, si id ob perfidiam, atq; per proditionem fecisse viderentur supplicia annua vivos in furca sambucca arbore fixos pependisse.

D

Guido Pap. decis. 238.

SI animal brutum delinquat, sicut quandoq; faciunt porci, qui comedunt pueros, an debeant mori? dico, quòd sic; casus est 15. q. 1. c. si mulier; & si homicidium committat debere per suum dominum tradi iustitiæ, vt moriatur. Exod. cap. 21. & secundum quòd alias delinquunt, debent puniri, vt ibid. habetur, & in cap. 9. Et alibi dicitur Leuit. cap. 20. Qui cum iumento coiuit, morte moriatur, pecusq; occidatur, *& in cap. 21. dicitur* iumentum si hominem interfecerit lapidibus occidatur. *Ista nòn vidi practicari in hac patria Delphin., sed in pratica Burgund. dùm ibam ad Ciuitatem Cathalani in Campaniam ad Regem, tùnc ibi existentem, vidi quemdam porcum in furca suspensum, qui dicebatur occidisse quendam puerum.*

E

Plin. natur. histor. lib. 8. cap. 16.

POlybius Æmiliani comes in senecta hominem appeti à leonibus refert, quoniam ad persequendas feras vires nòn suppetant, tunc obsidere Africæ vrbes, eaq; de causa crucifixos leones vidisse se cum Scipione, quia cæteri metu pænæ similis absterrerentur eadem noxa.

Carefully argued and replete with mock footnotes, this book satirizes corporal punishment. The image is an allegorical etching of the trial and judgment of beasts, indexed to citations from contemporary, ancient, and Biblical authority.

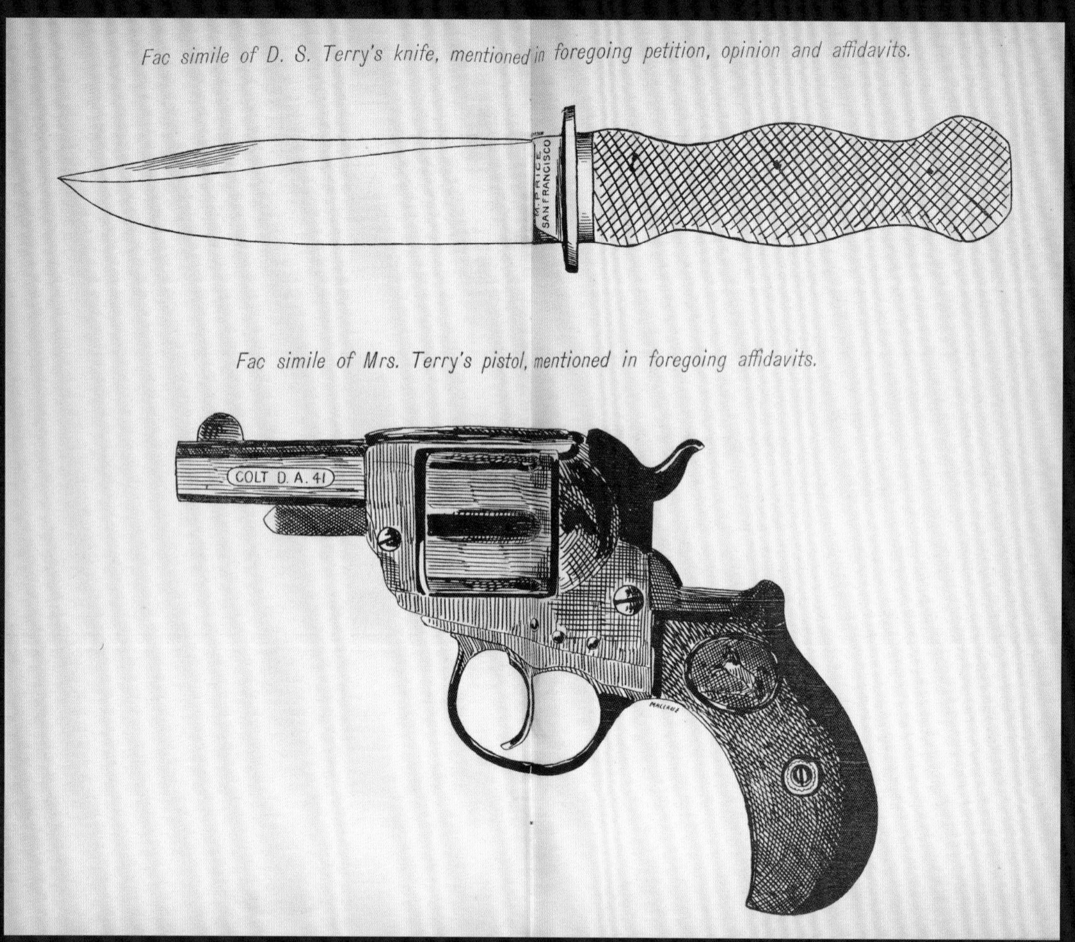
Fac simile of D. S. Terry's knife, mentioned in foregoing petition, opinion and affidavits.
M. PRICE SAN FRANCISCO
Fac simile of Mrs. Terry's pistol, mentioned in foregoing affidavits.
COLT D. A. 41

What knife did U.S. marshals seize from lawyer and former California Supreme Court Justice David S. Terry during a fracas in federal court? This one. Less than a year later, Terry was shot and killed for assaulting the judge who had him jailed for contempt that day: U.S. Supreme Court Justice Stephen J. Field. The controversy grew from a notorious divorce suit brought by the San Francisco socialite Sarah Alethea Hill (1850-1937).

The Terry contempt.
[San Francisco: s.n., 1888.]

Arguing the Law 7

In the nineteenth century, modern printing technologies enabled law book publishers to depict places, objects, and events at issue in litigation with greater accuracy than ever before. Illustrations and, in time, photographs, were used as courtroom evidence – as well as to influence public opinion and to supplement "true crime" literature. They are the least symbolic, most literal, type of law book image.

How did the body lie? How did the bullet fly? Where was the bone broken? And has the National Biscuit Company's trademark been infringed?

VERDADEIRA REPREZENTAÇAÕ DO HORROROZO ATENTADO SOCEDIDO NO NAVIO SUECO PATRISTEN, QUE SE PRATICOU NA NOUTE DE 2. DE JUNHO E NA MANHÃA DO DIA SEG.TE DO ANNO DE
I. Onavio Sueco encalha sem governo napraia d'Albofeira
II. Para se occultar odelicto abrem se sinco rombos de igual grandeza
III. Dois marinheiros occultando-se aos agreßores salvaõ as Vidas.
IV. Com as maos presas saõ mortos dois marinheiros de golpes horrorozos.
TEM PLVM JUS TITIÆ
A. Camera onde depois d'arrombada sevem os corpos de tantos infelices.
B. Ocapitaõ emcamiza, coberto do sangue das feridas mortaes.
C. Dom I. F. Perez se mostra cruelmente morto com as maos prezas.
D. Francisco Luiz com as mãos atadas morto de sete golpes de faca.
NEMINI PARCIT
Porta da Camara
V. I. L. Elizarde quazi moribundo com varios golpes penetrantes vive poucos dias.
VI. Marinheiros lansados ao mar p.a salvar as vidas, e excepto hũ, perecem todos.
VII. Batel dos agressores persegue o marinheiro q. demandava o auxilio d'outra embarcaçaõ.
VIII. Omarinheiro livre domar roga saõ ser restituido ao batel inimigo.
IX. Vista da terra onde se descobre onavio em perigo
E. Ant. de Lacovita com golpes horrorozos pelo corpo tendo as maos prezas.
F. Omenino Penco unido aseu Pay morrem de horrorozos golpes.
G. I. M. Penco experimenta com as mãos prezas a desgraça de seus parentes.
H. I. A. Gelardon tendo as mãos atadas morto de naõ poucas feridas.
I. Omarinheiro servente da camera com o corpo dilacerado morre cruelm
SETE ERAO OS AGRESSORES DESTE DELITO V CASTELHANOS E II. PORTUGUEZES
M. de Mattos delin. et s.
P. R.
Godinho

7.01

Dos autos da devaça das mortes, e roubos praticados no navio sueco Patristen.

Lisbon: Jozé de Aquino Bulhoens, 1781.
Engraving by Manuel da Silva Godinho.

Sailing from Lisbon, the Swedish ship *Patristen* was found wrecked on a beach in southern Portugal. Seven people, including the ship's captain, lay dead inside, their hands tied behind their backs – strangled by pirates. Before the advent of modern printing and photographic technologies, law book publishers were limited in their ability to depict the real. But in its detailed depiction of the victim's bodies, this eighteenth-century engraving can still send a chill up the spine.

7.02

Laurence Braddon.

Essex's innocency and honour vindicated.

London: Printed for the author and sold by most booksellers, 1690. Gift of Harold I. Boucher, 2008.

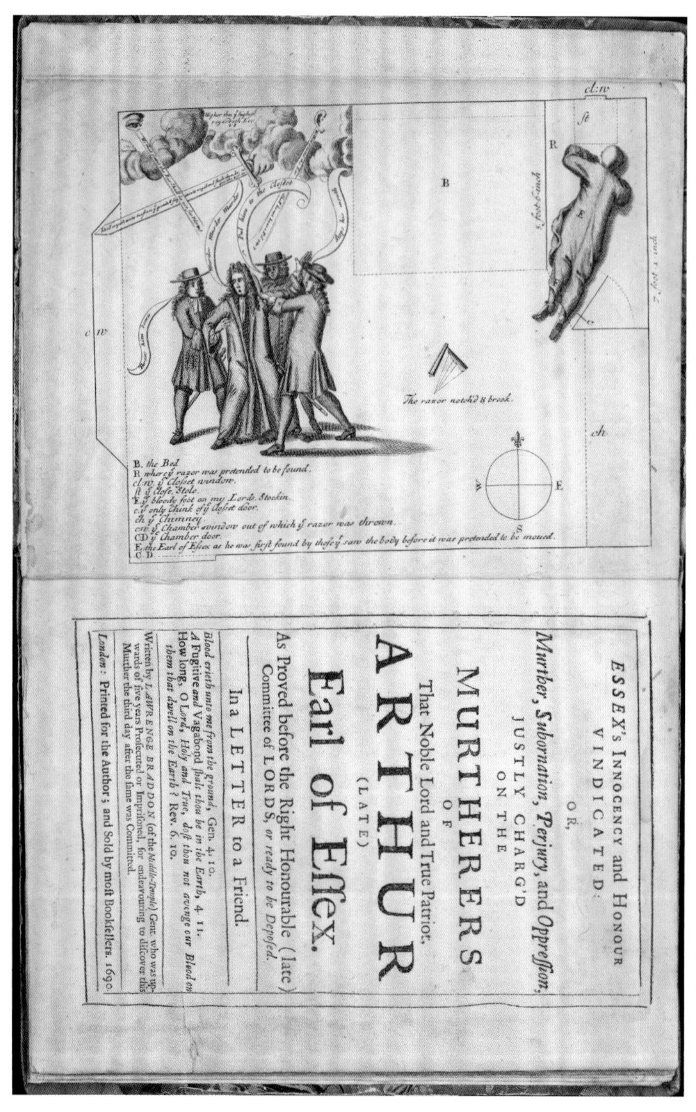

ESSEX's INNOCENCY and HONOUR
VINDICATED:
OR,
Murther, Subornation, Perjury, and Oppression,
JUSTLY CHARG'D
ON THE
MURTHERERS
OF
That Noble Lord and True Patriot,
ARTHUR
(LATE)
Earl of Essex.
As Proved before the Right Honourable (late) Committee of LORDS, *or ready to be Deposed.*
In a LETTER to a Friend.

Blood crieth unto me from the ground, Gen. 4. 10.
A Fugitive and Vagabond shalt thou be in the Earth, 4. 12.
How long, O Lord, *Holy and True, dost thou not avenge our Blood on them that dwell on the Earth?* Rev. 6. 10.

Written by LAWRENCE BRADDON (of the *Middle-Temple*) Gent. who was upwards of five years Prosecuted or Imprisoned, for endeavouring to discover this Murther the third day after the same was Committed.

London: Printed for the Author; and Sold by most Booksellers, 1690.

Did the Earl of Essex commit suicide in the Tower of London, where he had been imprisoned for taking part in a plot to assassinate Charles II, or was he murdered? The author of this book sought to prove murder by using an illustration that precisely reconstructed the scene of Essex's death, detailed down to the northeasterly angle at which his body lay. For his efforts, the author spent five years in prison.

The trial of Governor T. Picton, for inflicting the torture on Louisa Calderon, a free mulatto.

London: B. Crosby and Co., [1806].

7.03

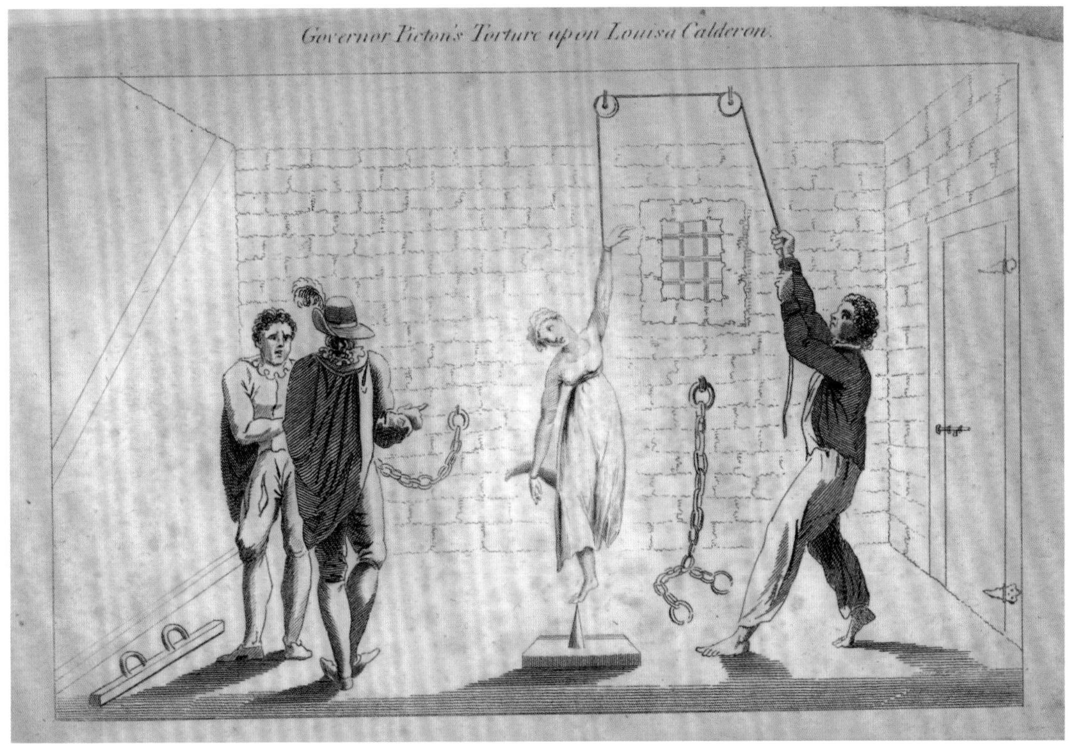

William Garrow (1760-1840) introduced this drawing as evidence in the trial against Thomas Picton, the former Governor of Trinidad, for torturing fourteen-year-old Louisa Calderon. It may have been the first time an image was introduced as evidence in an English court. Garrow used the illustration ostensibly to "explain" the method of torture to which Calderon had been subjected. Picton's counsel objected that the barrister was merely trying to whip up the passions of the jury.

7.04

Cases on appeals concerning the duties on houses and windows, servants and inhabited houses.

London: Fielding and Walker, 1780. From the collection of Anthony Taussig. Acquired with the support of the Oscar M. Ruebhausen Fund.

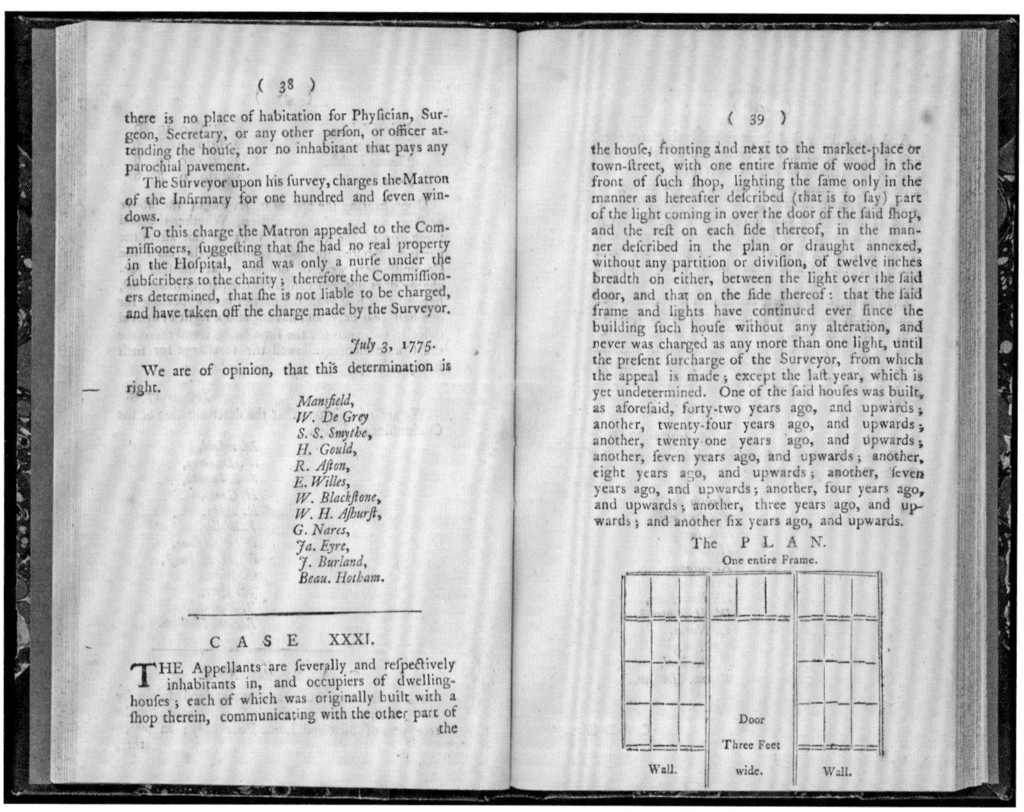

(38)

there is no place of habitation for Phyſician, Surgeon, Secretary, or any other perſon, or officer attending the houſe, nor no inhabitant that pays any parochial pavement.

The Surveyor upon his ſurvey, charges the Matron of the Infirmary for one hundred and ſeven windows.

To this charge the Matron appealed to the Commiſſioners, ſuggeſting that ſhe had no real property in the Hoſpital, and was only a nurſe under the ſubſcribers to the charity; therefore the Commiſſioners determined, that ſhe is not liable to be charged, and have taken off the charge made by the Surveyor.

July 3, 1775.

We are of opinion, that this determination is right.

Mansfield,
W. De Grey
S. S. Smythe,
H. Gould,
R. Aſton,
E. Willes,
W. Blackſtone,
W. H. Aſhurſt,
G. Nares,
Ja. Eyre,
J. Burland,
Beau. Hotham.

CASE XXXI.

THE Appellants are ſeverally and reſpectively inhabitants in, and occupiers of dwelling-houſes; each of which was originally built with a ſhop therein, communicating with the other part of the

(39)

the houſe, fronting and next to the market-place or town-ſtreet, with one entire frame of wood in the front of ſuch ſhop, lighting the ſame only in the manner as hereafter deſcribed (that is to ſay) part of the light coming in over the door of the ſaid ſhop, and the reſt on each ſide thereof, in the manner deſcribed in the plan or draught annexed, without any partition or diviſion, of twelve inches breadth on either, between the light over the ſaid door, and that on the ſide thereof: that the ſaid frame and lights have continued ever ſince the building ſuch houſe without any alteration, and never was charged as any more than one light, until the preſent ſurcharge of the Surveyor, from which the appeal is made; except the laſt year, which is yet undetermined. One of the ſaid houſes was built, as aforeſaid, forty-two years ago, and upwards; another, twenty-four years ago, and upwards; another, twenty-one years ago, and upwards; another, ſeven years ago, and upwards; another, eight years ago, and upwards; another, ſeven years ago, and upwards; another, four years ago, and upwards; another, three years ago, and upwards; and another ſix years ago, and upwards.

The PLAN.

One entire Frame.

Is there one window here, or forty-two? Windows were taxable, a stand-in for property value, and the answer mattered to the owner's pocketbook. The stellar panel of judges in this case included William Blackstone and Lord Mansfield.

Cases respecting assessed taxes determined by the judges, 1841.

7.05

London: Printed by W. Clowes and Sons, for Her Majesty's Stationery Office, 1841.
From the collection of Anthony Taussig.

Should the surgeon Samuel Parsley of Worle be taxed for thirteen windows or for twelve? From the text of case 1525: "The situation of the window is described in the accompanying plan." Illustrations like these have value not only for legal scholars, but also for architectural historians and preservationists.

7.06

Trial of Professor John W. Webster, for the murder of Doctor George Parkman.

New York: Stringer & Townsend ... printed at the Globe office, 1850. "Reported exclusively for the N.Y. Daily Globe." Gift of James Hillhouse (Yale 1875), 1931.

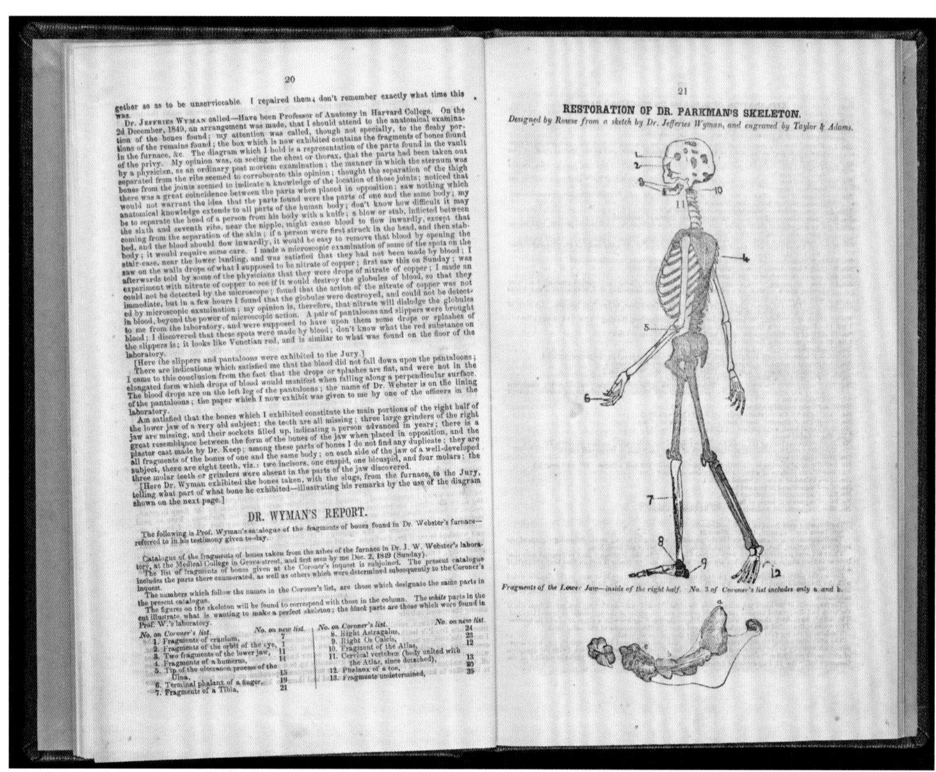

20

gether so as to be unserviceable. I repaired them; don't remember exactly what time this was.

Dr. JEFFRIES WYMAN called—Have been Professor of Anatomy in Harvard College. On the 2d December, 1849, an arrangement was made, that I should attend to the anatomical examination of the bones found; my attention was called, though not specially, to the fleshy portions of the remains found; the box which is now exhibited contains the fragments of bones found in the furnace, &c. The diagram which I hold is a representation of the parts found in the vault of the privy. My opinion was, on seeing the chest or thorax, that the parts had been taken out by a physician, as an ordinary post mortem examination; the manner in which the sternum was separated from the ribs seemed to corroborate this opinion; thought the separation of the thigh bones from the joints seemed to indicate a knowledge of the location of those joints; noticed that there was a great coincidence between the parts when placed in opposition; saw nothing which would not warrant the idea that the parts found were the parts of one and the same body; my anatomical knowledge extends to all parts of the human body; don't know how difficult it may be to separate the head of a person from his body with a knife; a blow or stab, inflicted between the sixth and seventh ribs, near the nipple, might cause blood to flow inwardly, except that coming from the separation of the skin; if a person were first struck in the head, and then stabbed, and the blood should flow inwardly, it would be easy to remove that blood by opening the body; it would require some care. I made a microscopic examination of some of the spots on the stair-case, near the lower landing, and was satisfied that they had not been made by blood; I saw on the walls drops of what I supposed to be nitrate of copper; first saw this on Sunday; was afterwards told by some of the physicians that they were drops of nitrate of copper; I made an experiment with nitrate of copper to see if it would destroy the globules of blood, so that they could not be detected by the microscope; found that the action of the nitrate of copper was not immediate, but in a few hours I found that the globules were destroyed, and could not be detected by microscopic examination; my opinion is, therefore, that nitrate will dislodge the globules in blood, beyond the power of microscopic action. A pair of pantaloons and slippers were brought to me from the laboratory, and were supposed to have upon them some drops or splashes of blood; I discovered that these spots were made by blood; don't know what the red substance on the slippers is; it looks like Venetian red, and is similar to what was found on the floor of the laboratory.

[Here the slippers and pantaloons were exhibited to the Jury.]

There are indications which satisfied me that the blood did not fall down upon the pantaloons; I came to this conclusion from the fact that the drops or splashes are flat, and were not in the elongated form which drops of blood would manifest when falling along a perpendicular surface. The blood drops are on the left leg of the pantaloons; the name of Dr. Webster is on the lining of the pantaloons; the paper which I now exhibit was given to me by one of the officers in the laboratory.

Am satisfied that the bones which I exhibited constitute the main portions of the right half of the lower jaw of a very old subject; the teeth are all missing; three large grinders of the right jaw are missing, and their sockets filled up, indicating a person advanced in years; there is a great resemblance between the form of the bones of the jaw when placed in opposition, and the plaster cast made by Dr. Keep; among these parts of bones I do not find any duplicate; they are all fragments of the bones of one and the same body; on each side of the jaw of a well-developed subject, there are eight teeth, viz.: two incisors, one cuspid, one bicuspid, and four molars; the three molar teeth or grinders were absent in the parts of the jaw discovered.

[Here Dr. Wyman exhibited the bones taken, with the slugs, from the furnace, to the Jury, telling what part of what bone he exhibited—illustrating his remarks by the use of the diagram shown on the next page.]

DR. WYMAN'S REPORT.

The following is Prof. Wyman's catalogue of the fragments of bones found in Dr. Webster's furnace—referred to in his testimony given to-day.

Catalogue of the fragments of bones taken from the ashes of the furnace in Dr. J. W. Webster's laboratory, at the Medical College in Grove-street, and first seen by me Dec. 2, 1849 (Sunday).

The list of fragments of bones given at the Coroner's inquest is subjoined. The present catalogue includes the parts there enumerated, as well as others which were determined subsequently to the Coroner's inquest.

The numbers which follow the names in the Coroner's list, are those which designate the same parts in the present catalogue.

The figures on the skeleton will be found to correspond with those in the column. The *white* parts in the cut illustrate what is wanting to make a perfect skeleton; the *black* parts are those which were found in Prof. W.'s laboratory.

No. on Coroner's list.	*No. on new list.*	*No. on Coroner's list.*	*No. on new list.*
1. Fragments of cranium,	7	8. Right Astragalus,	24
2. Fragments of the orbit of the eye,	1	9. Right Os Calcis,	23
3. Two fragments of the lower jaw,	11	10. Fragment of the Atlas,	12
4. Fragments of a humerus,	14	11. Cervical vertebra (body united with the Atlas, since detached),	13
5. Tip of the olecranon process of the Ulna,	15	12. Phalanx of a toe,	20
6. Terminal phalanx of a finger,	19	13. Fragments undetermined,	35
7. Fragments of a Tibia,	21		

21

RESTORATION OF DR. PARKMAN'S SKELETON.

Designed by Rowse from a sketch by Dr. Jefferies Wyman, and engraved by Taylor & Adams.

Fragments of the Lower Jaw—inside of the right half. No. 3 of Coroner's list includes only a and b.

The sensational trial of Prof. John W. Webster involved an early use of forensic science to identify the remains of Dr. George Parkman, which were found hidden in the privy of Harvard Medical College. From the text: "Here Dr. Wyman exhibited the bones taken, with the slugs, from the furnace, to the Jury, telling what part of what bone he exhibited – illustrating his remarks by the use of the diagram shown on the next page."

The American Print Works vs. Cornelius W. Lawrence.

New York: Collins, Bowne & Co., 1852. Acquired with the Charles A. Tanenbaum Fund.

7.07

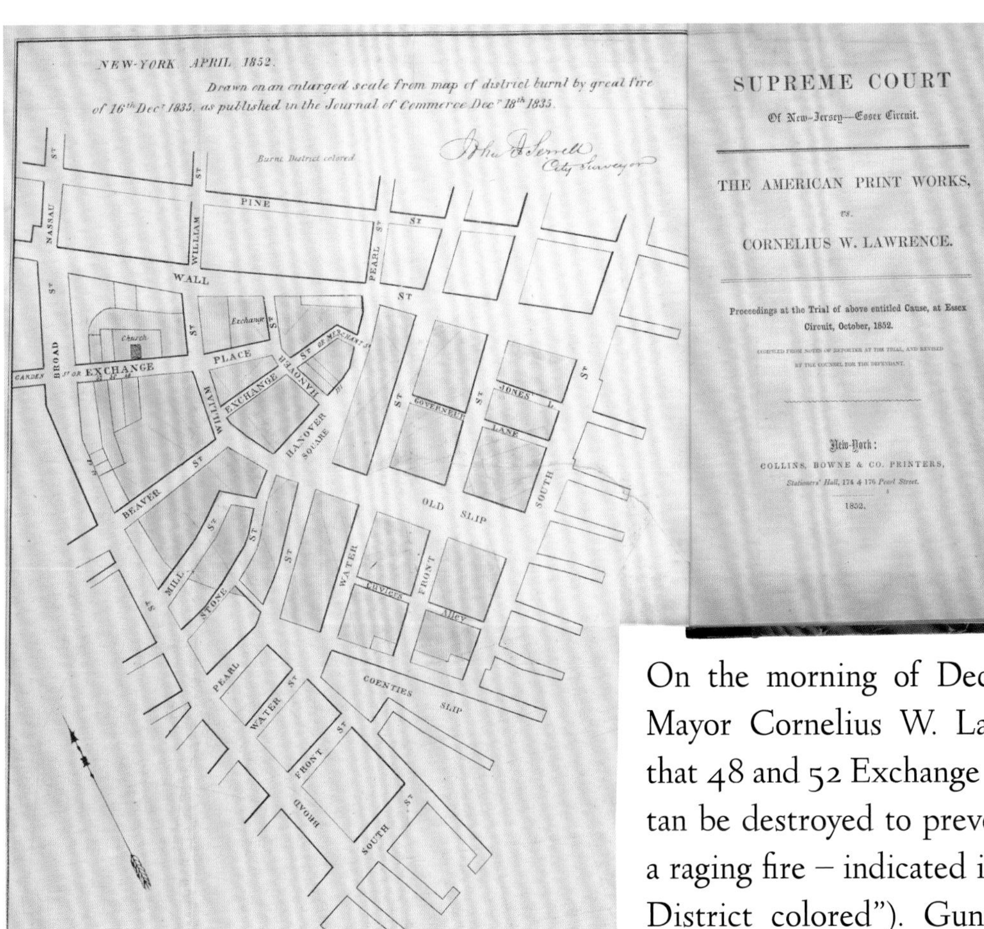

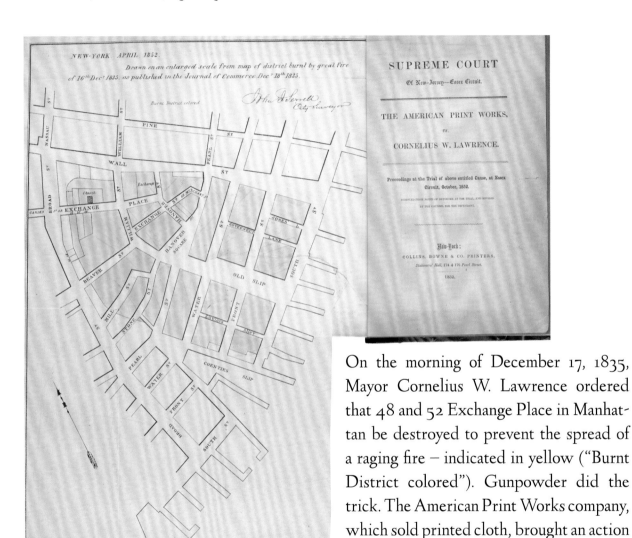

On the morning of December 17, 1835, Mayor Cornelius W. Lawrence ordered that 48 and 52 Exchange Place in Manhattan be destroyed to prevent the spread of a raging fire – indicated in yellow ("Burnt District colored"). Gunpowder did the trick. The American Print Works company, which sold printed cloth, brought an action for damages.

7.08

Francisco A. Serralde.

El crimen de Santa Julia: defensa gráfica que, sirviéndose de signos físicos encontrados en los cuerpos de las víctimas del crimen.

México: F.P. Hoeck y Compañía, 1899. Photographs by Agustín Jiménez.

FIG. 15.

The colorful "Colonel" Timoteo Andrade worked as both a police officer and a hired gun. Accused of murdering his son, he hired defense attorney Francisco A. Serralde, who used staged photography to prove his client's innocence. Serralde's ground-breaking work went beyond the common use of the medium, to record and classify evidence, and instead told a sequential narrative – a story that claimed to be an irrefutable proof of the event.

Amos E. Dolbear et al., appellants, v. the American Bell Telephone Co. ...

7.09

Oral argument of Mr. Storrow on the Bell patents.

Boston: A. Mudge & Son, 1887.

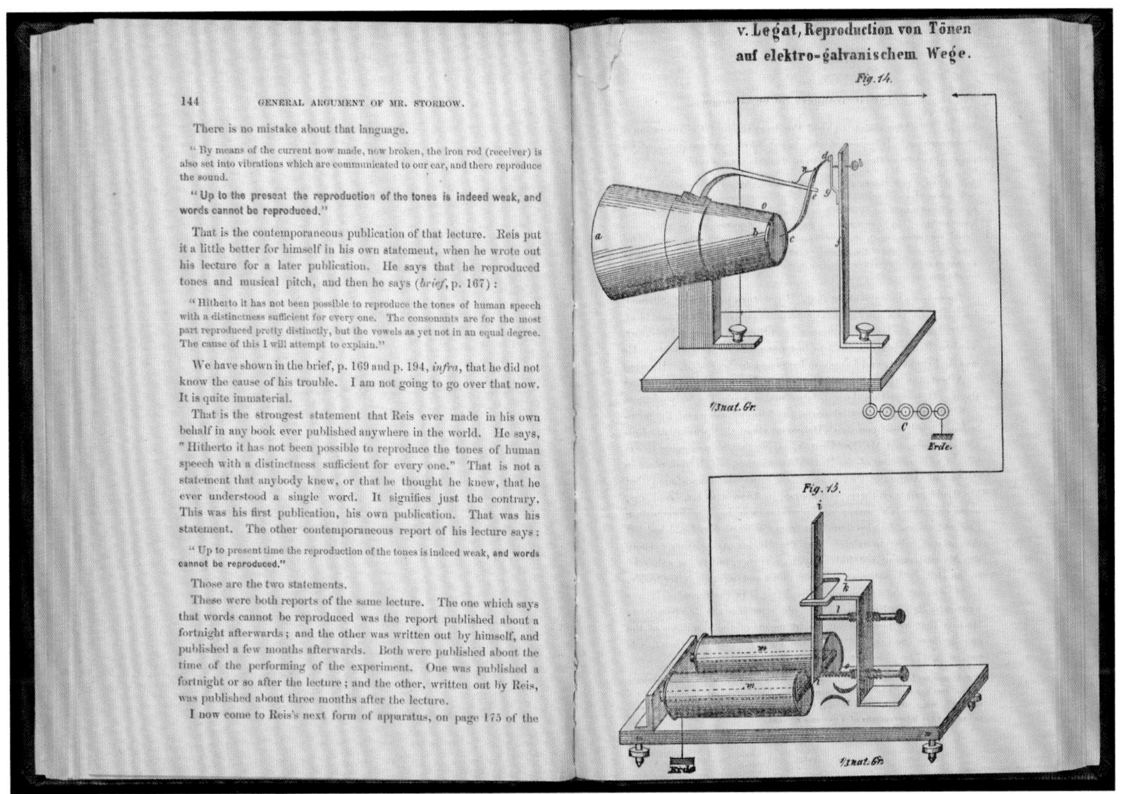

144 GENERAL ARGUMENT OF MR. STORROW.

There is no mistake about that language.

"By means of the current now made, now broken, the iron rod (receiver) is also set into vibrations which are communicated to our ear, and there reproduce the sound.

"Up to the present the reproduction of the tones is indeed weak, and words cannot be reproduced."

That is the contemporaneous publication of that lecture. Reis put it a little better for himself in his own statement, when he wrote out his lecture for a later publication. He says that he reproduced tones and musical pitch, and then he says (*brief*, p. 167):

"Hitherto it has not been possible to reproduce the tones of human speech with a distinctness sufficient for every one. The consonants are for the most part reproduced pretty distinctly, but the vowels as yet not in an equal degree. The cause of this I will attempt to explain."

We have shown in the brief, p. 169 and p. 194, *infra*, that he did not know the cause of his trouble. I am not going to go over that now. It is quite immaterial.

That is the strongest statement that Reis ever made in his own behalf in any book ever published anywhere in the world. He says, "Hitherto it has not been possible to reproduce the tones of human speech with a distinctness sufficient for every one." That is not a statement that anybody knew, or that he thought he knew, that he ever understood a single word. It signifies just the contrary. This was his first publication, his own publication. That was his statement. The other contemporaneous report of his lecture says:

"Up to present time the reproduction of the tones is indeed weak, **and words cannot be reproduced."**

Those are the two statements.

These were both reports of the same lecture. The one which says that words cannot be reproduced was the report published about a fortnight afterwards; and the other was written out by himself, and published a few months afterwards. Both were published about the time of the performing of the experiment. One was published a fortnight or so after the lecture; and the other, written out by Reis, was published about three months after the lecture.

I now come to Reis's next form of apparatus, on page 175 of the

The illustrations that made Ma Bell. The machine depicted here reproduces the human voice, but the illustration was used as evidence in a case of patent infringement. From the text: "I now come to Reis's next form of apparatus, on page 175."

7.10

National Biscuit Company.

Trade mark litigation: opinions, orders, injunctions, and decrees relating to unfair competition and infringement of trade marks.

5th ed. New York, 1915.

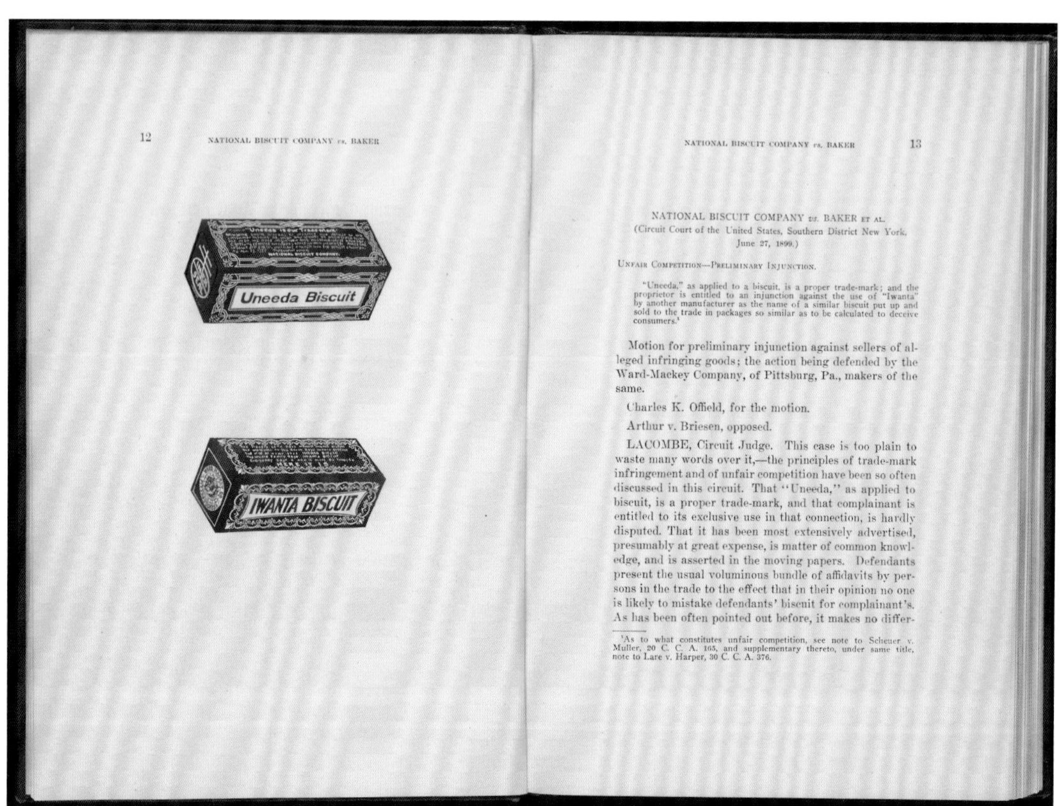
12 NATIONAL BISCUIT COMPANY *vs.* BAKER

NATIONAL BISCUIT COMPANY *vs.* BAKER 13

NATIONAL BISCUIT COMPANY *vs.* BAKER ET AL.
(Circuit Court of the United States, Southern District New York. June 27, 1899.)

UNFAIR COMPETITION—PRELIMINARY INJUNCTION.

"Uneeda," as applied to a biscuit, is a proper trade-mark; and the proprietor is entitled to an injunction against the use of "Iwanta" by another manufacturer as the name of a similar biscuit put up and sold to the trade in packages so similar as to be calculated to deceive consumers.[1]

Motion for preliminary injunction against sellers of alleged infringing goods; the action being defended by the Ward-Mackey Company, of Pittsburg, Pa., makers of the same.

Charles K. Offield, for the motion.

Arthur v. Briesen, opposed.

LACOMBE, Circuit Judge. This case is too plain to waste many words over it,—the principles of trade-mark infringement and of unfair competition have been so often discussed in this circuit. That "Uneeda," as applied to biscuit, is a proper trade-mark, and that complainant is entitled to its exclusive use in that connection, is hardly disputed. That it has been most extensively advertised, presumably at great expense, is matter of common knowledge, and is asserted in the moving papers. Defendants present the usual voluminous bundle of affidavits by persons in the trade to the effect that in their opinion no one is likely to mistake defendants' biscuit for complainant's. As has been often pointed out before, it makes no differ-

[1] As to what constitutes unfair competition, see note to Scheuer v. Muller, 20 C. C. A. 165, and supplementary thereto, under same title, note to Lare v. Harper, 30 C. C. A. 376.

A case "too plain to waste many words over" (see text, right) – especially in the face of a color illustration. This book was printed for the internal use of the National Biscuit Company, known today as Nabisco.

Order of reference of the Supreme Court ... State of Pennsylvania, complainant, against the Wheeling & Belmont Bridge Company.

7.11

Saratoga Springs [N.Y.]: George F. White, 1851. Lithographs by R. H. Peace.

State of Penn. vs. Wheeling & B. B. Company et al. 457

REPORT AND PLAN

FOR A

WIRE SUSPENSION BRIDGE,

PROPOSED TO BE ERECTED

OVER THE OHIO RIVER AT CINCINNATI.

BY JOHN A. ROEBLING, CIVIL ENGINEER.

To Robert Buchanan, Esq.; James Taylor, Esq.; Paul Anderson, Esq.; John K. McNickle, Esq.; Reuben R. Springer, Esq.; Charles A. Withers, Esq.

GENTLEMEN: Agreeably to your request, I have investigated the project of constructing a *Wire Cable Suspension Bridge* across the Ohio river between Cincinnati and Covington, with all that care and attention to which, from its magnitude and importance it appears to be entitled.

The following report and accompanying plan are the result of my labors, and are respectfully presented to your consideration.

As one of the great thoroughfares of the country, and spanning one of the great rivers of the west, this bridge, when constructed, will possess great claims as a national monument. As a splendid work of art and as a remarkable specimen of modern engineering, it will stand unrivalled upon this continent. Its gigantic features will speak loudly in favor of the energy, enterprise and wealth of the community which will boast of its possession.

With the sincere desire that this noble and eminently useful project may receive that general support, which it so richly merits,

I remain, gentlemen, respectfully,

Your obedient servant,

JOHN A. ROEBLING,

Civil Engineer.

Pittsburgh, September 1, 1846.

x 3

The height of the great Wheeling Suspension Bridge obstructed steamboat traffic on the Ohio River. Using the lithograph featured here, the U.S. Supreme Court determined that the bridge would need to be destroyed as an impediment to interstate commerce unless it could be raised 111 feet above low water – an impossible task. Congress saved the bridge in 1852 by declaring it to be a federal post road.

"The Paper Chase," circa 1495. The book in which this illustration appears includes a poem to help students memorize the titles of the papal decrees, or Decretals, of canon law. A distracted reader – possibly a bored student? – has added decorative elements to the original image.

Repertorium aureum continens titulos quinque librorum Decretalium. Cologne: Heinrich Quentell, 1495. Gift of Louis M. Rabinowitz, 1946.

Teaching the Law 8

ALTHOUGH THE LAW IS FULL OF LIFE, it is a complex subject, and many people – shockingly – find it dry. In teaching law, illustrations can help address this challenge. Illustrations can serve as mnemonic devices for committing intricate rules to memory, and they can make legal study more enjoyable by enlivening a relentlessly textual enterprise with visual interest, even some lightness of heart. Illustrations can also help bring critical legal information to marginalized communities. They play an especially important role in books for juveniles and young adults by nurturing their emotional attachment to the legal system, helping young people imagine themselves as actors in the rule of law.

8.01

Jacobus de Theramo.

Le procés de Belial a lencontre de Jhesus [leaf].

(Lyon: Johann Neumeister, 4 Mar. 1483/84).

nelle ⁊ nō pas equite ⁊ iustice contre ledit belial a ꝓffere sentēce dif finitiue laquelle belial dit estre nulle ou inique si elle a este daucūe vallue. d laqlle soy sentāt greue il a appelle deuāt nostre audiāce: pour la quelle chose no⁹ mandons que appelles ceulx q̄ doyuront estre appelles ⁊ les parties dune chescūe part ouyez en la causa tu ayes legitimemēt a proceder. ⁊ la dessusdicte sentēce tu aies a cōfer mer ou reuocquer toute appellatiō post pousee ainsi cōme d droit se deura faire ⁊ les tesmoigns ⁊ cetera. Donne en nostre grant palais de paradis le xxij. iour dauril.

Cōment belial presente son rescript a ioseph.

Quāt belial eust receu le rescript diuin incontināt sen ala a ioseph ⁊ se agenoilla deuāt luy ⁊ luy presenta son rescript en la forme dessus escripte. ⁊ aussi linstrumēt de son appel latiō les appostres ⁊ les ꝓces dessusditz en luy priāt que luy plai se de ꝓceder en la dicte cause cōme equite ⁊ iustice requierent. dit io seph voulentiers le feray. ⁊ que demādes que ie face en la dicte cause? dit belial mon seigneur ie vo⁹ prie q̄l soit inhibe ⁊ deffen du de par vo⁹ a salomon q̄ pendāt mon appellation q̄ plus il ne ꝓcede en la execution de sa sentēce. dit ioseph voulētiers le feray. ⁊ tantost māda au notaire ⁊ greffier d son audiēce. que incōtināt il fist escripre ladicte inhibicion selon lestille de la court. la quelle il fit en la maniere que sensuyt.

The wicked Belial, depicted here with cloven hoofs, presents Joseph with the written answer to a legal petition against Jesus. A notary sits below. This French translation of a fourteenth-century Latin text was used to teach legal procedure. The story of Belial's suit is analogous to the "hypotheticals" used to teach law today.

Giovanni d'Andrea.

Arbor consanguineitatis cum suis enigmatibus et figuris.

Nuremberg: Hieronymus Höltzel, 1506. Woodcuts attributed to Hans Baldung Grien.

Acquired with the Albert S. Wheeler Fund.

8.02

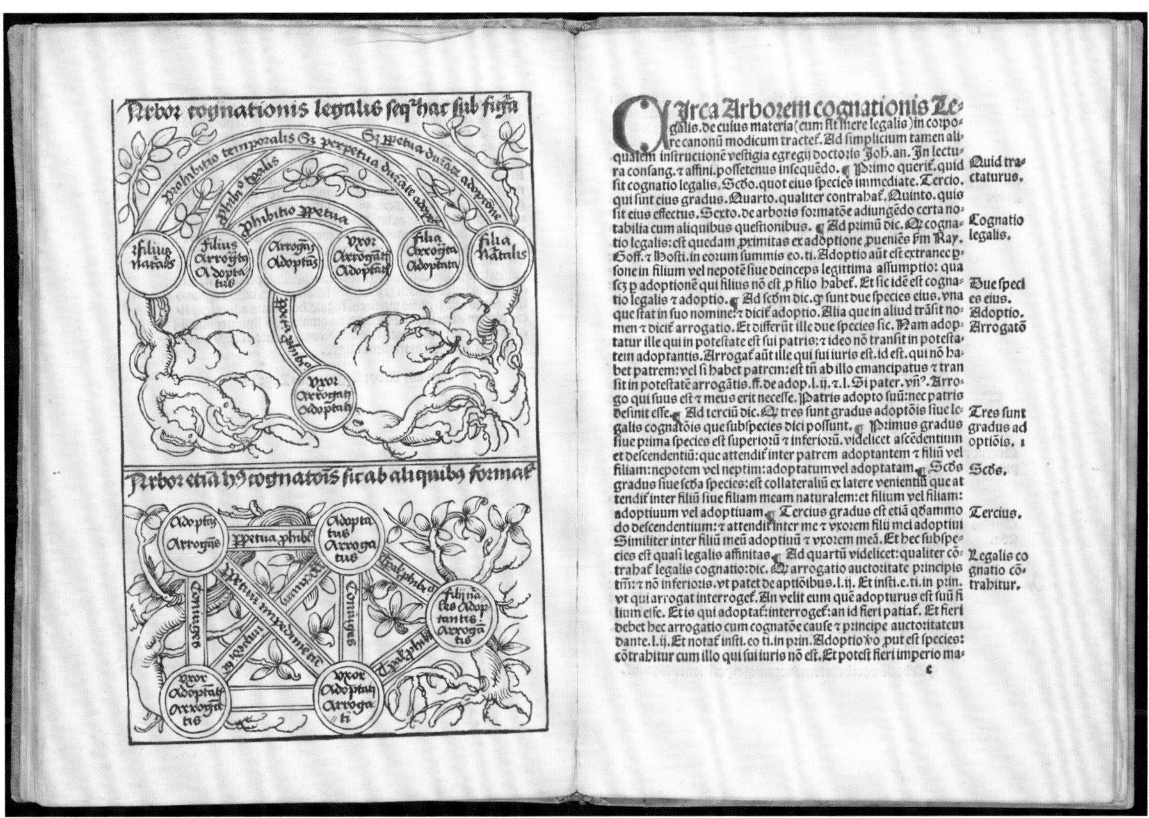

Circa Arborem cognationis Legalis. de cuius materia (cum sit mere legalis) in corpore canonũ modicum tractet. Ad simplicium tamen aliqualem instructionẽ vestigia egregij doctoris Joh. an. In lectura consang. et affini. possetenus insequẽdo. ¶ Primo querit. quid sit cognatio legalis. Scdo. quot eius species immediate. Tercio. qui sint eius gradus. Quarto. qualiter contrahat. Quinto. quis sit eius effectus. Sexto. de arboris formatõe adiungẽdo certa notabilia cum aliquibus questionibus. ¶ Ad primũ dic. q cognatio legalis: est quedam proximitas ex adoptione pueniẽs sm Ray. Goff. et Hosti. in eorum summis eo. ti. Adoptio aũt est extranee psone in filium vel nepotẽ siue deinceps legittima assumptio: qua scz p adoptionẽ qui filius nõ est p filio habet. Et sic idẽ est cognatio legalis et adoptio. ¶ Ad scdm dic. q sunt due species eius. vna que stat in suo nomine: et dicit adoptio. Alia que in aliud trãsit nomen et dicit arrogatio. Et differũt ille due species sic. Nam adoptatur ille qui in potestate est sui patris: et ideo nõ transit in potestatem adoptantis. Arrogat aũt ille qui sui iuris est. id est. qui nõ habet patrem: vel si habet patrem: est tñ ab illo emancipatus et transit in potestatẽ arrogãtis. ff. de adop. l. ij. et l. Si pater. vñ. Arrogo qui suus est et meus erit necesse. Patris adopto suũ: nec patris desinit esse. ¶ Ad terciũ dic. q tres sunt gradus adoptõis siue legalis cognatõis que subspecies dici possunt. ¶ Primus gradus siue prima species est superiorũ et inferiorũ. videlicet ascẽdentium et descendentiũ: que attendit inter patrem adoptantem et filiũ vel filiam: nepotem vel neptim: adoptatum vel adoptatam. ¶ Scds gradus siue scda species: est collateraliũ ex latere venientiũ que attendit inter filiũ siue filiam meam naturalem: et filium vel filiam: adoptiuum vel adoptiuam. ¶ Tercius gradus est etiã qdammodo descendentium: et attendit inter me et vxorem filiũ mei adoptiui Similiter inter filiũ meũ adoptiuũ et vxorem meã. Et hec subspecies est quasi legalis affinitas. ¶ Ad quartũ videlicet: qualiter cõtrahat legalis cognatio: dic. q arrogatio auctoritate principis tñ: et nõ inferioris. vt patet de aptiõibus. l. ij. Et insti. e. ti. in prin. vt qui arrogat interroget. An velit eum quẽ adopturus est suũ filium esse. Et is qui adoptat: interroget: an id fieri patiat. Et fieri debet hec arrogatio cum cognatõe cause et principe auctoritatem dante. l. ij. Et notat insti. eo ti. in prin. Adoptio vo put est species: cõtrahitur cum illo qui sui iuris nõ est. Et potest fieri imperio ma-

Quid tractaturus.

Cognatio legalis.

Due species eius.

Adoptio.

Arrogatõ

Tres sunt gradus adoptiõis.

Scds.

Tercius.

Legalis cognatio cõtrahitur.

The most popular legal textbook about consanguinity and affinity for centuries, this book by the great medieval canonist Giovanni d'Andrea (ca. 1270–1348) was later enhanced with a variety of charts to help students solve problems presented in the text. The balance between decorative and instructional elements in this tree diagram is especially fine.

8.03

Instituta novissime recognita aptissimisque figuris exculta.

Venice: Luca-Antonio Giunta, 1516.

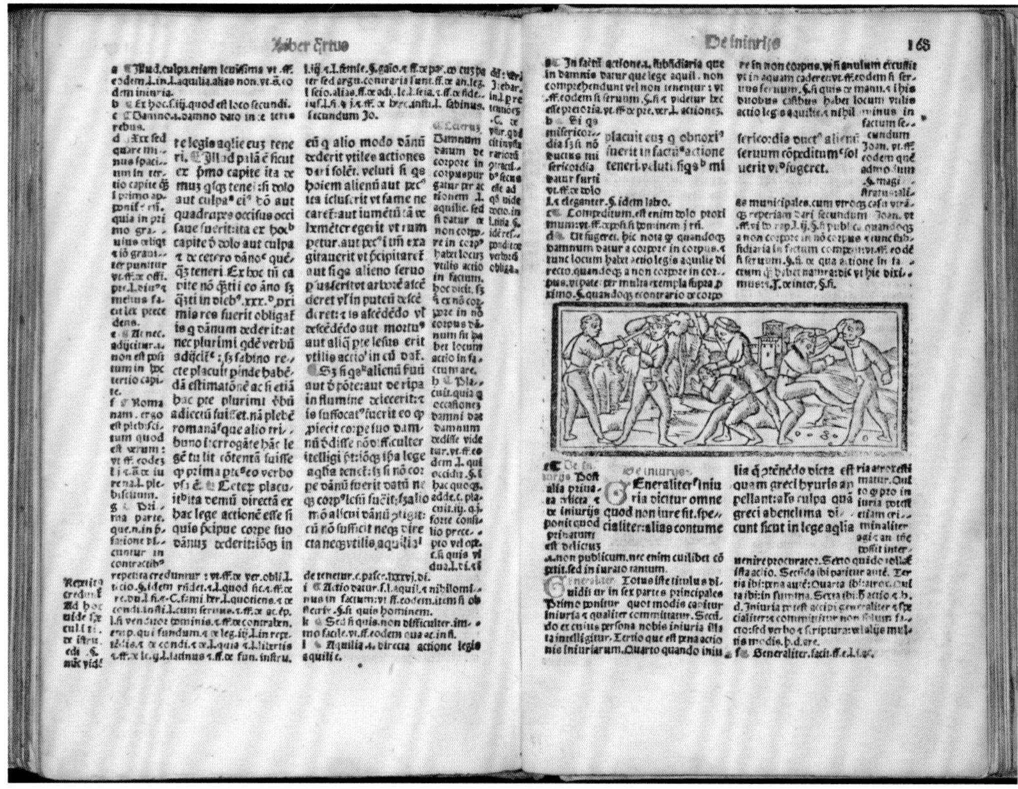

How does an exciting illustration like this one differ from those displayed in Section 2, "Depicting the Law"? Twenty-two woodcut vignettes introduce the chapters in this illustrated edition of Justinian's *Institutes*, the standard primer on Roman law for students throughout the medieval and early modern periods. This edition is published by a member of the Giunta printing dynasty of Venice, which also produced the books displayed as items 2.06 and 3.00.

Johann Moritz Werle.

Album juridicum.

Augsburg: Matthias Wolff, 1733.

Like many law students today, this sophisticated legal scholar in his library seems ready to pull an all-nighter. Pointing to a diagram outlining the book's contents – a collection of legal maxims arranged by topic – he announces that "the lion is on the way." At the top of the diagram is a Latin maxim, "Bibliotheca sola non sufficit; unde disce piger" – which, roughly translated, means "A library alone is not enough; learn, you lazy man!"

8.05

Juristische Ergötzlichkeiten vom Jung-Gesellen Rechte.

Frankfurt & Leipzig, 1723.

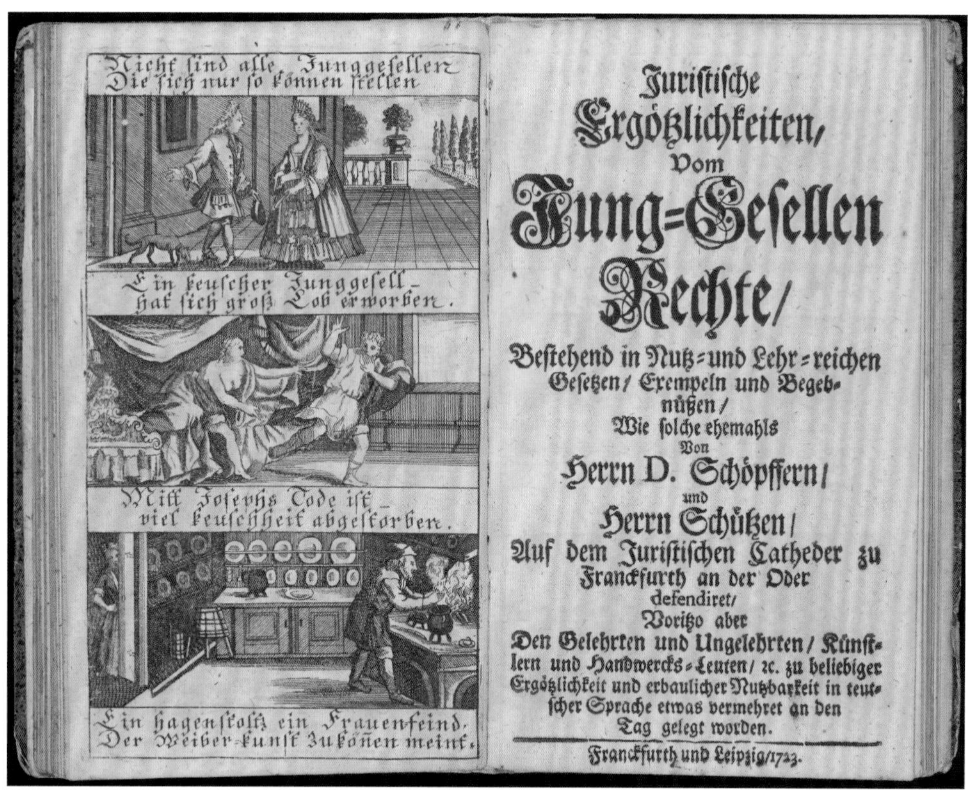

Nicht sind alle, Junggesellen
Die sich nur so können stellen

Ein keuscher Junggesell
hat sich groß Lob erworben.

Mitt Josephs Tode ist
viel keuschheit abgestorben.

Ein hagenstoltz ein Frauenfeind.
Der Weiber-kunst zu könen meint.

Juristische
Ergötzlichkeiten,
Vom
Jung=Gesellen
Rechte/
Bestehend in Nutz=und Lehr=reichen
Gesetzen/ Exempeln und Begeb-
nüssen/
Wie solche ehemahls
Von
Herrn D. Schöpffern/
und
Herrn Schützen/
Auf dem Juristischen Catheder zu
Franckfurth an der Oder
defendiret/
Voritzo aber
Den Gelehrten und Ungelehrten/ Künst-
lern und Handwercks-Leuten/ ꝛc. zu beliebiger
Ergötzlichkeit und erbaulicher Nutzbarkeit in teut-
scher Sprache etwas vermehret an den
Tag gelegt worden.
Franckfurth und Leipzig/1723.

Young men in eighteenth-century Germany might have found it advantageous to read this collection of "useful and instructive laws" for bachelors by two scholars from Frankfurt an der Oder. The book discusses the autonomy of men vis-à-vis their fathers, their obligations towards potential fathers-in-law, the legal consequences of confessing to rape, and considerations of the penalty of castration (happily, not illustrated here). A companion volume for young women appeared in same year.

Johann Friedrich Böckelmann.

Compendium Institutionum Caes. Justiniani.

Leiden: Felix López de Haro, 1681.

The frontispiece of this abbreviated edition of Justinian's *Institutes* is a product plug. The image depicts two ways to arrive at legal knowledge. The path on the right, in which a student carries a unwieldy basket of books, bears the motto "either slowly or never." The path on the left, in which students proceed at ever-increasing levels of skill with a single book in their hand – the author's – bears the motto "neither slowly, nor with difficulty."

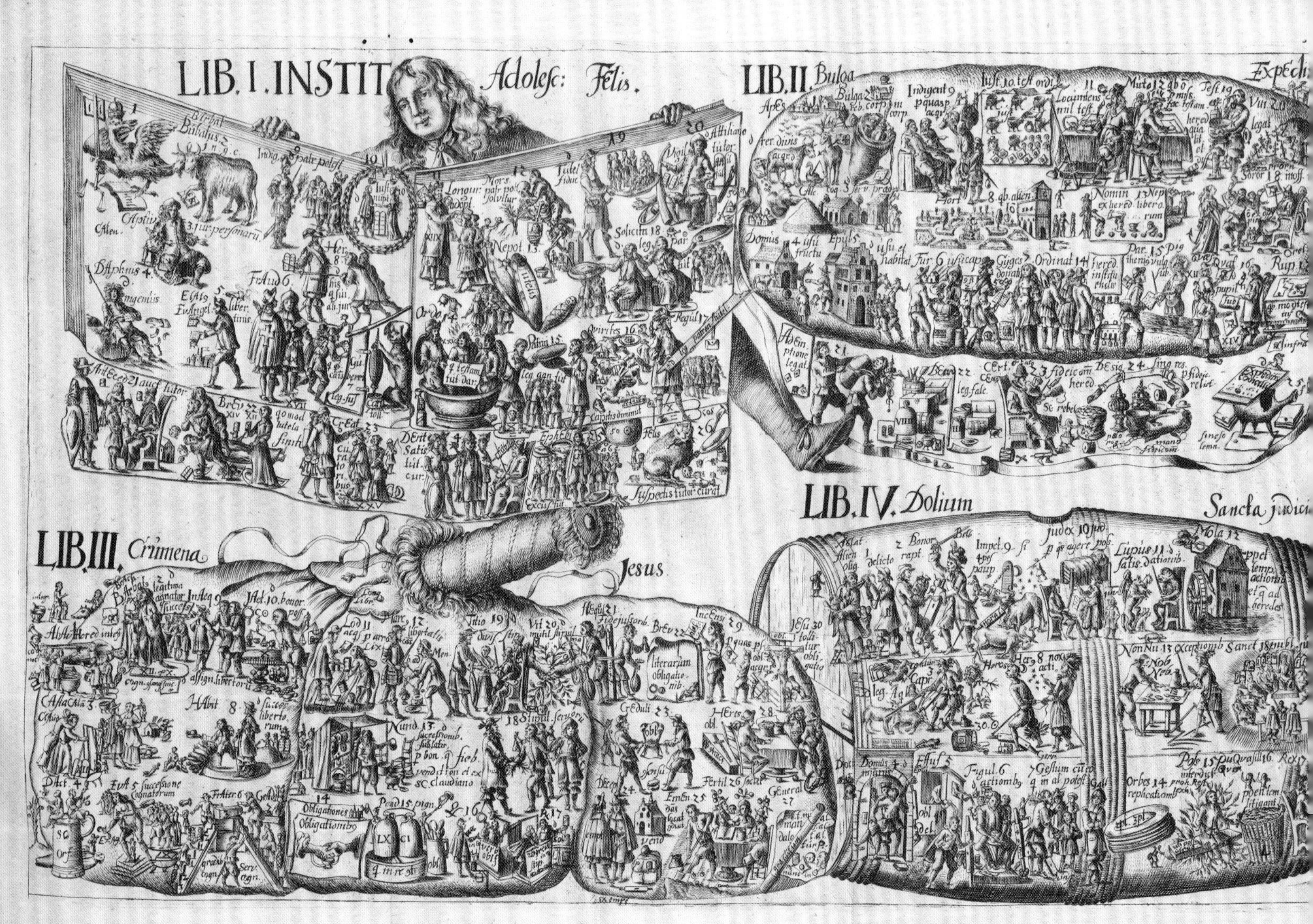
LIB. I. INSTIT
Adolesc: Felis.
LIB. II. Bulga
LIB. III. Crumena
Jesus
LIB. IV. Dolium

Johannes Buno.

Memoriale Institutionum juris.

Ratzeburg: Nicolaus Nissen, 1672. Foreign Law Collection of the Association of the Bar of the City of New York.

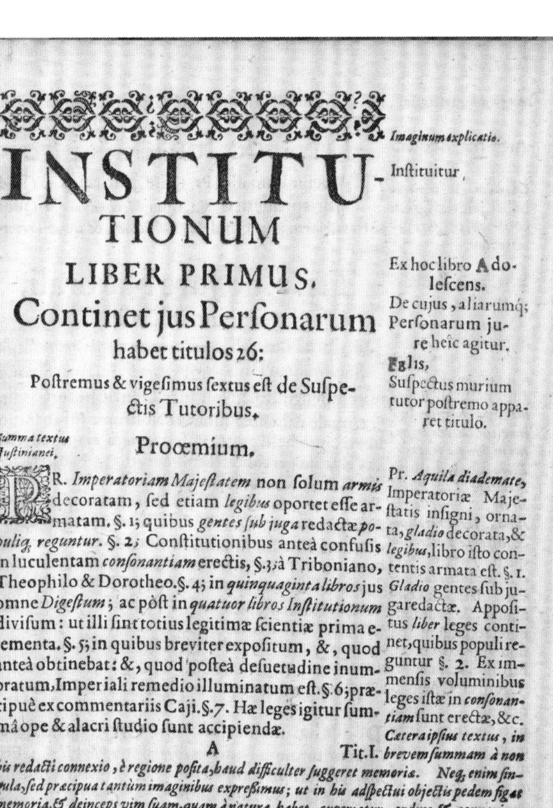

Imaginum explicatio.

INSTITU-
TIONUM
LIBER PRIMUS.
Continet jus Perſonarum
habet titulos 26:
Poſtremus & vigeſimus ſextus eſt de Suſpectis Tutoribus.

Inſtituitur,

Ex hoc libro Adoleſcens.
De cujus, aliarumq; Perſonarum jure heic agitur.
Fglis,
Suſpectus murium tutor poſtremo apparet titulo.

Summa textus Juſtinianei,

Prooemium.

PR. *Imperatoriam Majeſtatem* non ſolum *armis* decoratam, ſed etiam *legibus* oportet eſſe armatam. §. 1; quibus *gentes ſub juga* redactæ *populiq; reguntur.* §. 2; Conſtitutionibus anteà confuſis in luculentam *conſonantiam* erectis, §.3; à Triboniano, Theophilo & Dorotheo. §. 4; in *quinquaginta libros* jus omne *Digeſtum*; ac pòſt in *quatuor libros Inſtitutionum* diviſum: ut illi ſint totius legitimæ ſcientiæ prima elementa. §. 5; in quibus breviter expoſitum, &, quod anteà obtinebat: &, quod poſteà deſuetudine inumbratum, Imperiali remedio illuminatum eſt. §. 6; præcipuè ex commentariis Caji. §. 7. Hæ leges igitur ſummâ ope & alacri ſtudio ſunt accipiendæ.

Pr. *Aquila diademate,* Imperatoriæ Majeſtatis inſigni, ornata, *gladio* decorata, & *legibus*, libro iſto contentis armata eſt. §. 1. *Gladio* gentes ſub jugaredactæ. Appoſitus *liber* leges continet, quibus populi reguntur §. 2. Ex immenſis voluminibus leges iſtæ in *conſonantiam* ſunt erectæ, &c.

A Tit. I.

Cætera ipſius textus, in brevem ſummam à nobis redacti connexio, è regione poſita, haud difficulter ſuggeret memoriæ. Neq; enim ſingula, ſed præcipua tantùm imaginibus expreſſimus; ut in his adſpectui objectis pedem figat memoria, & deinceps vim ſuam, quam à natura habet, experiatur, ordine & connexione paragraphorum adjuta.

Johannes Buno (1617-1697) is known as the creator of the "emblematic teaching method," in which pictures and allegories are used as mnemonic devices. The subject of this illustration is Justinian's *Institutes.* The book also contains 1400 questions and answers about the *Institutes* produced for Buno's students at the St. Michaeli *Gymnasium* near Hannover.

8.08

George Billinghurst.

Arcana clericalia, or, The mysteries of clarkship.

London: Henry Twyford, 1674. From the collection of Anthony Taussig. Acquired with the John A. Hoober Fund.

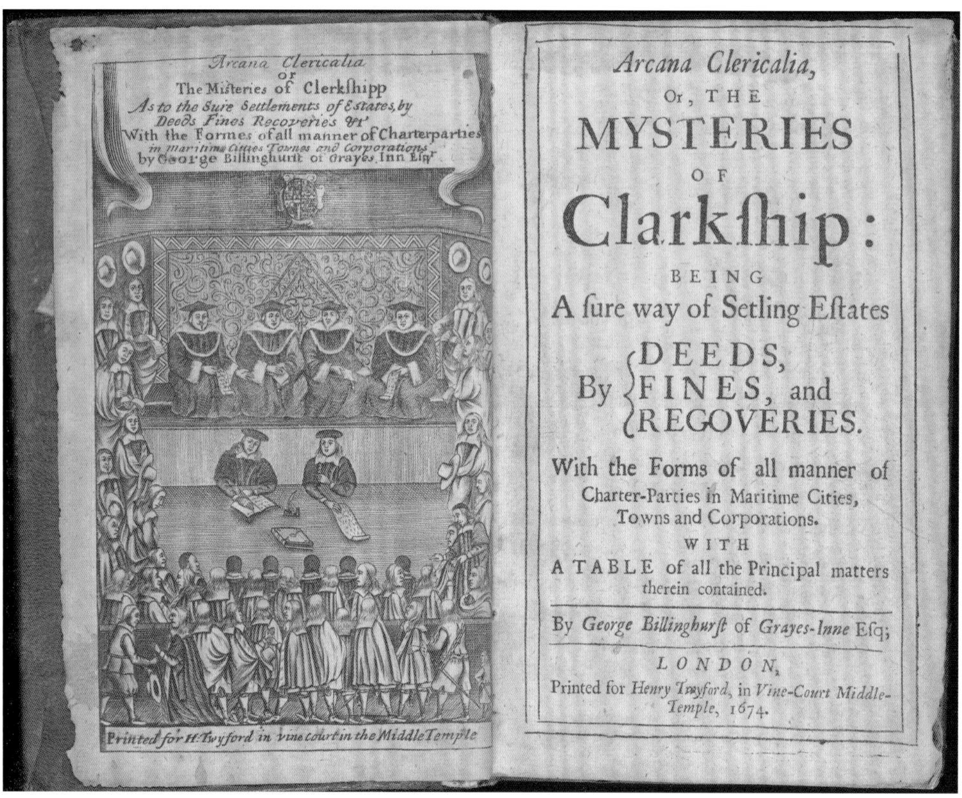

Arcana Clericalia
or
The Misteries of Clerkſhipp
As to the Sure Settlements of Estates, by
Deeds Fines Recoveries &c
With the Formes of all manner of Charterparties
in maritime Cities Townes and Corporations
by George Billinghurst of Grayes Inn Esqr

Printed for H: Twyford in vine court in the Middle Temple

Arcana Clericalia,
Or, THE
MYSTERIES
OF
Clarkſhip:
BEING
A ſure way of Setling Eſtates
By DEEDS, FINES, and RECOVERIES.
With the Forms of all manner of
Charter-Parties in Maritime Cities,
Towns and Corporations.
WITH
A TABLE of all the Principal matters
therein contained.

By *George Billinghurſt* of *Grayes-Inne* Eſq;

LONDON,
Printed for *Henry Twyford*, in *Vine-Court Middle-Temple*, 1674.

Instructional law books often promise to reveal mysteries – including those contained in other law books, like the one laying at the center of the table, at left.

8.09

Maud Hoestlandt.

La justice à petit pas.

Paris: Actes Sud Junior, 2004. Illustrations by Nicolas Hubesch.

Justice in small, French steps – from chocolate cake to the Code Civil. Illustrations can help young people see law as their own. In the varied works shown here, comic art is an instrument of active citizenship and the democratization of legal knowledge, whether in a collection of "legal amusements" from eighteenth-century Germany, "parlor commentaries" from nineteenth-century England, or delightful comic illustrations like this one.

8.10

Hagamos valer nuestros derechos.

San Salvador, El Salvador: Ministerio de Educación, Dirección Nacional de Educación, 1997.
Illustrated by Daniel Saravia. Gift of Morris L. Cohen, 2009.

Hagamos Valer
Nuestros Derechos
Guía didáctica sobre los derechos, deberes y libertades de los niños y niñas de primero y segundo ciclos de Educación Básica.
MINISTERIO DE EDUCACION
Dirección Nacional de Educación
1997.
Rädda Barnen
de Suecia

"Let's assert our rights" – from the Ministry of Education in El Salvador. Books like these teach children about their legal interests in a language appropriate to their level of development.

8.11

Syl Sobel.

The U.S. Constitution and you.

Hauppauge, N.Y.: Barron's Educational Series, 2001. Illustrated by Denise Gilgannon.
Gift of Morris L. Cohen, 2009.

♪ "This law is my law,
this law is your law." ♪

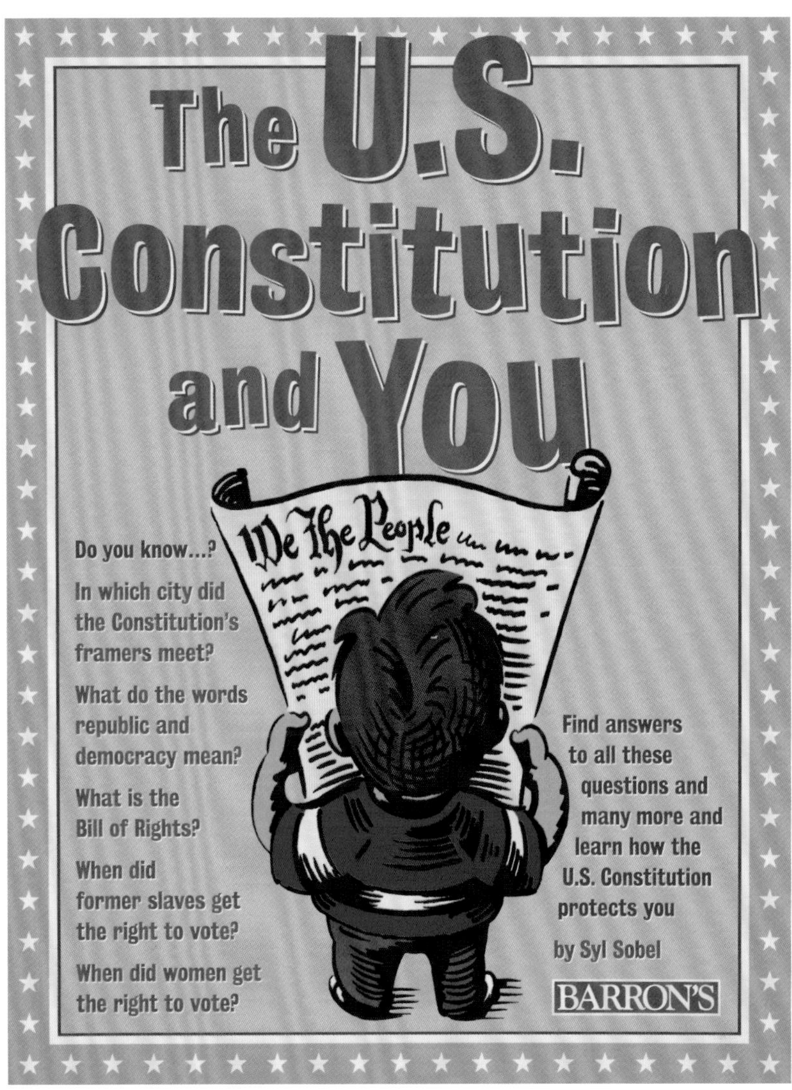

8.12

Yuki Nakamichi & Yamanaka Masahiro. *Osaru no tomasu keiho o shiru: saruyama kyowakoku no jikenbo [Thomas Monkey learns the criminal law].*

Tokyo: Tarojiroshaeditasu, 2014. Acquired with the Charles J. Tanenbaum Fund.

All students can benefit from the example of Thomas Monkey! Hopefully they won't learn about law in quite the way that Thomas does – the hard way.

Illiustrirovannaia Konstitutsiia Rossiiskoi Federatsii. = The illustrated Constitution of the Russian Federation.

8.13

Moscow: Izdatel M.IU. Gorelov, 2012. Illustrated by Natalia Khudyakova & Maxim Gorelov.
Gift of William E. Butler, 2013.

An award-winning work of graphic design, this illustrated Russian constitution was produced for the twentieth anniversary of the document. From the publisher: "It is illustrated article-by-article with colorful pictures and diagrams, thus making the sophisticated legal language of the Fundamental Law much easier to comprehend. This volume can be a perfect gift or a Russian souvenir. The text of the Constitution of the Russian Federation is given both in Russian and English language."

8.14

Keith Aoki, James Boyle, & Jennifer Jenkins.

Bound by law? Tales from the public domain.

Durham, N.C.: Duke Center for the Study of the Public Domain, 2006. Illustrations by Keith Aoki.

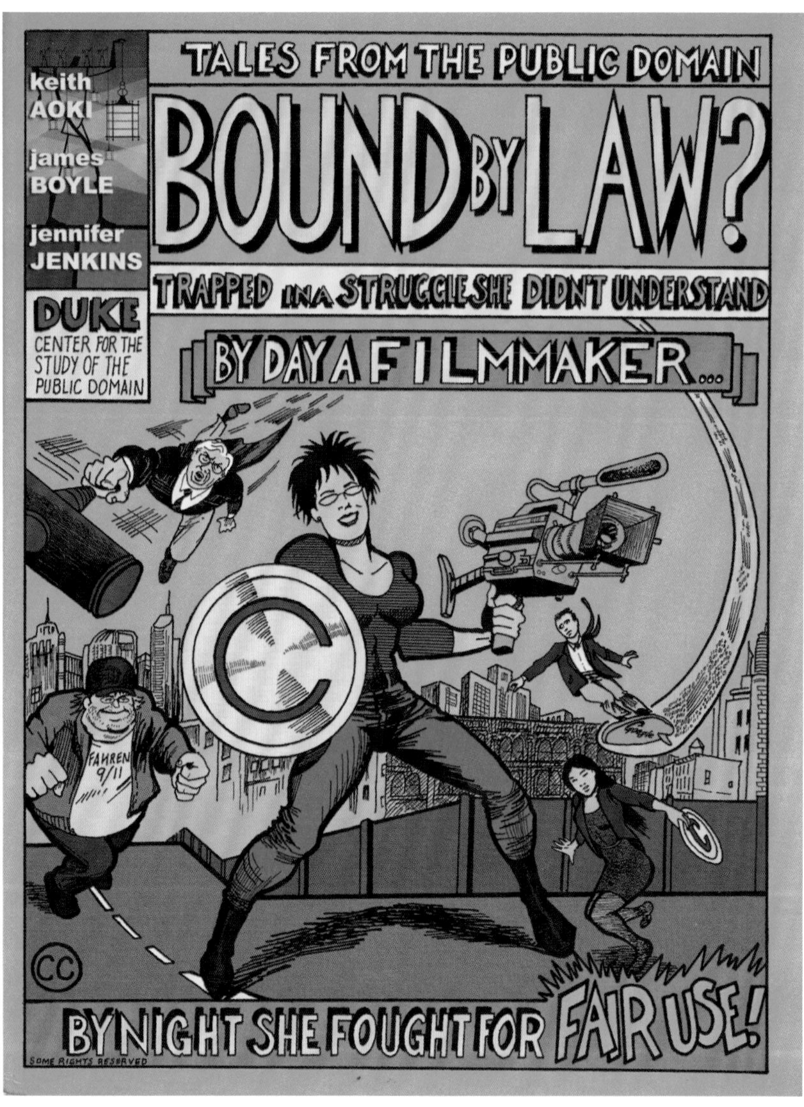

Three law professors teamed up to create this guide to copyright law. In the spirit of their analysis, the authors placed the work in the public domain and made it freely available on line.

8.15

Jefferys Taylor.

Parlour commentaries on the Constitution and laws of England.

London: John Harris, 1825. Gift of Morris L. Cohen, 2009.

A female judge presides over the parlor game of "Judge & Jury," at left, while a girl holds forth at an improvised lectern. Books lay about the floor. Is the cat testifying or merely observing? And what is its knowledge of the constitution and the laws of England?

8.16

Jehoshaphat Aspin.

The constitution of England, or, Magna-charta, Bill of Rights, Habeas Corpus, and all the other laws of England.

London: A.K. Newman & Co., 1810. Acquired with the Ford Motor Company Fund.

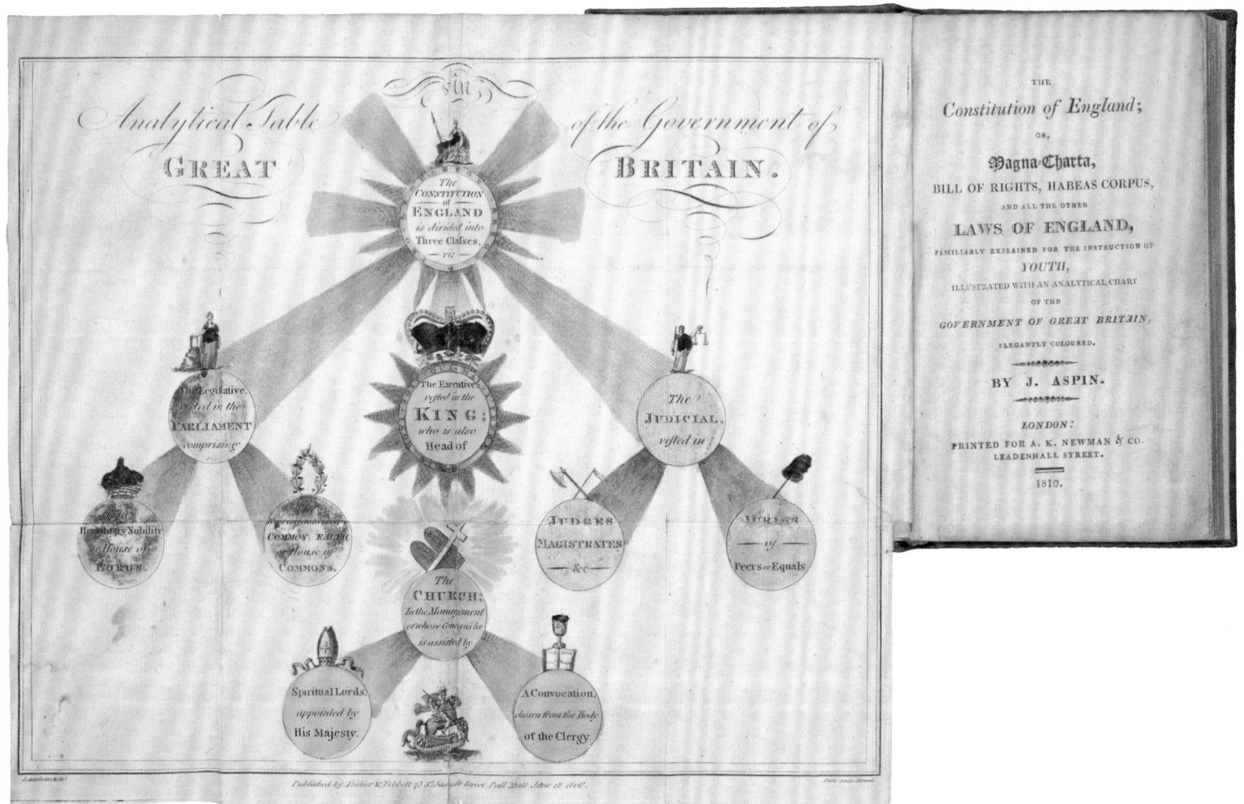

Like other books on display in this section, this "elegantly colored" volume on English law, "familiarly explained for the instruction of youth," is part of the Yale Law Library's Juvenile Jurisprudence Collection.

8.17

NATHANIEL BURNEY.

The illustrated guide to criminal procedure.

New York: Ivers Morgan, 2014.

Whether in the United States, as in this book, or in Brazil [8.18], the subject of criminal law seems to lend itself especially well to comic illustration. Why would that be?

8.18

Denise Cardia Saraiva.

Direito penal ilustrado: parte geral.

Rio de Janeiro: Edições Illustradas, 1999.

Acquired with the Gordon Bradford Tweedy Memorial Fund.

The section of the illustrated guide to Brazilian criminal law featured here deals with intentional acts.

Youth & law: legal advice for youth.

8.19

[San Francisco?: High School Committee, National Lawyers Guild, undated.
Acquired with the Charles J. Tanenbaum Fund.

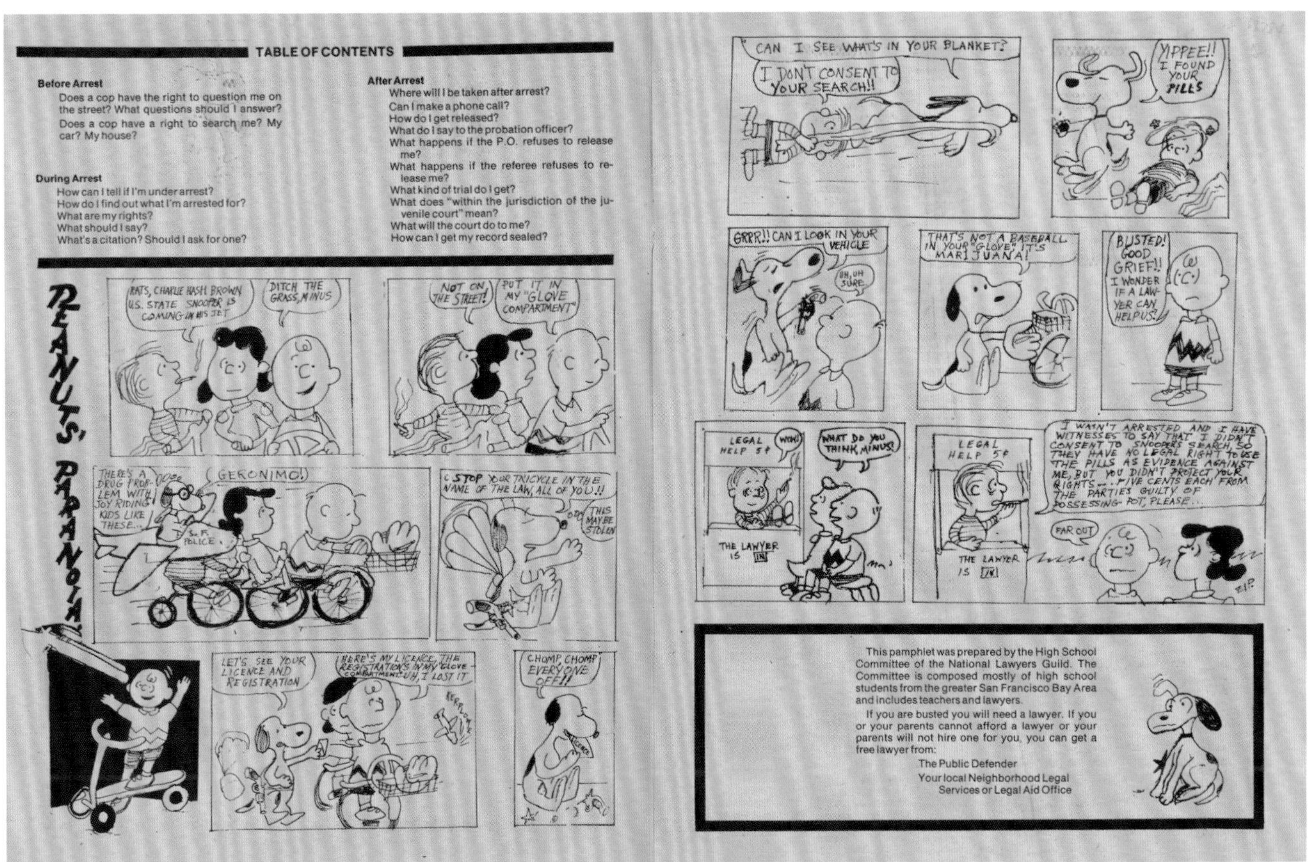

TABLE OF CONTENTS

Before Arrest
Does a cop have the right to question me on the street? What questions should I answer?
Does a cop have a right to search me? My car? My house?

During Arrest
How can I tell if I'm under arrest?
How do I find out what I'm arrested for?
What are my rights?
What should I say?
What's a citation? Should I ask for one?

After Arrest
Where will I be taken after arrest?
Can I make a phone call?
How do I get released?
What do I say to the probation officer?
What happens if the P.O. refuses to release me?
What happens if the referee refuses to release me?
What kind of trial do I get?
What does "within the jurisdiction of the juvenile court" mean?
What will the court do to me?
How can I get my record sealed?

This pamphlet was prepared by the High School Committee of the National Lawyers Guild. The Committee is composed mostly of high school students from the greater San Francisco Bay Area and includes teachers and lawyers.

If you are busted you will need a lawyer. If you or your parents cannot afford a lawyer or your parents will not hire one for you, you can get a free lawyer from:

The Public Defender
Your local Neighborhood Legal Services or Legal Aid Office

The National Lawyers Guild, the nation's oldest and largest progressive bar association, put mainstream comic characters in unlawful situations in this pamphlet from the 1970s – an artistic strategy characteristic of counter-culture literature. The pamphlet was produced by the NLG's high school committee of the San Francisco Bay Area.

8.20

The Legal Self-Defense Group presents: Mr. Natural in "Bailed out."

Boston, Mass., 1971?. "Story & drawings by a follower of R. Crumb".

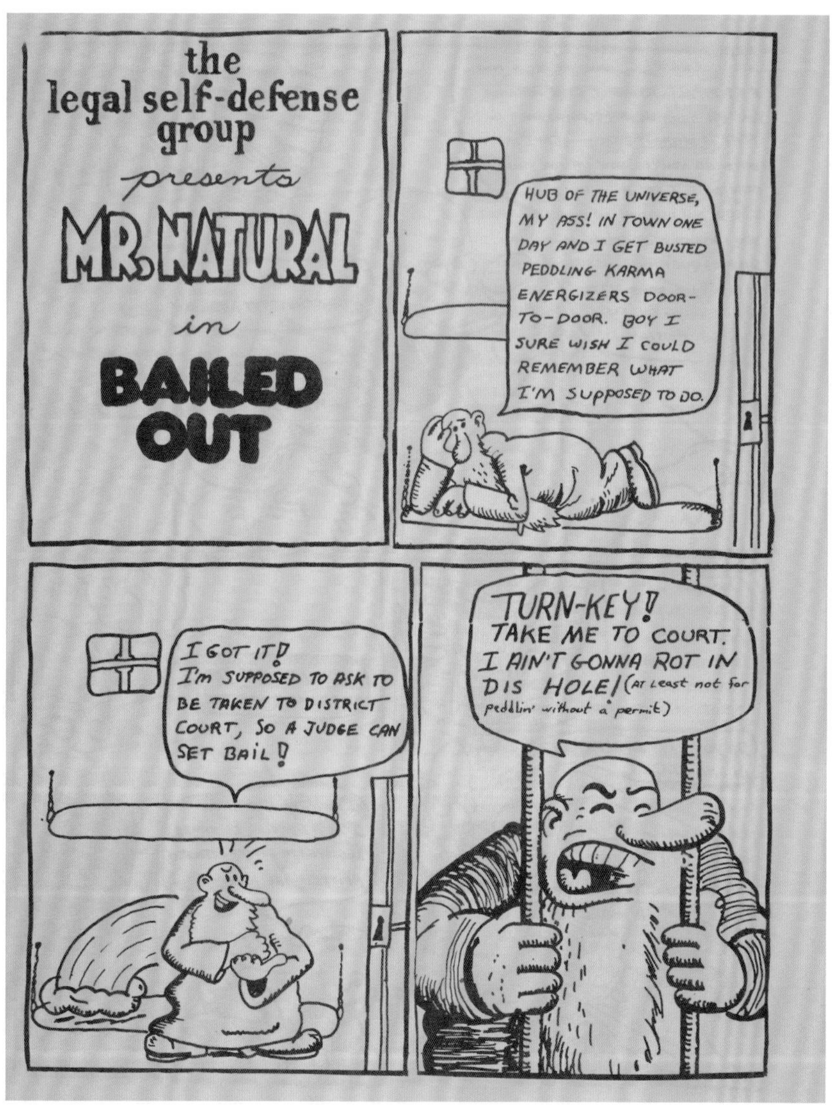

These leaflets offer legal self-defense strategies in cases of unlawful search and seizure and following arrest. They are drawn in the style of two popular underground cartoon characters of the day: Robert Crumb's "Mr. Natural" and Gilbert Shelton's "The Fabulous Furry Freak Brothers." The Legal Defense Group was a project of the Massachusetts Lawyers Guild, a left-wing legal consortium devoted to civil liberties.

The Legal Self-Defense Group presents: "Search and seizure."

8.21

Boston, Mass., 1971?.

An illustrated criminal code by the great French illustrator Joseph Hémard (1880-1961) describes its images as "picture comments" – or "illustrated commentary."

France.
Code penal: commentaires imagés de Joseph Hémard.
Paris: Editions Littéraires de France, [192u?]). "Commentaires imagés de Joseph Hémard."

Laughing – and Crying – at the Law

9

Because law is so serious, it begs to be satirized. Publishers have eagerly responded to this need with a wealth of figurative illustrations – biting, mocking, aggressive, droll, or simply funny and entertaining. These illustrations lift readers above the legal texts in which they appear, placing them in a critical relationship to legal rules and the language of the law. They also point to the importance of the legal profession for human life by depicting the foibles of the poor, blind, hapless creatures that law serves.

9.01

François Marchant.

La constitution en vaudevilles: suivie des Droits de l'homme, de la femme & de plusieurs autres vaudevilles constitutionnels.

Paris: Libraires Royalistes, 1792.

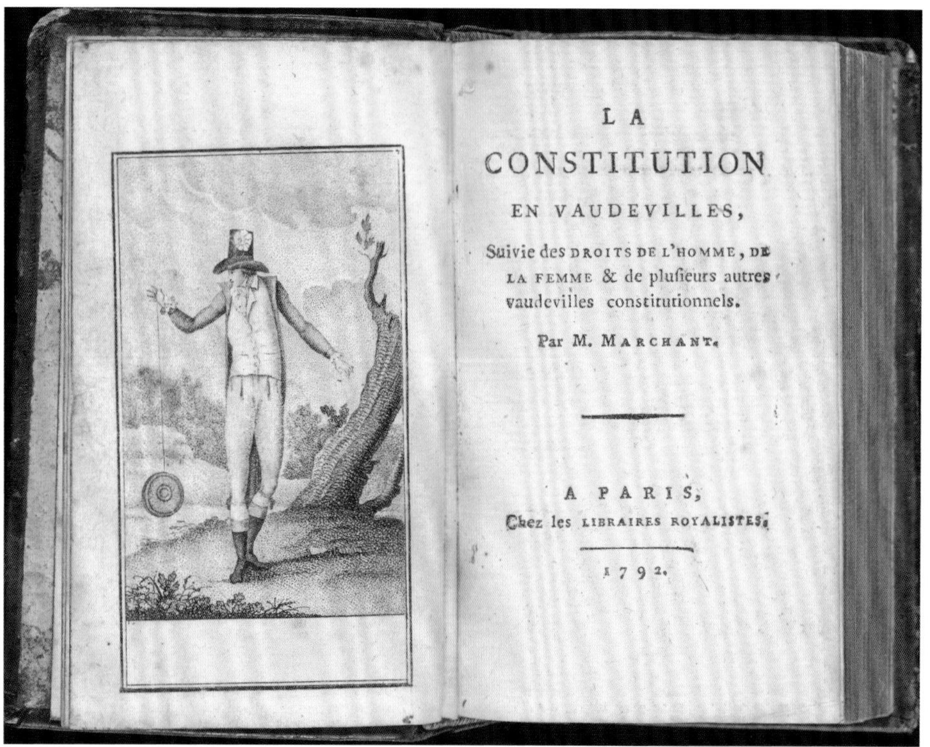

LA
CONSTITUTION
EN VAUDEVILLES,
Suivie des DROITS DE L'HOMME, DE LA FEMME & de plusieurs autres vaudevilles constitutionnels.
Par M. MARCHANT.
A PARIS,
Chez les LIBRAIRES ROYALISTES.
1792.

Note the publisher of this volume, which mocks the French constitution as a series of "vaudevilles" – and which features an early illustration of a yo-yo. Yo-yos were popular among the French aristocracy, and were known as émigrettes.

Charles Dumercy.

Exegése biblique au point de vue du droit belge.

Antwerp: J.E. Buschmann, 1895.

9.02

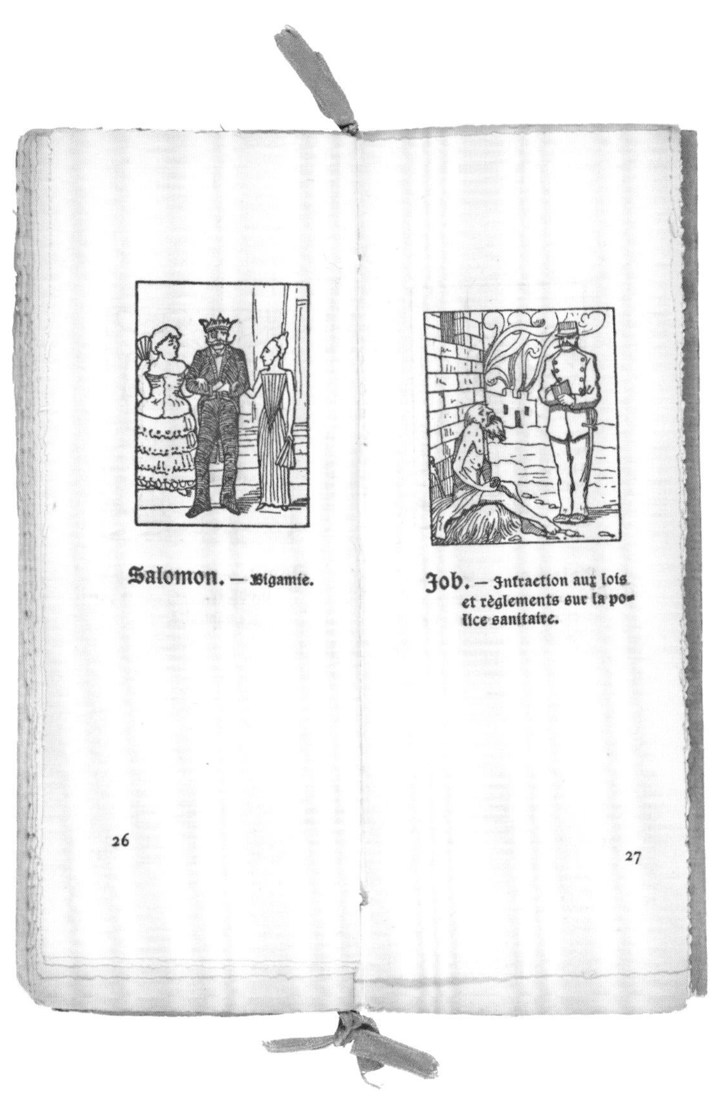

A rare Belgian pamphlet indicts figures of the Bible for contemporary crimes, placing ancient characters in contemporary settings. Solomon is depicted as a bigamist, and Job is charged with violating the rules of public sanitation. In works like these, illustrations are weapons in an ideological criticism of both the past and present.

CODE GÉNÉRAL

DES

IMPOTS DIRECTS

ET TAXES ASSIMILÉES

TEXTE INTÉGRAL DES LOIS, DÉCRETS, DÉCRETS-LOIS, DÉCRET DE CODIFICATION, SUIVI D'UN FORMULAIRE ADMINISTRATIF

AUX DÉPENS

DES ÉDITIONS LITTÉRAIRES ET ARTISTIQUES

13, rue des Saints-Pères, PARIS (6e)

DE LA LIBRAIRIE « LE TRIPTYQUE »

80, boulevard du Port-Royal, PARIS (5e)

pendant trois mois suivant celui de la mise en recouvrement du rôle suivant.

En ce qui concerne les rôles subséquents, les propriétaires sont admis à réclamer pendant les trois mois suivant celui de la mise en recouvrement de chaque rôle lorsque, par suite de circonstances exceptionnelles, leur immeuble a subi une dépréciation.

(*D. L.* 30 *juillet* 1937 *et* 21 *avril* 1939). Pour l'application de l'alinéa précédent, est considérée notamment comme résultant de circonstances exceptionnelles toute diminution durable de la valeur locative d'un immeuble ayant pour effet de ramener cette valeur locative au-dessous des quatre cinquièmes de la valeur locative cadastrale.

Art. 179 *bis* (*D. C.* 18 *février* 1943). — Par dérogation aux dispositions du premier alinéa de l'article précédent, le calcul, dans les conditions fixées par l'article 4 de la loi du 15 mars 1942, des nouvelles bases de cotisation applicables, à partir de 1943 aux établissements industriels ne peut valablement être contesté par les propriétaires, dans les délais prévus audit alinéa, que dans le cas d'erreur matérielle.

Art. 180 (*D. C.* 18 *février* 1943). — En dehors des cas prévus aux

Art. 179. — *Dépréciation d'immeuble.*

151

LIVRE II

IMPOSITIONS DÉPARTEMENTALES ET COMMUNALES

LIVRE III

DISPOSITIONS DIVERSES

ROLES — RÉCLAMATIONS

RECOUVREMENT

France.

Code général des impôts directs et taxes assimilées.

9.03

Paris: Editions Littéraires et Artistiques; Librairie "Le Triptyque," 1944.
"Illustré par Joseph Hémard." Gift of Farley P. Katz, 2007.

The work of the great Joseph Hémard epitomizes a tradition of comic illustration that is especially strong in France. Wonderfully, the illustrations here appear within ordinary texts of the criminal and tax codes – their humor derives from playing the text straight.

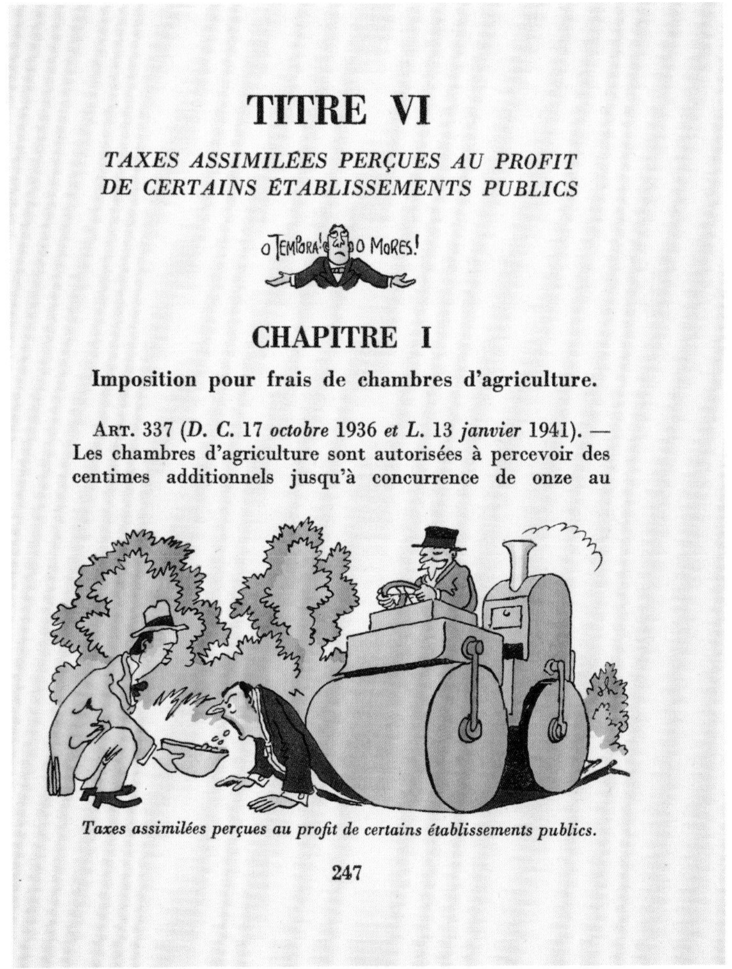

TITRE VI

TAXES ASSIMILÉES PERÇUES AU PROFIT DE CERTAINS ÉTABLISSEMENTS PUBLICS

CHAPITRE I

Imposition pour frais de chambres d'agriculture.

ART. 337 (*D. C.* 17 *octobre* 1936 *et L.* 13 *janvier* 1941). — Les chambres d'agriculture sont autorisées à percevoir des centimes additionnels jusqu'à concurrence de onze au

Taxes assimilées perçues au profit de certains établissements publics.

247

9.04

France.

Code de la route: texte officiel et complet.

Paris: Maurice Gonon, 1956. "Illustrations en couleurs de Dubout."
Acquired with the Gary and Brian Bookman Literature and Arts Fund.

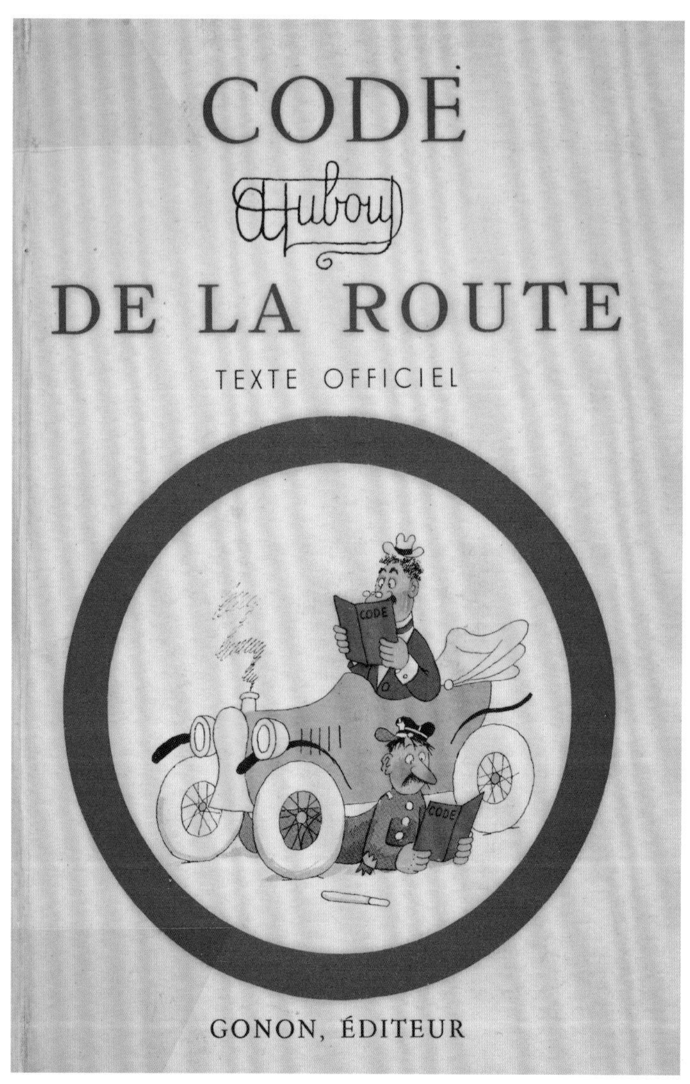

France has given birth to an especially rich tradition of comic legal illustration, as in this illustrated traffic code. Both driver and police officer seem befuddled by their reading material.

FRANCE.

9.05

Code penal: commentaires imagés de Joseph Hémard.

Paris: Editions Littéraires de France, [192u?]). "Commentaires imagés de Joseph Hémard."

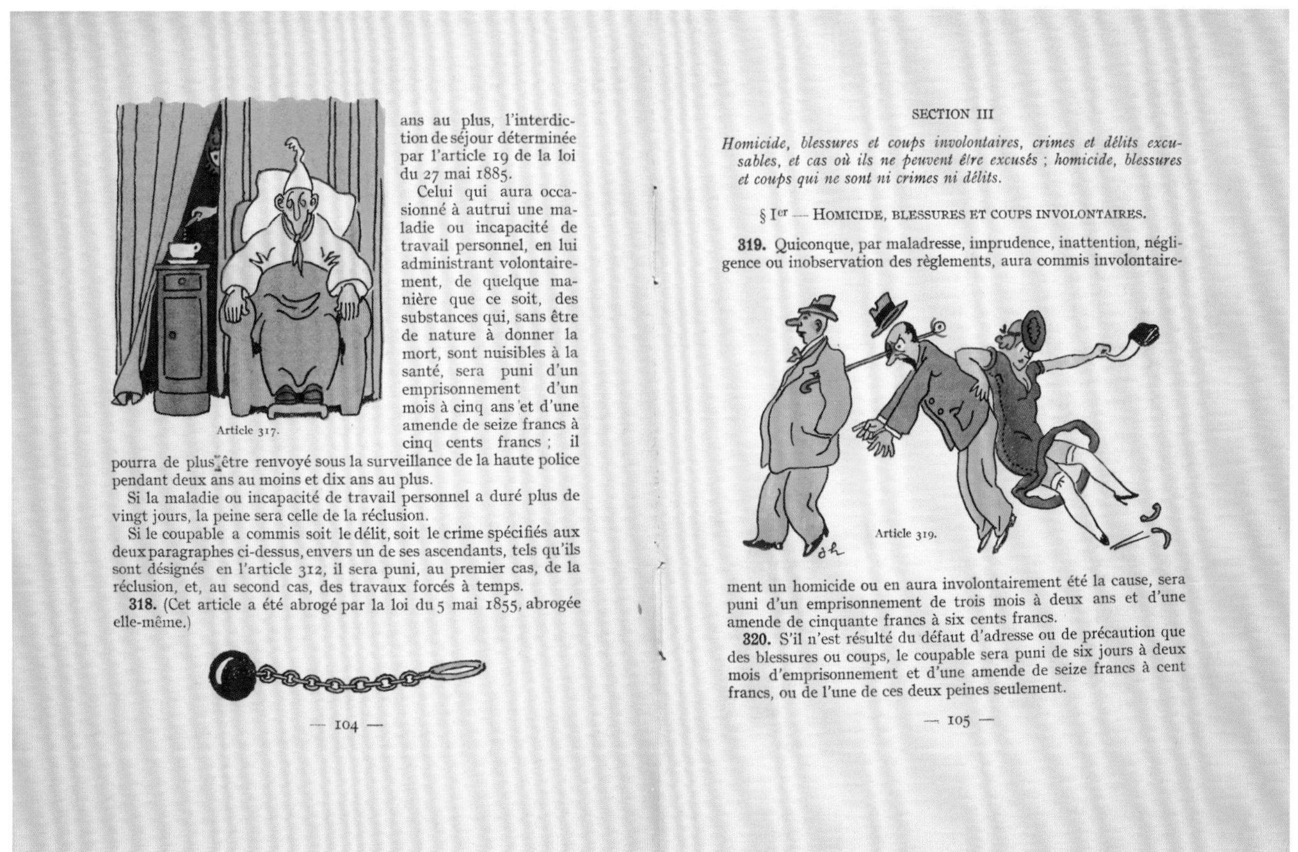

Article 317.

ans au plus, l'interdiction de séjour déterminée par l'article 19 de la loi du 27 mai 1885.

Celui qui aura occasionné à autrui une maladie ou incapacité de travail personnel, en lui administrant volontairement, de quelque manière que ce soit, des substances qui, sans être de nature à donner la mort, sont nuisibles à la santé, sera puni d'un emprisonnement d'un mois à cinq ans et d'une amende de seize francs à cinq cents francs; il pourra de plus être renvoyé sous la surveillance de la haute police pendant deux ans au moins et dix ans au plus.

Si la maladie ou incapacité de travail personnel a duré plus de vingt jours, la peine sera celle de la réclusion.

Si le coupable a commis soit le délit, soit le crime spécifiés aux deux paragraphes ci-dessus, envers un de ses ascendants, tels qu'ils sont désignés en l'article 312, il sera puni, au premier cas, de la réclusion, et, au second cas, des travaux forcés à temps.

318. (Cet article a été abrogé par la loi du 5 mai 1855, abrogée elle-même.)

— 104 —

SECTION III

Homicide, blessures et coups involontaires, crimes et délits excusables, et cas où ils ne peuvent être excusés ; homicide, blessures et coups qui ne sont ni crimes ni délits.

§ Ier — HOMICIDE, BLESSURES ET COUPS INVOLONTAIRES.

319. Quiconque, par maladresse, imprudence, inattention, négligence ou inobservation des règlements, aura commis involontairement un homicide ou en aura involontairement été la cause, sera puni d'un emprisonnement de trois mois à deux ans et d'une amende de cinquante francs à six cents francs.

Article 319.

320. S'il n'est résulté du défaut d'adresse ou de précaution que des blessures ou coups, le coupable sera puni de six jours à deux mois d'emprisonnement et d'une amende de seize francs à cent francs, ou de l'une de ces deux peines seulement.

— 105 —

Can even involuntary manslaughter be humorous? It can in the hands of Hémard.

9.06

France.

Code pénal: texte officiel.

Neuilly-sur Seine: M. Gonon, 1959. "Illustré par Siné."
Acquired with the Gary and Brian Bookman Literature and Arts Fund.

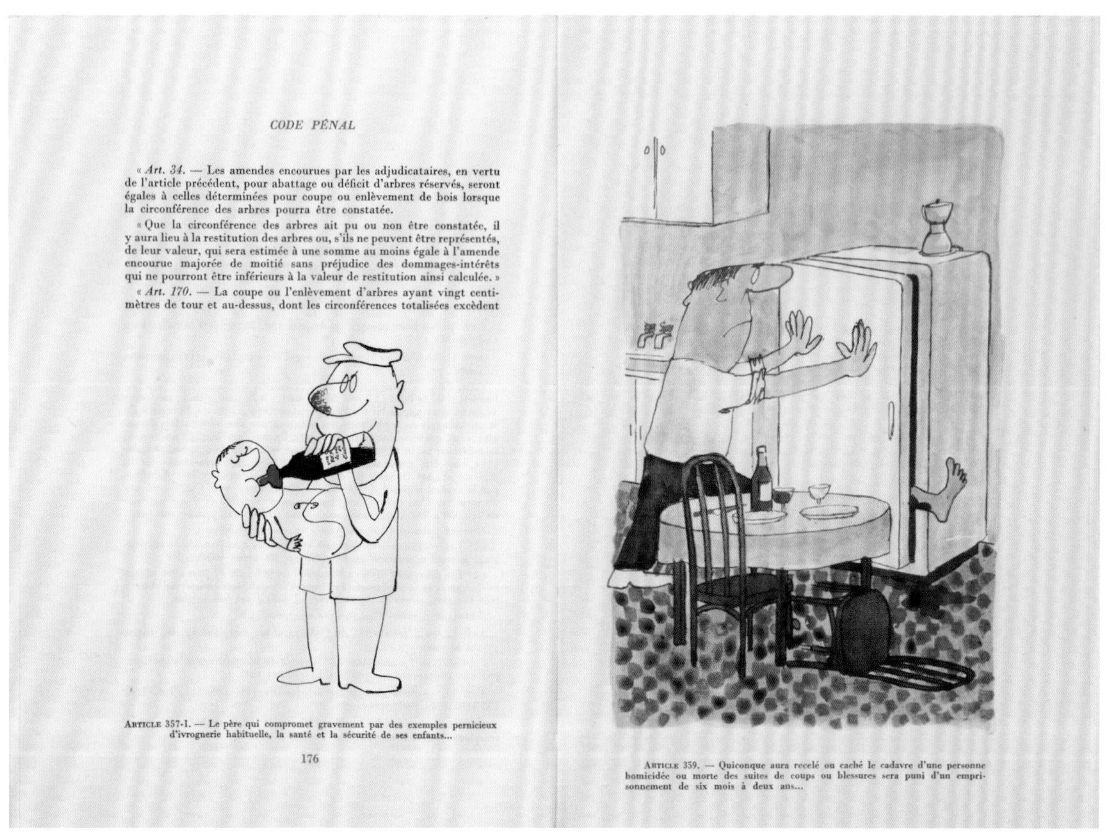

CODE PÉNAL

« *Art. 34.* — Les amendes encourues par les adjudicataires, en vertu de l'article précédent, pour abattage ou déficit d'arbres réservés, seront égales à celles déterminées pour coupe ou enlèvement de bois lorsque la circonférence des arbres pourra être constatée.

« Que la circonférence des arbres ait pu ou non être constatée, il y aura lieu à la restitution des arbres ou, s'ils ne peuvent être représentés, de leur valeur, qui sera estimée à une somme au moins égale à l'amende encourue majorée de moitié sans préjudice des dommages-intérêts qui ne pourront être inférieurs à la valeur de restitution ainsi calculée. »

« *Art. 170.* — La coupe ou l'enlèvement d'arbres ayant vingt centimètres de tour et au-dessus, dont les circonférences totalisées excèdent

ARTICLE 357-1. — Le père qui compromet gravement par des exemples pernicieux d'ivrognerie habituelle, la santé et la sécurité de ses enfants...

176

ARTICLE 359. — Quiconque aura recelé ou caché le cadavre d'une personne homicidée ou morte des suites de coups ou blessures sera puni d'un emprisonnement de six mois à deux ans...

The images in this illustrated criminal code take a decidedly different comic approach to their subject from the work of Joseph Hémard. The image at left illustrates an injunction against fathers compromising the health and safety of their children through their own habitual drunkenness. The image at right illustrates a provision against concealing the body of a murder victim.

Johann Friedrich Hertel.

9.07

Politische Schnupf-Tobacs-Dose vor die wächserne Nase der Justitz.

Frankfurt & Leipzig [i.e. Jena: Verlegts Christian Friedrich Gollner], 1739.

Acquired with the Arthur Hobson Dean Purchase Fund in International Law.

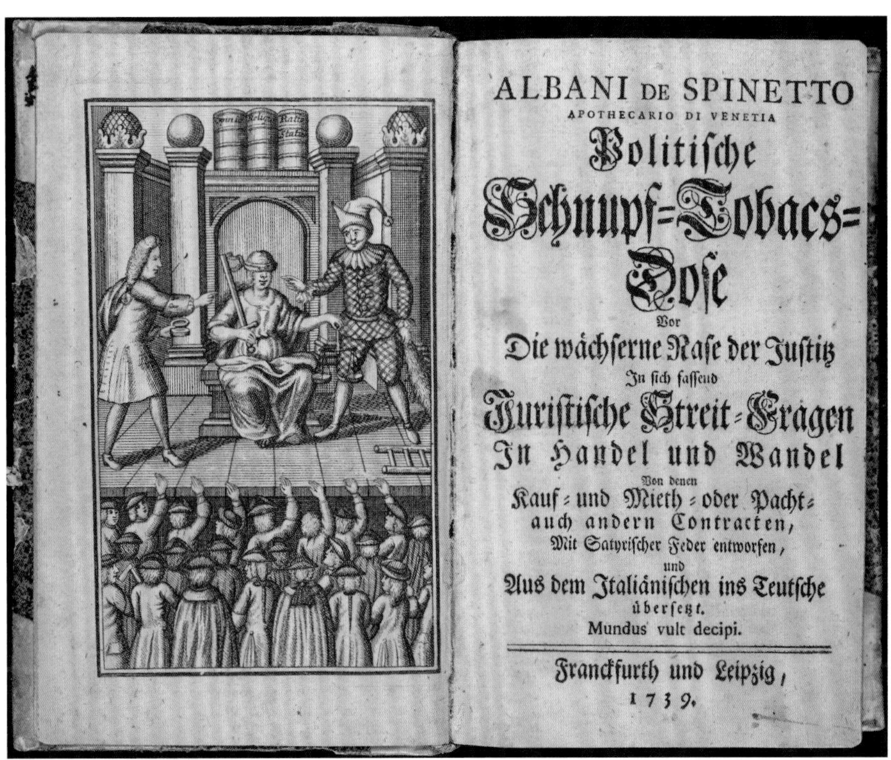

ALBANI DE SPINETTO
APOTHECARIO DI VENETIA
Politische
Schnupf=Tobacs=
Dose
Vor
Die wächserne Nase der Justitz
In sich fassend
Juristische Streit=Fragen
In Handel und Wandel
Von denen
Kauf= und Mieth= oder Pacht=
auch andern Contracten,
Mit Satyrischer Feder entworfen,
und
Aus dem Italiänischen ins Teutsche
übersetzt.
Mundus vult decipi.

Franckfurth und Leipzig,
1739.

In this eighteenth-century German lampoon of the intricacies of legal argument, over two hundred legal questions are depicted as "snuff," while the "growing nose of justice" expels a solution from each nostril. The book purports to be a translation from Italian, but it was written by a German law professor. A large number of the cases concern commercial transactions, especially sales, bad debts, money-lending, interest charges, and usury.

9.08

Johann Georg Döhler.

Processualische Mause-Fallen.

Coburg: Paul Gunther Pfolenhauer und Sohn, 1723.

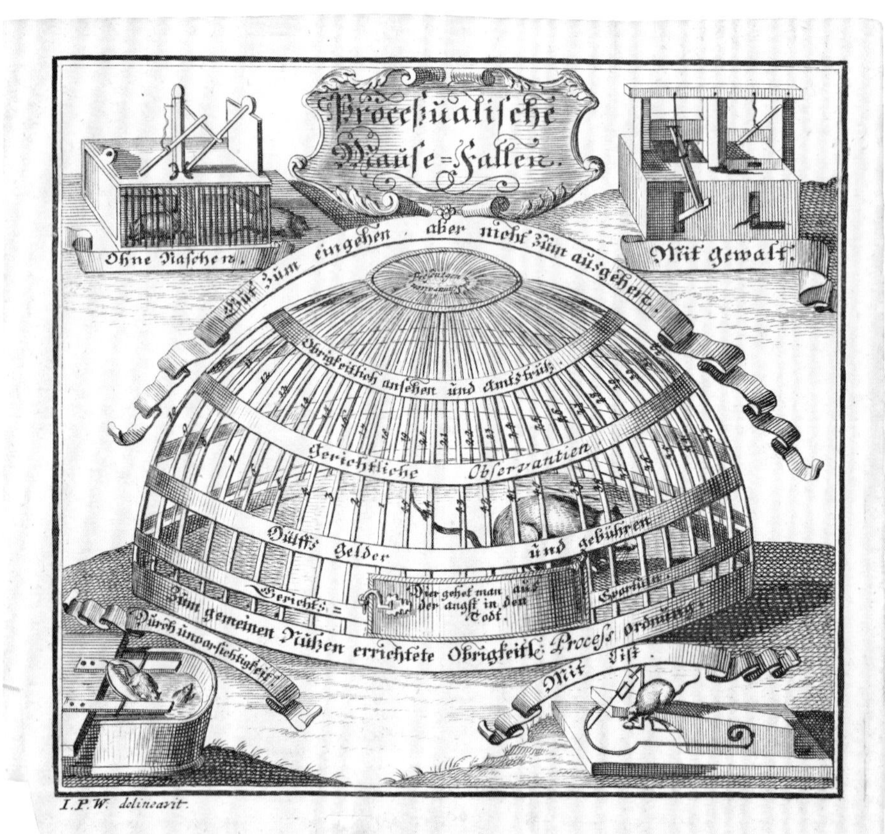

This practical work depicts various pitfalls that can befall a litigant as "mousetraps." The author was a German lawyer and popular writer, hoping to pass on the wisdom of his experience to young lawyers. Will the mice escape from their text-inscribed cage?

Johann Christian Lünig.

Vade mecum juridicum.

Basel: Johann Rudolf Im Hof, 1750-1752. Volume 2 of 3.

9.09

If you were the innocent man at right, would you trust these worthy gentleman with your case? Perhaps instead you ought to read this trusty handbook on legal self-representation.

9.10

GILBERT ABBOTT À BECKETT.

The comic Blackstone.

London: Bradbury, Agnew, & Co., 1887. "New and revised edition ... with ten full-page coloured illustrations & others by Harry Furniss." Acquired with the Charles J. Tanenbaum Fund.

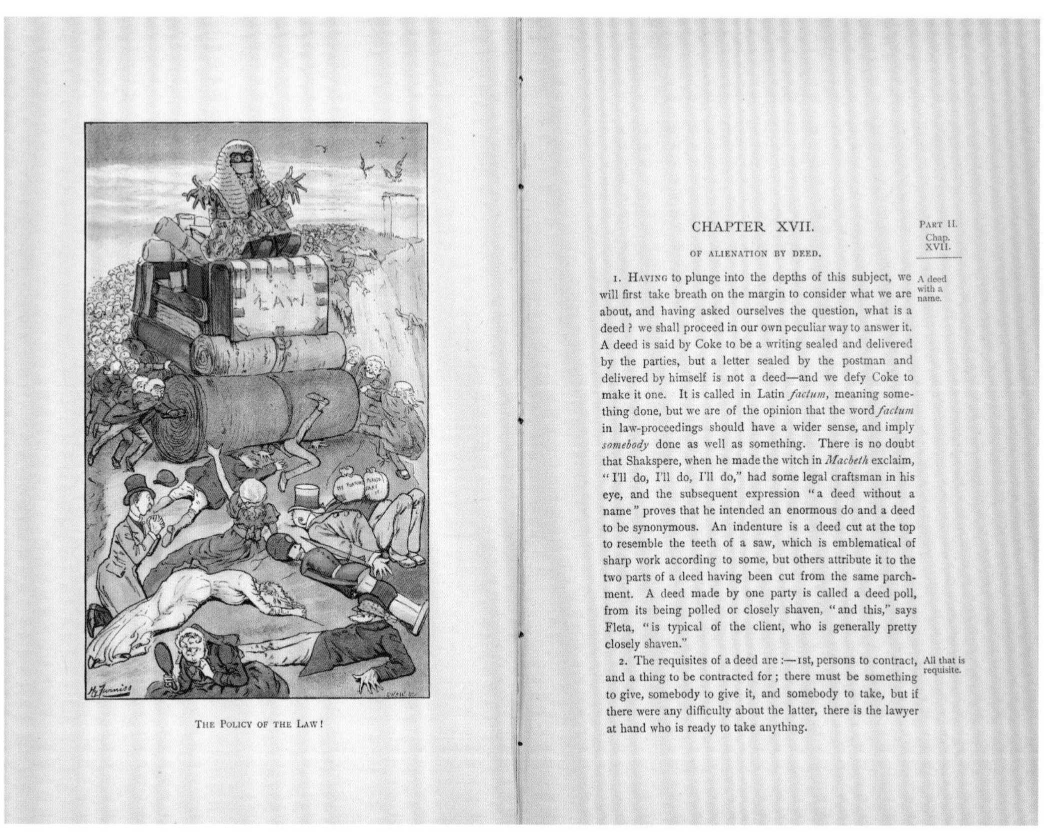

THE POLICY OF THE LAW!

PART II. Chap. XVII.

CHAPTER XVII.

OF ALIENATION BY DEED.

A deed with a name.

1. HAVING to plunge into the depths of this subject, we will first take breath on the margin to consider what we are about, and having asked ourselves the question, what is a deed? we shall proceed in our own peculiar way to answer it. A deed is said by Coke to be a writing sealed and delivered by the parties, but a letter sealed by the postman and delivered by himself is not a deed—and we defy Coke to make it one. It is called in Latin *factum*, meaning something done, but we are of the opinion that the word *factum* in law-proceedings should have a wider sense, and imply *somebody* done as well as something. There is no doubt that Shakspere, when he made the witch in *Macbeth* exclaim, "I'll do, I'll do, I'll do," had some legal craftsman in his eye, and the subsequent expression "a deed without a name" proves that he intended an enormous do and a deed to be synonymous. An indenture is a deed cut at the top to resemble the teeth of a saw, which is emblematical of sharp work according to some, but others attribute it to the two parts of a deed having been cut from the same parchment. A deed made by one party is called a deed poll, from its being polled or closely shaven, "and this," says Fleta, "is typical of the client, who is generally pretty closely shaven."

All that is requisite.

2. The requisites of a deed are:—1st, persons to contract, and a thing to be contracted for; there must be something to give, somebody to give it, and somebody to take, but if there were any difficulty about the latter, there is the lawyer at hand who is ready to take anything.

Humorously illustrated legal codes and treatises are popular on the continent, but they are almost unknown in the Anglo-American tradition. *The Comic Blackstone* is a rare exception. As in many such comic works, law books themselves are objects of satire. Previously published serially in *Punch*, this popular volume is written in the style of a layman's guide.

Read Hodshon.

The honest man's companion, or, The family's safeguard.

9.11

Newcastle upon Tyne: Printed for the author, and sold by M. Bryson, 1736. From the collection of Anthony Taussig. Acquired with the support of the Oscar M. Ruebhausen Fund.

THE

Honeſt Man's Companion:

OR, THE

FAMILY'S SAFEGUARD.

Illuſtrated with COPPER PLATES, and done at the Requeſt of ſeveral Gentlemen and others, occaſion'd by an Attorney's defying any Perſon to paint him or his Brotherhood in their proper Colours, or to propoſe any Method to regulate them, or their Practice.

AS ALSO

Remarks upon Roman-Catholick Lawyers Practiſing as Chamber-Counſel and Conveyancers, and the Danger and Conſequences attending it; with the Author's own CASE.

LIKEWISE

Some Hints relating to the Clergy, Pleading Lawyers, Work-Houſes, our Plantations, Priſons, Priſoners, Pawnbrokers, Bailiffs, and Felons; together with the Dying Speech of WREATHOCKE the Attorney.

Recommended to every Houſe-Keeper to have one always in the Houſe by him, it being a ſurer Protection to his Perſon, Houſes, Money, Goods, and Lands, than if he kept a Guard of Muſqueteers, or a Dozen of Maſtiffs; that every honeſt Man may have one to remind him and his Family what they ought to do in Caſe they are attack'd, and may be left as a very good Legacy to his Children.

NEWCASTLE upon *TYNE*:
Printed for the AUTHOR, and ſold by *Martin Bryſon*, Bookſeller in *Newcaſtle*, 1736.

Client Sheep may not receive the best advice from Attorney Wolf, Lawyer Fox, or Bailiff Bear. And Griffin Jailer (Goaler) would like to "come in for snacks." Poor Sheepie seems not to grasp what his counselors are saying – but then, how could he possibly understand the language contained in those books and case files on the wall?

"THE MEETING OF CREDITORS."
They refuse to listen to anything — even to themselves.

"COOKS A BALANCE SHEET."

After being severely reprimanded by the Court, his certificate is suspended for "12 months" but this terrible punishment is somewhat mitigated by "his protection being also granted". In this painful situation he of course avoids the public notice.

Mr. Sampson Lynx gives great encouragement but the unfortunate bankrupt nearly sinks under the impending disgrace.

Watts Phillips.

A case in bankruptcy.

London: D. Bogue, [18--].

A mocking face bursts through a legal document – an apt symbol of comic legal illustrations, which often take aim at the language and literature of law.

9.13

Kathi Linz.

Chickens may not cross the road and other crazy (but true) laws.

Boston: Houghton Mifflin, 2002. "Illustrated by Tony Griego."

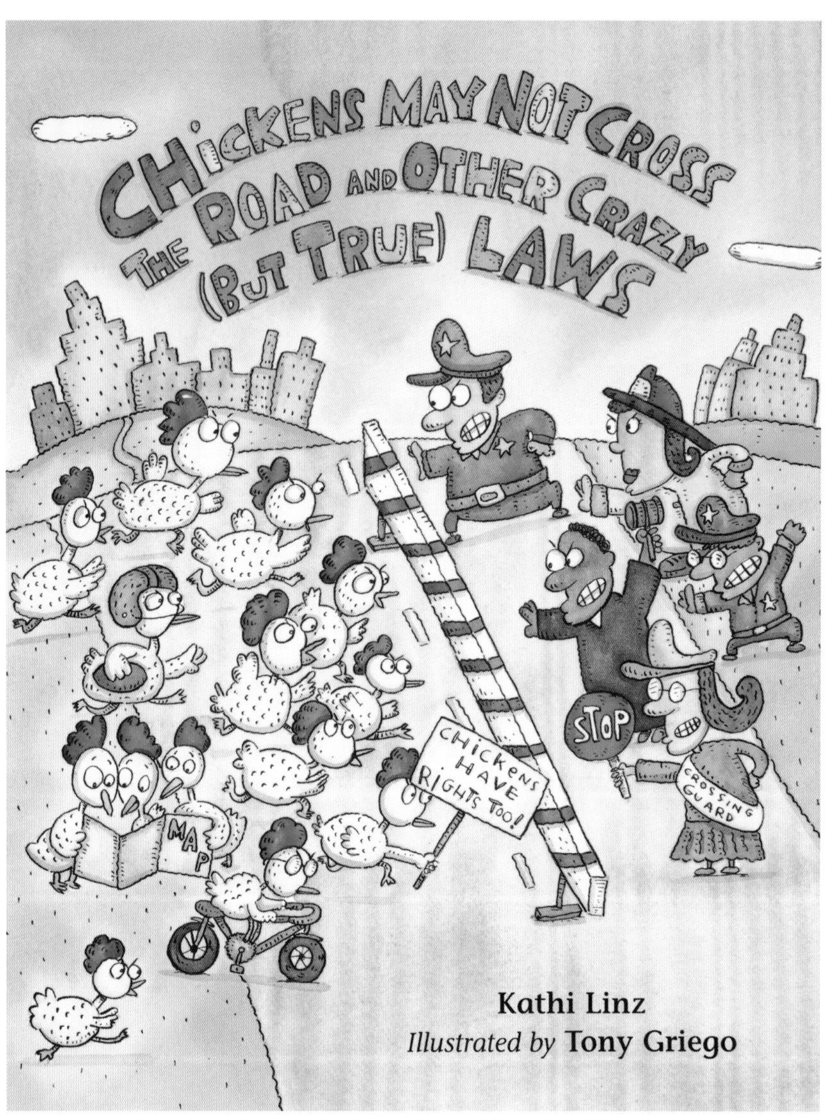

From the publisher: "A collection of humorous laws from across the country, along with information on why we have laws, how they are established, and why some of these may not be as funny as they seem."

Batton Lash.

Supernatural law, no. 35.

San Diego, CA: Exhibit A Press, July 2002.
Acquired with the Gary and Brian Bookman Literature and Arts Fund.

9.14

"Beware the creatures of the night – they have lawyers!" This long-running comic by Brooklyn-based artist Batton Lash was originally published as *Wolff and Byrd, Counselors of the Macabre*, of which the Yale Law Library has a complete collection. The series ran from 1979-1996 in *The Brooklyn Paper* and from 1983-1997 in *The National Law Journal*.

PRE-ORDERS

By pre-ordering products, you are authorizing the Services to automatically charge your account and download the product when it becomes available.

You may cancel your pre-order prior to the time the item becomes available.

FAMILY SHARING

Family Sharing allows you to share eligible iTunes, App Store, Mac App Store, and iBooks Store products with up to six members (including yourself) of a "Family."

If you set up or join a Family, you may view the eligible products of other Family members and download such products to your compatible device or computer.

You can also choose to hide purchases so that other Family members will not be able to view or download them from you.

You can share information such as photos and videos via the Photos app,

events via your Family Calendar, reminders via the Reminders app,

location information via Find My Friends, and device location via Find My iPhone. Family Sharing is for personal, non-commercial use only.

iTunes and iCloud accounts are required;

iOS 8 and/or OS X Yosemite are required to start and join a Family.

Certain transactions and features may not be compatible with earlier software and may require a software upgrade.

If you join a Family, the features of Family Sharing are enabled on your compatible devices and computers automatically.

The "Organizer" of a Family can invite other members to participate in the Family. The Organizer must be 18 years or older and must have an eligible payment method registered with iTunes.
If you are an Organizer, you represent that you are the parent or legal guardian of any Family member under age 13.

The Organizer's payment method is used to pay for any purchase initiated by a Family member in excess of any store credit in such initiating Family member's account.

Products are associated with the account of the Family member who initiated the transaction.

BY INVITING FAMILY MEMBERS TO JOIN A FAMILY, THE ORGANIZER AGREES THAT ALL FAMILY MEMBER PURCHASES ARE AUTHORIZED BY AND ARE THE RESPONSIBILITY OF THE ORGANIZER, EVEN IF THE ORGANIZER WAS UNAWARE OF ANY PARTICULAR PURCHASE, IF A FAMILY MEMBER EXCEEDED HIS OR HER AUTHORITY AS GRANTED BY THE ORGANIZER, OR IF MULTIPLE FAMILY MEMBERS PURCHASE THE SAME PRODUCT.

THE ORGANIZER IS RESPONSIBLE FOR COMPLIANCE WITH ANY AGREEMENT WITH ITS PAYMENT METHOD PROVIDER,
AND ASSUMES ALL RISK IN THE EVENT THAT SHARING ACCESS TO SUCH PAYMENT METHOD LIMITS ANY PROTECTION OFFERED BY THE PAYMENT METHOD PROVIDER.

The Organizer can change the payment method on file at any time.
A record of the purchase will be sent to the initiating Family member and the Organizer, even if the purchase is hidden by the Family member;

please use Report a Problem on your receipt

if you or your Family members do not recognize charges on your receipt or payment method statement.

The unabridged graphic adaptation iTunes terms and conditions.

9.15

Birdcage Bottom Books, 2015. 2 volumes. "Artwork, R. Sikoryak."

This unusual work sets the text of the iTunes consumer contract in the style of over ninety illustrators from comic history. The book stars Steve Jobs, depicted in his signature black turtleneck as Snoopy, SpongeBob SquarePants, and other well-known comic characters. The book suggests the absurdity of such contracts by placing its legal language in an entirely new context, breaking its sentences to accommodate the flow of a purely visual narrative.

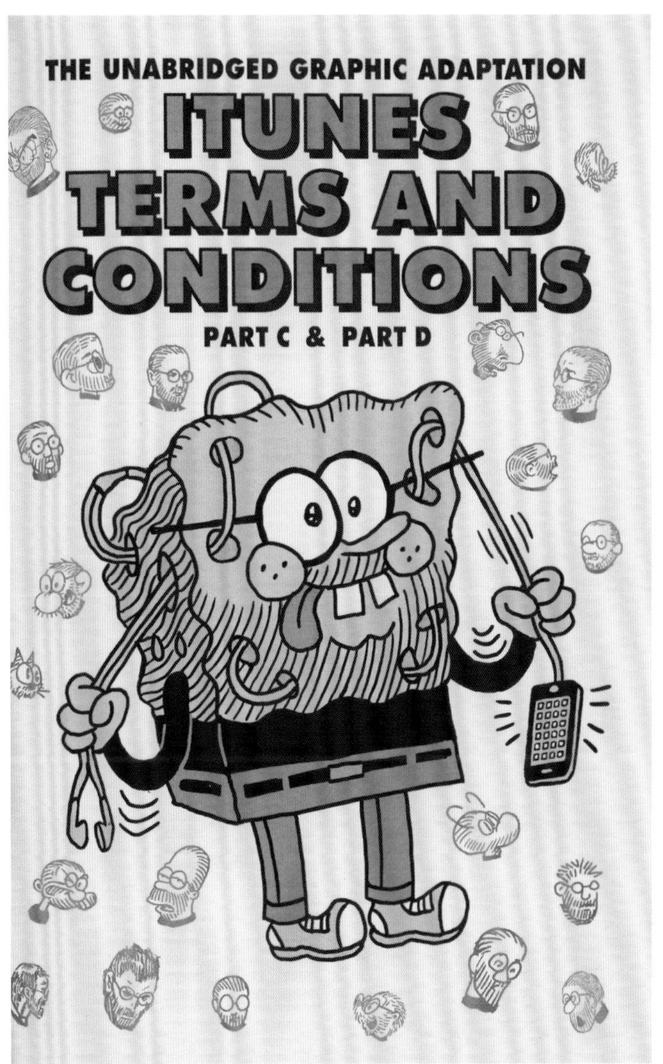

9.16

Allen Ginsberg.

Chicago trial testimony.

San Francisco: City Lights, 1975. Illustration by Pat Ryan.
Acquired with the Gary and Brian Bookman Literature and Arts Fund.

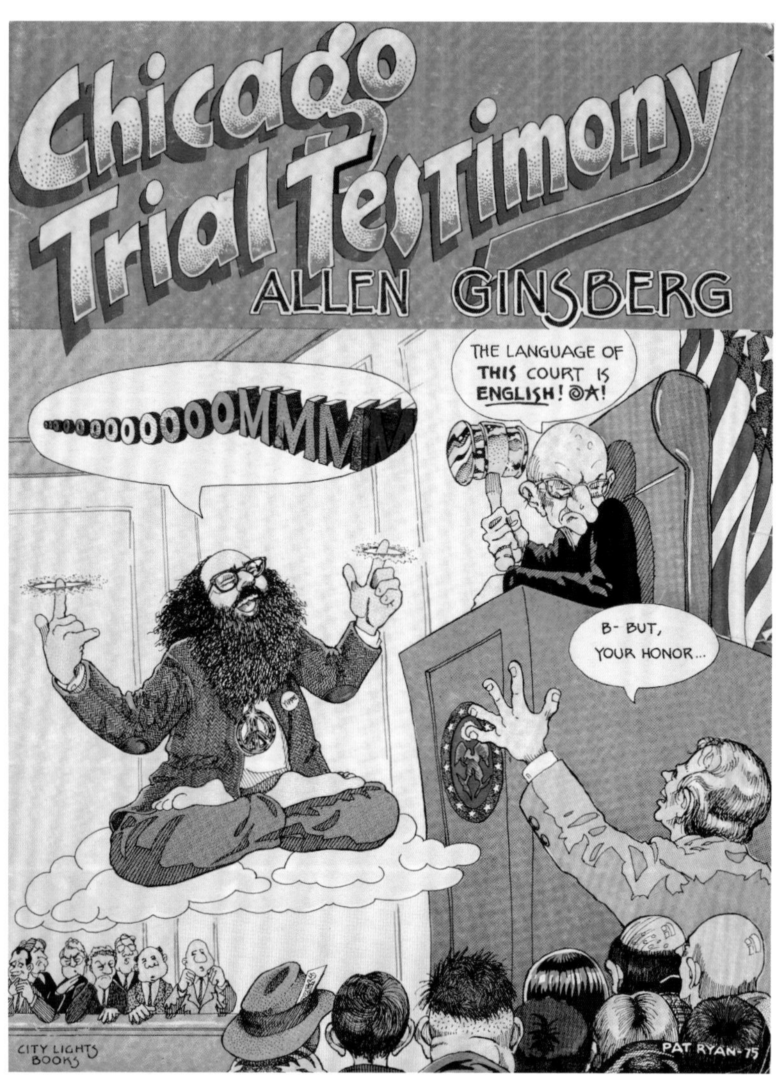

Legal arguments are often conflicts about words. The illustration here renders a fundamental conflict about legal legitimacy – the legitimacy of American legal procedure in the trial of political radicals – into an image about the nature of language and its intelligibility.

Russia (Federation).

Illiustrirovannyi ugolovnyi kodeks Rossiiskoi Federatsii.

9.17

Moscow: Izdatel'stvo "Mann, Ivanov i Ferber", 2013. Illustrations by Aleksei Merinov. Gift of William E. Butler, 2013.

Раздел VIII Преступления в сфере экономики

Ст. 179

Статья 179. Принуждение к совершению сделки или к отказу от ее совершения

1. Принуждение к совершению сделки или к отказу от ее совершения под угрозой применения насилия, уничтожения или повреждения чужого имущества, а равно распространения сведений, которые могут причинить существенный вред правам и законным интересам потерпевшего или его близких, при отсутствии признаков вымогательства — наказывается штрафом в размере до трехсот тысяч рублей или в размере заработной платы или иного дохода осужденного за период до двух лет, либо ограничением свободы на срок до двух лет, либо принудительными работами на срок до двух лет, либо арестом на срок до шести месяцев, либо лишением свободы на срок до двух лет со штрафом в размере до восьмидесяти тысяч рублей или в размере заработной платы или иного дохода осужденного за период до шести месяцев либо без такового.
2. То же деяние, совершенное:

а) *утратил силу*;
б) с применением насилия;
в) организованной группой, —
наказывается лишением свободы на срок до десяти лет.

264

Глава 22 Преступления в сфере экономической деятельности

Статья 180. Незаконное использование товарного знака

Ст. 180

1. Незаконное использование чужого товарного знака, знака обслуживания, наименования места происхождения товара или сходных с ними обозначений для однородных товаров, если это деяние совершено неоднократно или причинило крупный ущерб, —
наказывается штрафом в размере до двухсот тысяч рублей или в размере заработной платы или иного дохода осужденного за период до восемнадцати месяцев, либо обязательными работами на срок до четырехсот восьмидесяти часов, либо исправительными работами на срок до двух лет.
2. Незаконное использование предупредительной маркировки в отношении не зарегистрированного в Российской Федерации товарного знака или наименования места происхождения товара, если это деяние совершено неоднократно или причинило крупный ущерб, —
наказывается штрафом в размере до ста двадцати тысяч рублей или в размере заработной платы или иного дохода осужденного за период до одного года, либо обязательными работами на срок до трехсот шестидесяти часов, либо исправительными работами на срок до одного года.
3. Деяния, предусмотренные частями первой или второй настоящей статьи, совершенные группой лиц по предварительному сговору или организованной группой, —
наказываются штрафом в размере от пятисот тысяч до одного миллиона рублей или в размере заработной платы или иного дохода осужденного за период от трех до пяти лет, либо принудительными работами на срок до пяти лет, либо лишением свободы на срок до шести лет со штрафом в размере до пятисот тысяч рублей или в размере заработной платы или иного дохода осужденного за период до трех лет или без такового.

265

References to children's stories and folklore provide a wry perspective on the Russian criminal code. In this section on economic crimes, Pinocchio – highly popular in Russia – illustrates contractual duress as he prepares to outwit the fox and cat. At right, a matryoshka doll is opened to reveal the witch Baba Yaga – illustrating improper use of a trademark. For more work by Aleksei Merinov, see item 2.11.

Who could be more stylish than this lawyer, with his elegant posture, surrounded by the tools of his trade – books? In such illustrations, law is depicted as a profession at once learned and beautiful. Indeed, the learned and the beautiful are shown to be one.

Joan L. Blasius. *Nederlandts versterf-recht.* Amsterdam: Voor Doornick, 1671.

Nederlandts

Verſterf-Recht/

Waer na de Erf-goederen, ſonder Teſtament, in de 7 Vereenighde Provintien worden verdeelt.

IDEM

't Rechte gebruyck om in te ſtellen alderhande Contracten/ Huwelijkſe Voorwaerden/ Teſtamenten/ Obligatien/ Koop- en Huur-cedullen/ &c.

t'Amſterdam, voor Marcus Doornick, op de Middel-dam. 1671.

Beautifying the Law 10

Law book illustrations serve many practical purposes. Yet they also can be items of simple beauty. This catalogue closes with books in which the bridge between abstraction and the real opens onto a view of the aesthetic. In this magic space of the imagination, law gives birth to art that stands on its own.

These books gently overflow the boundaries of law as a field of knowledge and the law book as a category of publishing. They thereby pay tribute to law and to the publishing of books as endeavors that implicate our deepest humanity.

650
Brächsen
Mas
649
Karpffen
Mas

Bavaria (Duchy). 10.01

Landrecht, Policeÿ-, Gerichts-, Malefitz- und andere Ordnungen des Fürstenthumben Obern und Nidern Baÿrn.

Munich: Nicolaus Henricus, 1616.

These striking depictions of carp were once utilitarian tools to enforce Bavaria's fishing regulations. Now the images are the main attractions. In legal publishing, images may detach dramatically from their original practical context, allowing the purely beautiful to emerge over time.

10.02

Austria.

Handbuch aller unter der Regierung des Kaisers Joseph des II.

Vienna: J.G. Moesle, 1785-1790. Volume 15 (1789) of 18. Acquired with the Albert S. Wheeler Fund.

pag. 307.

Die Bella Donna die Wolfsbeere oder Wolfs Kirsche.

15ten Band.

(307)

Sanitätssachen. N. XXIII.

Die diesfälligen erschienenen älteren Gesetze mit ihren Beziehungen. Sieh im 13. B. S. 287 — 295.

Da die Pflanze bella donna, welche von dem Landvolk gemeiniglich Wolfsbeere genannt wird, unter die giftigsten Pflanzen gehöret, und der Genuß ihrer Beere bei den Menschen die gefährlichsten Zufälle, und sogar, wenn nicht gleich anfangs ausgiebige Hilfe geleistet wird, den elendesten Tod verursachet; so wird um allen übeln Folgen, die daraus entstehen können, vorzubeugen, nicht nur derselben Beschaffenheit und Eigenschaft, nebst der Heilungsart der hierdurch verunglückten Personen zur allgemeinen Wissenschaft bekannt gemacht, sondern auch noch zu mehrerer Kennbarkeit derselben die Abbildung hievon beigefüget.

Die Beschreibung der giftigen Wurzel bella donna oder Wolfsbeere.

Die bella donna, welche Pflanze auch Tollkirsche, Wolfskirsche, Tollkraut, und Waldnachtschatten genannt wird, und unter die giftigen Pflanzen gehöret, wächst in schattigten, und hohen Wäldern, auch wird sie in einigen Gärten gepflanzet, und blühet im Monat Julius, und August.

X 2 Die

Bella donna poisoning had become a problem for school children on outings in the Austrian Alps. With its beautiful hand-coloring, this image would have helped in identifying the deadly nightshade. The *Handbuch* is part of a multi-volume, systematic treatment of law under the Hapsburg monarchy. The loveliness of the image belies the gruesomeness of its accompanying text – a feature of many illustrated law books.

Lorenzo Mascambrone.

Degli asili de Christiani ragionamento.

Rome: Camera Appostolica, 1731.

10.03

This image depicts an argument, and its beauty is an argument in itself. In a vigorous defense of the institution of sanctuary, the author, an Augustinian friar, compares the Church's obligation to sanctuary seekers to a mother's protection of her child. Seated in peaceful Nature, a female cherub points out the scales of Justice to her male counterpart. Holding a Roman symbol of magistrate authority, he cowers amidst the ruins of human civilization.

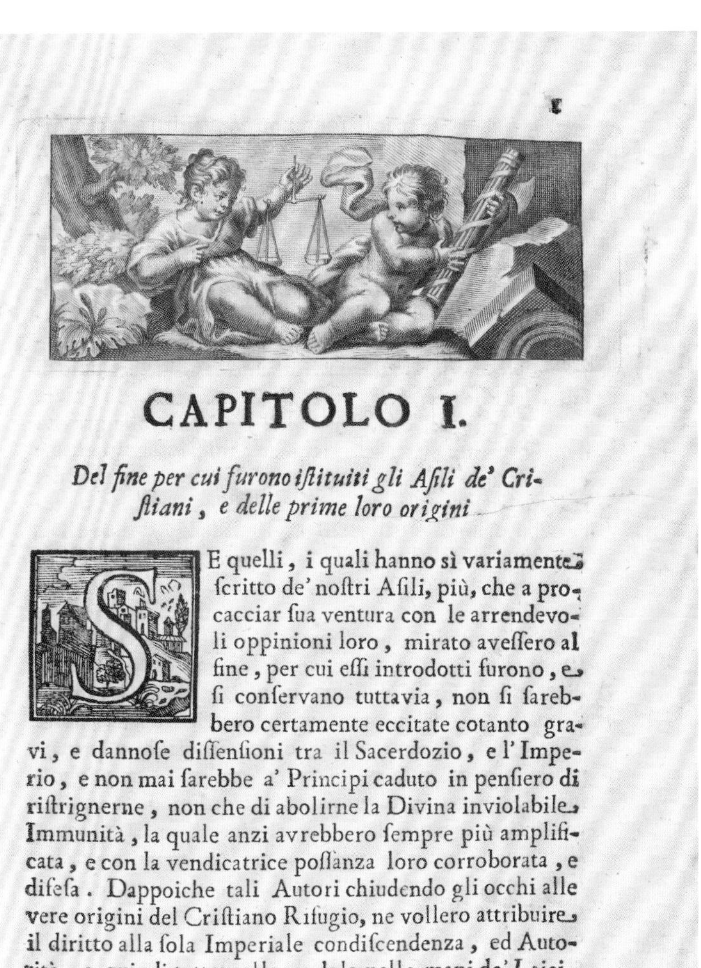

1

CAPITOLO I.

Del fine per cui furono istituiti gli Asili de' Cristiani, e delle prime loro origini.

SE quelli, i quali hanno sì variamente scritto de' nostri Asili, più, che a procacciar sua ventura con le arrendevoli oppinioni loro, mirato avessero al fine, per cui essi introdotti furono, e si conservano tuttavia, non si sarebbero certamente eccitate cotanto gravi, e dannose dissensioni tra il Sacerdozio, e l'Imperio, e non mai sarebbe a' Principi caduto in pensiero di ristrignerne, non che di abolirne la Divina inviolabile Immunità, la quale anzi avrebbero sempre più amplificata, e con la vendicatrice possanza loro corroborata, e difesa. Dappoiche tali Autori chiudendo gli occhi alle vere origini del Cristiano Rifugio, ne vollero attribuire il diritto alla sola Imperiale condiscendenza, ed Autorità, e quindi tutto collocandolo nelle mani de' Laici,

A bal-

10.04

Knights of Malta.

Statuta Hospitalis Hierusalem.

Rome, 1586. Engravings by Philippe Thomassin. Acquired with the John A. Hoober Fund.

31

DE HOSPITALITATE
TITVLVS QVARTVS.

QVOD FRATRES HOſpitalitatem exerceant.

CONSVETVDO.

INTER cætera pietatis atque humanitatis officia, communi totius populi Chriſtiani cõſenſu, Hoſpitalitas præcipuum locum obtinet, vtpotè quæ alia omnia complectatur. Ea ſi à bonis omnibus magno ſtudio colenda eſt, quanto maiori ab ijs qui Hoſpitalariorum Militum appellatione & cognomento ſe notos eſſe volunt? Quapropter nihil potius nobis faciendum eſt, quàm quod in nomine proferimus, re & actis præſtemus. I.

DE PROBIS HOMINIBVS Infirmariæ.

F. IOANNES DE LASTICO.

VT Infirmariæ noſtræ ſtatus rectius & diligentius adminiſtretur, ſtatuimus, vt per Magiſtrum & Concilium quotannis eligantur duo probi homines ex diuerſis linguis, qui quolibet die, ſumma cura & ſtudio; vnà cum Infirmario ægrotos viſitent. Et ſi quid ad eorum curam deeſſe compererint, exactè reparent. Quibus ſingulis quoque menſibus, Infirmarius rationem impenſarũ, quæ in ipſa infirmaria fiunt, in ſcriptis reddere teneatur. Quod ſi facere omiſerint, is per quem ſteterit quominus id fiat, eo ipſo priuatus officio intelligatur. II.

QVALITER PROBI HOMINES, ET ſcriba Infirmariæ, & Commendatarius paruæ commendæ ſe gerere debent.

F. FABRITIVS DE CARRETO.

AD euitanda ſiniſtra, quæ facile committi poſſunt, ſtatuimus, quod probi homines infirmariæ poſtquam à Magiſtro & concilio ordinario fuerint electi, in eodem concilio ſolemne ſacramentum faciant de bene & fide- III.

liter

A major military and political force in the sixteenth century, the Knights of Malta never abandoned their mission of serving the poor. The 1586 edition of their statutes is graced with copper-plate engravings by Philippe Thomassin (1562-1622), set within woodcut borders. The section on hospital regulations opens with a view of a ward, with the Order's motto above – sometimes translated as "care given to the sick."

10.05

England.

Statuta Angliae nova.

Manuscript on vellum, in law French, and Latin. 1444-1483/1484.
Acquired with the John A. Hoober Fund.

This ornate manuscript features iconography strongly associated with portraits of King David. The image depicts Henry VI illumined by the face of God, shown as a blue circle with golden rays. A collection of English statutes, it was commissioned for Henry's heir apparent, the Prince of Wales, by the Prince's mother, Queen Margaret of Anjou.

Wiewol ein Erber Rate der Stat
Nüremberg vergangner zeit/Nem
lich in dem Vierundachtzigiſtenn
iar/der myndern zal Chriſti nechſt=
verruckt/vmb gemeynes nutz vñ
notturfft willen/auſz beweglichen
guten vrſachen ein Reformacion
Irer Statut vnnd geſetz/ſouil ſich
nach Irer Stat Nüremberg gele=
genheit herkomen alter gewon=
heyt/vnd der lewffte hat erleyden
mogen gemacht/drucken vnd auſz
geen laſſen/mit vorbehaltnus/dar=
innen erklerung/lewterunng/en=
drung vnd peſſerung zethun/Auch
newe vnd meer andere geſetz fürze
nemen ꝛc. Demſelben nach hat ein
Erber Rate auſz fürgefalner guter
bewegnuſz/gemeynem nutz züſtat
ten in etlichen Titteln vnd geſetzen
gemelter Reformacion abermaln
nach gehabtem Rat/gut endrung/
vnd peſſerung fürgenomen vnd ge=
macht/Dieſelbenn Reformacion
Aa ij

Nuremberg (Germany). 10.06

Reformacion der Stat Nüremberg.

Nüremberg: Fridrich Peypus, 1522. Woodcut attributed to Albrecht Dürer.

Albrecht Dürer's woodcut, originally issued as a print in 1521, glorifies this revised legal code of the city of Nuremberg – the heart of the German Renaissance. Dürer (1471-1528) placed Lady Justice and Charity over the city's arms.

10.07

Paolo Attavanti.

Breviarium totius juris canonici.

Milan: Leonhard Pachel & Ulrich Scinzenzeler, 1479. Acquired with the John A. Hoober Fund.

A portrait of Paolo Attavanti (1445?-1499), a Servite monk, is believed to be the first author portrait in a printed book – it's the great-great-grandfather of photos on today's book jacket flaps. In this detail, the author is depicted at work in front a shelf of casually-arranged books. This particular volume is a summary of canon law.

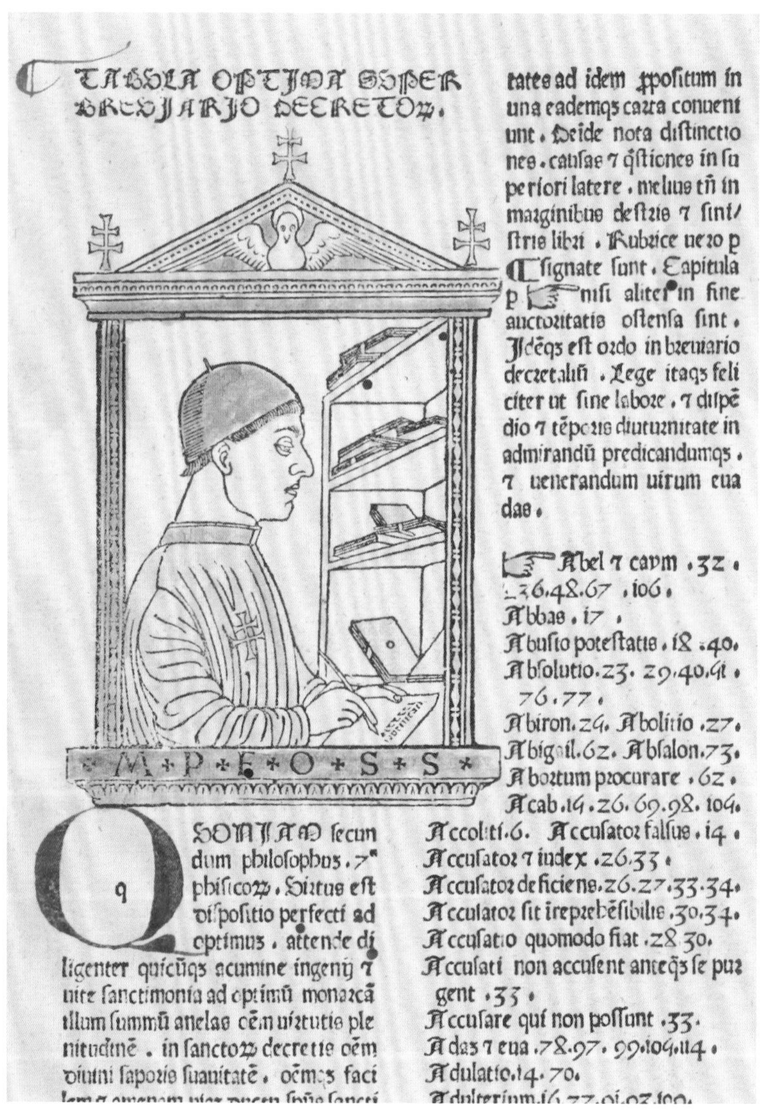
TABOLA OPTIMA SOPER BREVIARIO DECRETOR.

M · P · F · O · S · S

Quoniam secundum philosophos. 7 phisicorum. Situs est dispositio perfecti ad optimum. attende diligenter quicũqꝫ acumine ingenij 7 uite sanctimonia ad optimũ monarcã illum summũ anelas cẽm uirtutis plenitudinẽ. in sanctorum decretis oẽm diuini saporis suauitatẽ. oẽmqꝫ faci

tates ad idem ꝓpositum in una eademqꝫ causa conueniunt. Deinde nota distinctiones. causas 7 q̃stiones in superiori latere. melius tñ in marginibus dextris 7 sinistris libri. Rubrice uero p signate sunt. Capitula p nisi aliter in fine auctoritatis ostensa sint. Ideoqꝫ est ordo in breuiario decretaliũ. Lege itaqꝫ feliciter ut sine labore. 7 dispẽdio 7 tẽporis diuturnitate in admirandũ predicandumqꝫ. 7 uenerandum uirum euadas.

Abel 7 caym .32. 36.48.67 .106.
Abbas. 17.
Abusio potestatis. 18 .40.
Absolutio. 23. 29.40.41. 76.77.
Abiron. 24. Abolitio .27.
Abigail. 62. Absalon. 73.
Abortum procurare. 62.
Acab. 14. 26. 69. 98. 104.
Accoliti. 6. Accusator falsus. 14.
Accusator 7 iudex. 26.33.
Accusator deficiens. 26.27.33.34.
Accusator sit irreprehẽsibilis. 30.34.
Accusatio quomodo fiat. 28 30.
Accusati non accusent anteqꝫ se purgent. 33.
Accusare qui non possunt. 33.
Adam 7 eua. 78.97. 99.104.114.
Adulatio. 14. 70.

John Anthony Scott, ed.

10.08

The defense of Gracchus Babeuf before the High Court of Vendôme.

Northampton, Mass.: Gehenna Press, 1964. With 21 etched portraits by Thomas Cornell.
Acquired with the Ford Motor Company Fund.

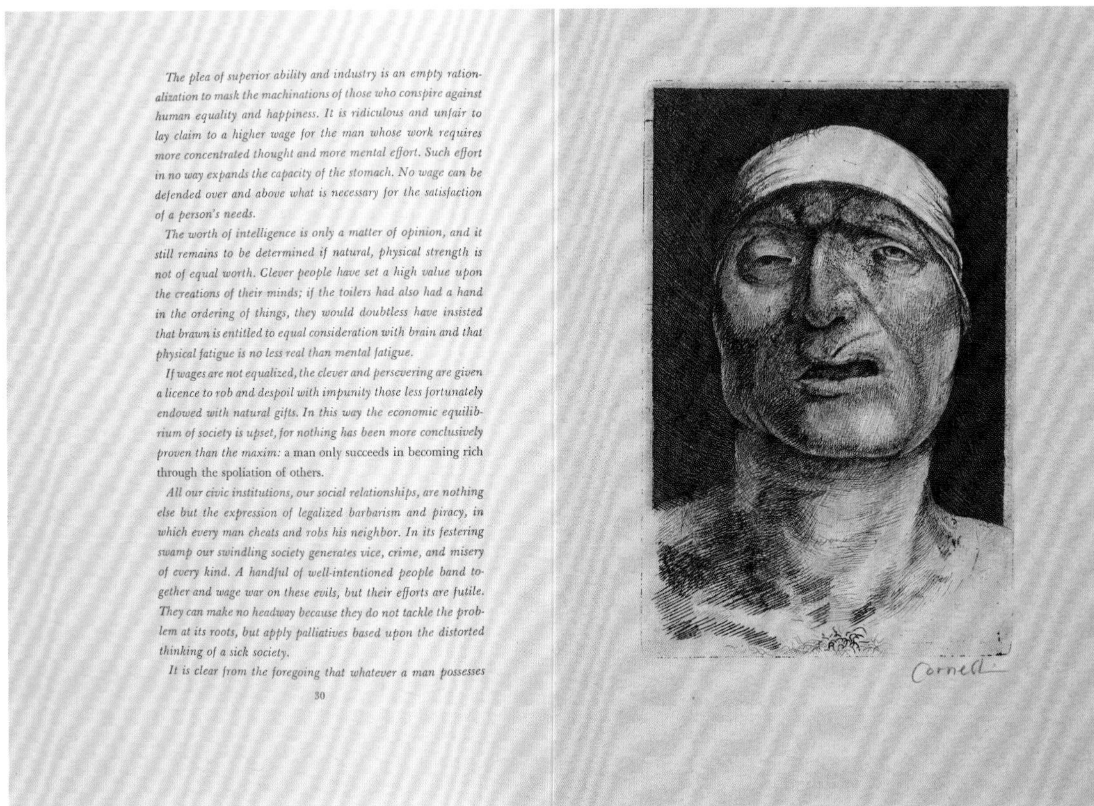

The plea of superior ability and industry is an empty rationalization to mask the machinations of those who conspire against human equality and happiness. It is ridiculous and unfair to lay claim to a higher wage for the man whose work requires more concentrated thought and more mental effort. Such effort in no way expands the capacity of the stomach. No wage can be defended over and above what is necessary for the satisfaction of a person's needs.

The worth of intelligence is only a matter of opinion, and it still remains to be determined if natural, physical strength is not of equal worth. Clever people have set a high value upon the creations of their minds; if the toilers had also had a hand in the ordering of things, they would doubtless have insisted that brawn is entitled to equal consideration with brain and that physical fatigue is no less real than mental fatigue.

If wages are not equalized, the clever and persevering are given a licence to rob and despoil with impunity those less fortunately endowed with natural gifts. In this way the economic equilibrium of society is upset, for nothing has been more conclusively proven than the maxim: a man only succeeds in becoming rich through the spoliation of others.

All our civic institutions, our social relationships, are nothing else but the expression of legalized barbarism and piracy, in which every man cheats and robs his neighbor. In its festering swamp our swindling society generates vice, crime, and misery of every kind. A handful of well-intentioned people band together and wage war on these evils, but their efforts are futile. They can make no headway because they do not tackle the problem at its roots, but apply palliatives based upon the distorted thinking of a sick society.

It is clear from the foregoing that whatever a man possesses

30

Fine press publishers have produced a number of legal texts of transcendental human significance, such as this limited-edition work about the trial of revolutionary French socialist Gracchus Babeuf, publisher of *Le Tribun du people*. Babeuf was guillotined in 1797 for his part in the Conspiracy of Equals to overthrow the bourgeois *Directoire*.

IOannes. gratiosū hoc nomē p interpretatiōes deriuationes vel etymologias extollē nō ē meū. suspitiōis rō patz. Esset ēt hoc refricare notissima. i apostolatu tñ hoc nomē sup cetera viguit. xxij. Est. n. ipe qui loquit: cū tñ reliqua romanoꝝ pontificū noīa. xi. nō trāscēderūt numerum: ad quē ēt solius bene dicti nomē ascēdit Inter canōistas ēt commētarios hoc nomen viguit. Habuim⁹. n. ioannem theotonicū pferendū nō ex ordie: sz ex fructu. ioannez galeñ. vulteranuz. Jo. hispanuz. Jo. fauētinum. Jo. de saucona. Jo. ð acona. Jo. de deo etiā hispanū. Jo. de lāgucella cesenateñ. Jo. monachuz cardinalē: ego ēt q minor sū iter. xij. doctōes collegij bononieñ. me quartū susisse ioannem: nunc iter eos ꝯmētatōes solus: sz iſ ꝯmētatores decimus: ⁊ de nigro forte papyꝛ ñ dignū occupare mēbranā. Et quia put patet hic in exordio ēt ꝯpositōes iurium vix pñt taz claꝝ certūqꝫ statuere: quin dubia mlta relinquant: excusabilis ero: q i hac prima lectione uel glosatione singula non pfecte rimant. Nā ēt ī rebus expimur: q̄ nāliter gñant: q ī eis paulatī de īperfecto ad pfectū venit: sic ⁊ qui de veritatis cognitione a principio parum attingunt: postea quasi pedetentim ad quādam pleniorem veritatis mensuram puenīunt. Igitur sub hoc excusationis clypeo: licet varijs occupatus p fiduciam clementie diuine has clementinas glosandas aggredior. Est autem sciendū q iste dñs ioannes pontifex idustriosus ⁊ mūdus simoniam fugans et iustitiam amans: scientia magnus statura pusillus: conceptu magnanimus prius iacobus vocabat. De hac vero mutatione nominis ⁊ alijs que ad salutationez hanc respiciūt

est propter duo. Primo quia ius positiuum quātūcunqꝫ mature certe et clare compositum non sufficit ad casus emergentes: propter quod opportuna est ⁊ necessaria declaratio principis. Secūdo quia homo pronus ad malum facile mores subuertit: propter quod est necessaria pricipis potestas ad inserendas virtutes ⁊ vicia extirpāda. Patet ergo q in his tribus exordijs nulla ē inculcatio sup pfluitas vel repetitio. quo modo autem exordicanti um proposito pdicta cōueniant: per se patet.

c ¶ Juris humani. positiui sit canonicum vel ciuile synodale uel municipale. naturale vero vel diuinuz morale est immutabile. v. di. i prin. Et est perfectum: q manau͛t ab illo qui nō nouit imperfectum opus: de bap. maiores. ꝟ. sed adhuc

d ¶ Sanctio. hic ⁊. ī. ꝟ. hec sane. late sumitur. nam ponitur stricte pro constitutione penali: ut nō. iij. di. i sūma.

e ¶ Perpenso. quasi pfecte pēsato ⁊ deliberato. habetur simile uerbuz ð pac. c. vlt. circa mediū li. vi.

f ¶ Digesta. alibi dr̄ decocta. xxxv. q. ix. aplice. ⁊ hec bene ꝯueniunt. de cōse. di. v. ne tales ⁊. c. pelt. io. an.

g ¶ Uarietatem. sumi potuit de coꝛ. auf. de re. ec. non alie. §. ut autem i prin coll. ij. ⁊ de instru. caute. p⁹ pn. coll. vi.

h ¶ Machinatiōes. quasi astuta ingenia. quid est enī q homo semel dedit mali cie non adinueniat: i auf. ut hi qui se ob. phi. p⁹ pn. coll. vi.

Incipiunt constitutiones clementis pape quinti vna cum apparatu domini ioannis andree.

IOANNES EPIscopus seruus seruoꝝ dei. dilectis filijs doctoribus et scholaribus vniu͛sis bononie cōmorātib⁹ salutē ⁊ aplicam benedictōem. ¶ Quoniā nulla iuris sanctio quātūcūqꝫ perpēso digesta cōsilio ad humane nature varietatem ⁊ machinationes eius inopinabiles sufficit: nec ad decisionez lucidam sue nodose ambiguitatis attigit: eo psertim q vix aliqd adeo certū clarūqꝫ statuit: quin ex causis emergentibus quib⁹ iura iam posita mederi non pñt: i dubiū reuocet. ¶ Quia etiaz ab adolescētia viri ꝓcliui ad maluz sensualitas humana declinat: p qð moꝝ subuersio in clero ⁊ pplo frequenter obrepit: necessaria ē superioris auctas: ut tā p determinatōis opportune suffragium tollat ābigua: lites auferat: altcatōes dirimat: ⁊ obscura succidat: qꝫ p cultoris ꝓuidi sarculū extirpet vicia: ⁊ virtutes inserat: corrigat excessus: moresqꝫ reformet. ¶ Hec sane felicis recordationis clemens papa qntus predecessor noster prudent attēdēs ⁊ prouide cupiens deformatorum reformationē ꝓspicere: soluere difficilia: ac sanctiones questionibus et

i ¶ Nodose. de vbo. sig. cum olim ⁊ de reliqui. c. vno i pn. li. vi.
k ¶ Ambiguitat. de triplici ābiguitate iuris facti ⁊ psone nō. xxxiij. di. c. fi.
l ¶ Uix. innuit fieri posse: de cog. spi. c. ij.
m ¶ Mederi. facit in auf. hec ꝯstitutio inno. cō. i pn. coll. viij.
n ¶ Procliui. xx. q. iij. ꝓcliuus: facit. xij. q. i. c. i. ⁊ i auf. de mo. §. siqs igitur ad fi. coll. i. ⁊ dr̄ ꝓcliuus quasi preceps: ꝓmpta facilis vel inclinabilis.
o ¶ Sēsualitas. de hac de sacra vnc. c. vno. ꝟ. in vtice: ⁊ p hāc appetimus delectabilia corpori ⁊ fugimus nocua: nec oīo pōt extingui: ut dicā. ī. de bē. ad nostrum. ꝟ. ij.

Catholic Church.

Clementis V. papae Constitutiones.

10.09

Venice: Nicolaus Jenson, 1479. Acquired with the John A. Hoober Fund.

Pope Clement V (d.1314) blesses a compilation of his papal legislation, the *Constitutions of Clement V* – the very book in which this image appears. Decorative elements common in manuscripts, such as miniatures and illuminated initials, persisted in the new medium of the printed book. According to musicologist Flynn Warmington, the unknown artist is the same one who decorated the two earliest known manuscripts of polyphony, now in the Vatican Library.

10.10

Franz Albrecht, Count of Oettingen.

Philosophia legalis, sive, Quaestiones dialecticae, physicae et metaphysicae, ad scientiam juris accommodatae.

Dillingen: Johann Caspar Bencard for Johann Federle, [1682?].

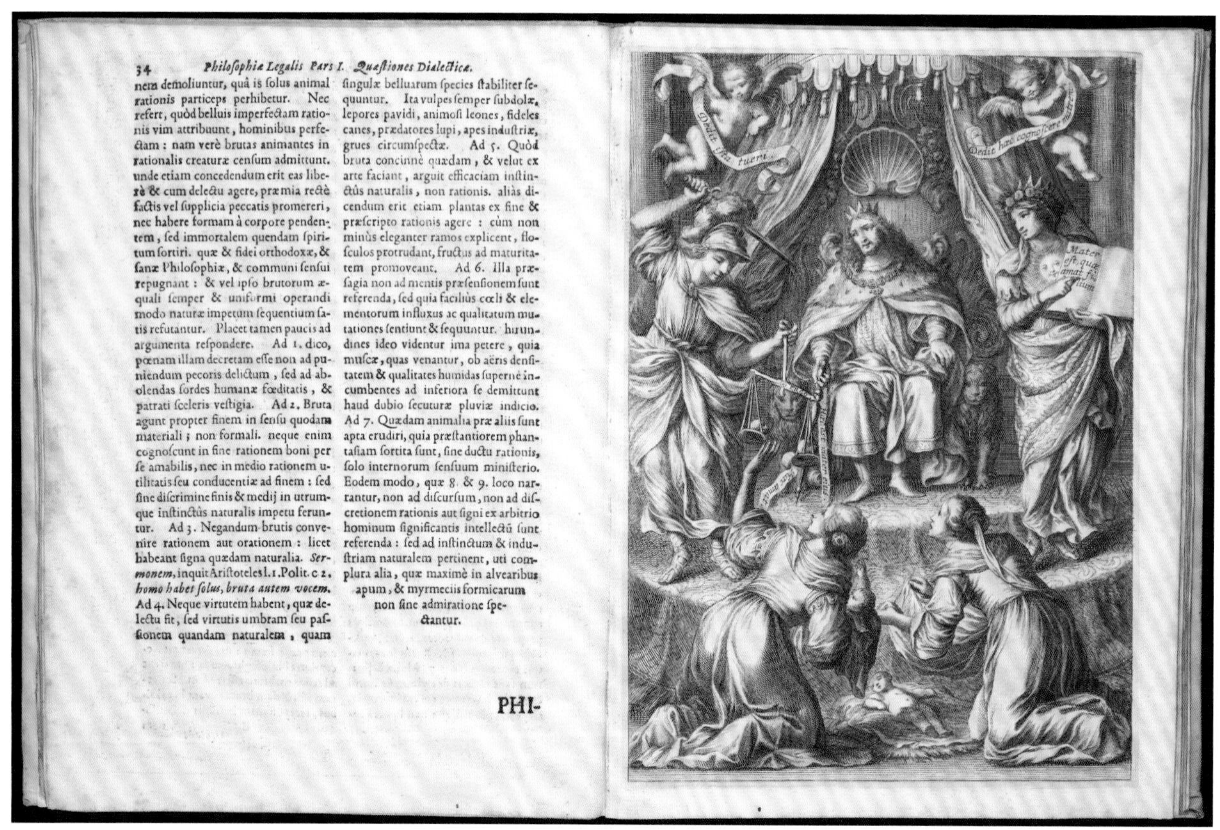

34 *Philoſophiæ Legalis Pars I. Quæſtiones Dialecticæ.*

nem demoliuntur, quâ is ſolus animal rationis particeps perhibetur. Nec refert, quòd belluis imperfectam rationis vim attribuunt, hominibus perfectam: nam verè brutas animantes in rationalis creaturæ cenſum admittunt. unde etiam concedendum erit eas liberè & cum delectu agere, præmia rectè factis vel ſupplicia peccatis promereri, nec habere formam à corpore pendentem, ſed immortalem quendam ſpiritum ſortiri. quæ & fidei orthodoxæ, & ſanæ Philoſophiæ, & communi ſenſui repugnant: & vel ipſo brutorum æquali ſemper & uniformi operandi modo naturæ impetum ſequentium ſatis refutantur. Placet tamen paucis ad argumenta reſpondere. Ad 1. dico, pœnam illam decretam eſſe non ad puniendum pecoris delictum, ſed ad abolendas ſordes humanæ fœditatis, & patrati ſceleris veſtigia. Ad 2. Bruta agunt propter finem in ſenſu quodam materiali; non formali. neque enim cognoſcunt in fine rationem boni per ſe amabilis, nec in medio rationem utilitatis ſeu conducentiæ ad finem: ſed ſine diſcrimine finis & medij in utrumque inſtinctûs naturalis impetu feruntur. Ad 3. Negandum brutis convenire rationem aut orationem: licet habeant ſigna quædam naturalia. *Sermonem*, inquit Ariſtoteles l. 1. Polit. c. 2. *homo habet ſolus, bruta autem vocem.* Ad 4. Neque virtutem habent, quæ delectu fit, ſed virtutis umbram ſeu paſſionem quandam naturalem, quam ſingulæ belluarum ſpecies ſtabiliter ſequuntur. Ita vulpes ſemper ſubdolæ, lepores pavidi, animoſi leones, fideles canes, prædatores lupi, apes induſtriæ, grues circumſpectæ. Ad 5. Quòd bruta concinnè quædam, & velut ex arte faciant, arguit efficaciam inſtinctûs naturalis, non rationis. aliàs dicendum erit etiam plantas ex fine & præſcripto rationis agere: cùm non minùs eleganter ramos explicent, floſculos protrudant, fructus ad maturitatem promoveant. Ad 6. Illa præſagia non ad mentis præſenſionem ſunt referenda, ſed quia faciliùs cœli & elementorum influxus ac qualitatum mutationes ſentiunt & ſequuntur. hirundines ideo videntur ima petere, quia muſcæ, quas venantur, ob aëris denſitatem & qualitates humidas supernè incumbentes ad inferiora ſe demittunt haud dubio ſecuturæ pluviæ indicio. Ad 7. Quædam animalia præ aliis ſunt apta erudiri, quia præſtantiorem phantaſiam ſortita ſunt, ſine ductu rationis, ſolo internorum ſenſuum miniſterio. Eodem modo, quæ 8. & 9. loco narrantur, non ad diſcurſum, non ad diſcretionem rationis aut ſigni ex arbitrio hominum ſignificantis intellectû ſunt referenda: ſed ad inſtinctum & induſtriam naturalem pertinent, uti complura alia, quæ maximè in alvearibus apum, & myrmeciis formicarum non ſine admiratione ſpectantur.

PHI-

An elegant copperplate engraving of the Judgment of Solomon graces a deluxe doctoral dissertation in legal philosophy by a German nobleman.

10.11

Juan Eugenio de Ochoa.
Manual del abogado americano.

Arequipa: Imprenta del Gobierno Administrada por Pedro Benavides, 1830. Volume 2 of 2.

324 *Titulo diez y siete*

juro &a.=(auto)=*traslado y autos.*

Pedimento solicitando un reo se le tome la confesion—J vecino de esta ciudad y preso en la carcel publica, como mejor proceda digo: que hace tantos dias me hallo en uno de los calabosos de esta, sin saber la causa de mi prision; por lo que=A U. pido se sirva mandar que siendo la causa civil se me entreguen los autos, y si criminal se me reciba la confesion (ó declaracion instructiva) ponga la acusacion en forma, y se me dé traslado para alegar lo conveniente á mi derecho. Pido justicia, juro &a =(auto)=*Como lo pide.*

Sentencia—En la causa que es entre partes, de la una F, vecino de esta ciudad actor querellante, y de la otra B, reo demandado, M, y D, procuradores en sus nombres—vista: fallo atento á la causa y meritos del proceso, (en el Perú hemos dicho que se causan las sentencias, y se dirá: atendiendiendo: 1.° á que tal cosa: 2.° á que &a.) á lo que en caso necesario me refiero, que F probó bien y cumplidamente su accion y querella, como probar le convino: declárola por bien probada, y que B reo, no probó sus escepciones y

Juicio criminal. 325

defensas como debió; en cuya consecuencia debo condenar y condeno al referido B en tal pena (aqui se espresa la pena, y si fuere de muerte se concluye asi:) y mando que esta sentencia se consulte: 1.° con la I. C. S. de Justicia, de tal parte, y por esta mi sentencia difinitivamente juzgando, asi lo pronuncio mando y firmo. (si hubiese costas en las que se le deba condenar, se espresará).

FIN.

Our feathered friend may be a red jungle fowl, a commonly domesticated food source. Striding beneath hand-drawn curlicues, the bird marks the conclusion of a Peruvian lawyer's manual – and of this catalogue.

Author-Title Index

charg'd on the murtherers of that noble lord and true patriot, Arthur (late) Earl of Essex. London: Printed for the author and sold by most booksellers, 1690. 7.02

Buno, Johannes (1617-1697). *Memoriale Institutionum juris*. Ratzeburg: Nicolaus Nissen, 1672. 8.07

Burney, Nathaniel. *The illustrated guide to criminal procedure*. New York: Ivers Morgan, 2014. 8.17

California. Commission to Revise the Laws of California. *Revised laws of the State of California, in four codes: Political, Civil, Civil Procedure and Penal*. [Volume 2] *Civil Code*. Sacramento: D.W. Gelwicks, State Printer, 1871. 3.13

California. *The civil codes of the State of California, published under authority of law, by Creed Haymond, John C. Burch [and] John H. McKune, commissioners to revise the laws*. Sacramento: T.A. Springer, State Printer, 1872. 3.05

Cardoso da Costa, Vicente José Ferreira (1765-1834). *Explicação da arvore que representa o prospecto do Codigo Civil Portuguez: offerecido ao soberano congresso nacional pela maõ do seu ill.mo deputado o Sr. José Joaquim Rodrigues de Bastos*. Lisbon: Antonio Rodrigues Galhardo, 1822. 3.11

Carmagnola, Giuseppe. *Trattato delle alluvioni: diviso in ragionamenti teorico-pratici sopra l'origine, il diritto, e la divisione degli incrementi fluviali*. Torino: Nella Stamperia Soffietti, 1793. 4.02

Carpzov, Benedict (1595-1666). *Verhandeling der lyfstraffelyke misdaaden en haare berechtinge, naar 't voorschrift des gemeenen rechts*. 2 vols. Rotterdam: Jan Daniel Beman, 1752. 1.02

Cases on appeals concerning the duties on houses and windows, servants and Inhabited houses: with determinations of the commissioners, and opinions of the judges thereon. London: Fielding and Walker, 1780. 7.04

Cases respecting assessed taxes determined by the judges, 1841 [nos. 1476-1564]. London: Printed by W. Clowes and Sons, for Her Majesty's Stationery Office, 1841. 7.05

Castile (Kingdom). *Las siete partidas del sabio rey D. Alfonso el Nono*. 7 vols. Valencia: J.T. Lucas, 1758. 3.14

Catholic Church. *Clementis V. papae Constitutiones*. Venice: Nicolaus Jenson, 1479. 10.09

Ceremonial for the trial of a peer, in Westminster-Hall with Garter's list of the peerage, as it now stands, April 1776, and a plan of the court. London: T. Payne, 1776. 5.01

Chasseneuz, Barthélemy de (1480-1541). *Le grant coustumier de Bourgogne*. Paris: Francois Regnault, 1534. 3.04

Coke, Sir Edward (1552-1634). *The first part of the Institutes of the lawes of England: or, A commentarie upon Littleton*. London: Societie of Stationers, 1628. 3.10

Consultatien, advysen en advertissementen, gegeven ende geschreven by verscheyden treffeljcke rechts-geleerden in Hollandt. 7 vols. Rotterdam: J. Naeranus, 1648-1666. 5.06

Damhoudere, Joost de (1507-1581). *La practique et enchiridion des causes criminelles*. Louvain: Etienne Wauters & Johan Bathen, 1555. 2.04

Damhoudere, Joost de (1507-1581). *Practycke in civile saecken*. The Hague: Hillebrant Jacobsz van Wouw, 1626. 1.09

Damhoudere, Joost de (1507-1581). *Practycke in criminele saecken*. Rotterdam: Jean van Waesberge, 1628. 2.05

Damhoudere, Joost de (1507-1581). *Practycke in criminele saken*. Rotterdam: Pieter van Waesberge, 1650. 2.00

Damhoudere, Joost de (1507-1581). *Praxis rerum criminalium*. Antwerp: Jean Beller, 1556. 2.03

Damhoudere, Joost de (1507-1581). *Praxis rerum criminalium.* Frankfurt: Johann Wolff, 1565. 6.03

Damhoudere, Joost de (1507-1581). *Pupillorum patrocinium.* Antwerp: Jean Beller, 1564. 5.00

De haereditatibus quae ab intestato deferunt. Manuscript, Italy?, 17th century?. 3.03

De Sarno, Agnello. *Novissima praxis criminalis, et civilis: cum observationibus as nonnullas ex regiis pragmaticis, ac singulari tractatu inscripto il Medico fiscale pro optima cognitione delictorum in genere ... Doctoris Horatii Graeci.* Naples: Michael Monaco, 1687. 6.02

Decretales Domini pape Gregorij noni. Venice: Luca-Antonio Giunta, 1514. 2.06

Diz Antonio Alvares Gil, escrivaõ proprietario da correiçaõ do crime do Bairro Alto, e dos autos da devaça das mortes, e roubos praticados no navio succo Patristen, que para requerimentos que tem, pertende extrahir por certidaõ a sentença. Lisbon: Jozé de Aquino Bulhoens, 1781. 7.01

Döhler, Johann Georg (1667-1749). *Processualische Mause-Fallen.* Coburg: Paul Gunther Pfolenhauer und Sohn, 1723. 9.08

Dumercy, Charles. *Exegése biblique au point de vue du droit belge.* Antwerp: J.E. Buschmann, 1895. 9.02

Eike von Repgow (1180?-1233?). *Vollstandige Faksimile-Ausgabe im Originalformat des Wolfenbütteler Sachsenspiegels* [facsimile]. Graz: Akademische Druck- und Verlagsanstalt, 2006. 2.01

England. *Statuta Angliae nova.* Manuscript on vellum, in law French, and Latin. 1444-1483/1484. 10.05

Fitch, A. Norton. *A treatise on commercial law: with forms of ordinary legal and business documents, and copious questions with references.* Rochester, N.Y.: E.R. Andrews, 1889. 3.12

France. *Code de la route: texte officiel et complet.* Paris: Maurice Gonon, 1956. "Illustrations en couleurs de Dubout." 9.04

France. *Code général des impôts directs et taxes assimilées: text intégral des lois, décrets, décrets-lois, décret de codification, suivi d'un formulaire administratif.* Paris: Editions Littéraires et Artistiques; Librairie "Le Triptyque," 1944. "Illustré par Joseph Hémard." 9.03

France. *Code penal: commentaires imagés de Joseph Hémard.* Paris: Editions Littéraires de France, [192u?]). 9,.00, 9.05

France. *Code pénal: texte officiel.* Neuilly-sur Seine: M. Gonon, 1959. "Illustré par Siné." 9.06

Gamboa, Francisco Javier de (1717-1794). *Comentarios a las ordenanzas de minas.* Madrid: Joaquín Ibarra, 1761. 4.04

Gelderland (Netherlands). *Water-recht waar nae een yder in het Furstendom Gelre en Graafschap Zutphen.* Arnhem: Wed. de Haas, 1715. 4.05

Genoa (Italy). *Prohibitione de coltelli.* Genoa: Giovanni Maria Farroni, 1646. 2.09

Genoa (Republic). *Criminalium iurium serenissimae reipublicae Genuensis.* Genoa: Ioannes Baptista Tiboldus, 1669. 1.00

Ginsberg, Allen (1926-1997). *Chicago trial testimony.* San Francisco: City Lights, 1975. 9.16

Giovanni d'Andrea (1270-1348). *Arbor consanguineitatis cum suis enigmatibus et figuris.* Nuremberg: Hieronymus Höltzel, 1506. 8.02

Giovanni d'Andrea (1270-1348). *De arbore consanguineitatis et affinitatis.* Manuscript on vellum, Italy, 14th century. 3.01

Giovanni d'Andrea (1270-1348). *Super arboribus consanguinitatis et affinitatis.* Nuremberg: Friedrich Creussner, ca. 1473. 3.02

Glafey, Adam Friedrich (1692-1753). *Vollständigen Geschichte des Rechts der Vernunfft*. Leipzig: Christoph Riegel, 1739. 1.03

Glassbrenner, Adolf (1810-1876). *Eine Volks-Jury in Berlin*. Leipzig: Verlag von Ignaz Jackowitz, 1848. 5.10

Göbler, Justinus (1503?-1567). *Statutenbuch, Gesatz, Ordnungen und Gebrauch, keyserlicher, allgemeyner, und etlicher besonderer Landt und Stett Rechten*. Frankfurt: Christian Egenolff, 1572. 2.07

Guggenberger, Veit (active 17th c.). *Ayd-Buch: warinnen findig das ayd, und ayd-schwur seyen, wie mancherley derselben gefunden*. Munich: Heinrich Theodor von Cöllen, 1738. 2.08

Hagamos valer nuestros derechos: guía didáctica sobre los derechos, deberes y libertades de los niños y niñas de primero y segundo ciclos de Educación Básica. San Salvador, El Salvador: Ministerio de Educación, Dirección Nacional de Educación, 1997. 8.10

Hayes, H. G. *A complete history of the trial of Guiteau, assassin of President Garfield*. Philadelphia: Hubbard Bros.; San Francisco: A.L. Bancroft; St. Louis, Mo.: J. Burns, 1882. 5.09

Hertel, Johann Friedrich (1667-1743). *Politische Schnupf-Tobacs-Dose vor die wächserne Nase der Justitz*. Frankfurt & Leipzig [i.e. Jena: Verlegts Christian Friedrich Gollner], 1739. 9.07

Hilgendorf, Eric. *Dtv-Atlas Recht*. 2 vols. Munich: Deutscher Taschenbuch Verlag, 2003-2008. 3.15

Hodshon, Read. *The honest man's companion, or, The family's safeguard*. Newcastle upon Tyne: Printed for the author, and sold by M. Bryson, 1736. 9.11

Hoestlandt, Maud. *La justice à petit pas*. Paris: Actes Sud Junior, 2004. 8.09

Hommel Karl Ferdinand (12722-1781). *Iurisprudentia numismatibus illustrata*. Leipzig: Johann Wendler, 1763. 5.04

Hungary. *In causa Fisci Regii, contra Abbatem Josephum Ignatium Martinovits, ex crimine laesae majestatis seu perduellionis promota*. Pest: Michael Landerer de Füskút, 1795. 3.09

Illiustrirovannaia Konstitutsiia Rossiiskoi Federatsii. = The illustrated Constitution of the Russian Federation. Moscow: Izdatel M.IU. Gorelov, 2012. 8.13

Instituta novissime recognita aptissimisque figuris exculta. Venice: Luca-Antonio Giunta, 1516. 8.03

Jacobus de Theramo (1350-1417). *Le procés de Belial a lencontre de Jhesus* [leaf]. (Lyon: Johann Neumeister, 4 Mar. 1483/84). 8.01

Juristische Ergötzlichkeiten vom Jung-Gesellen Rechte. Frankfurt & Leipzig, 1723. 8.05

Justice is waiting. [Los Angeles?] Mooney Defense of Southern California, 1930. 1.07

Knaust, Heinrich (d. ca 1577). *De D. Ivonis juris consulti laudibus et vita oratio*. Cologne: Maternus Cholinus, 1574. 1.11

Knights of Malta. *Statuta Hospitalis Hierusalem*. Rome, 1586. 10.04

Lash, Batton. *Supernatural law, no. 35*. San Diego, CA: Exhibit A Press, July 2002. 9.14

Lawrence, William (1614-1682). *Marriage by the morall law of God vindicated against all ceremonial laws of popes and bishops destructive to filiation aliment and succession and the government of familyes and kingdomes*. [London: s.n.], 1680. 1.10

Le Rouillé, Guillaume (1494-1550?). *Justicie atque iniusticie descriptionum compendium*. Paris: Claude Chevallon, 1520. 1.15

The Legal Self-Defense Group presents: Mr. Natural in "Bailed out." Boston, Mass., 1971?. 8.20

The Legal Self-Defense Group presents: "Search and seizure." Boston, Mass., 1971?. 8.21

Lehmann, Ignaz. *Amerika's Gesetze.* St. Louis, Mo.: C. Witter, 1857. 1.08

Leiser, Christian Gottfried (1647-1700). *Jus georgicum, sive, Tractatus de praediis = Von Land-Güthern.* Leipzig: heirs of Friedrich Lanckisch, 1698. 4.07

Liber sextus Decretalium D. Bonifacii Papae VIII; Clementis Papae V. Constitutiones; Extravagantes tum vigenti D. Ioannis Papae XXII, tum communes. Venice: Giunta, 1600. 3.00

The life, trial & defence, of Her Most Gracious Majesty, Caroline, Queen of Great-Britain: including every proceeding in her case, both in and out of Parliament. London: Dean & Munday, 1820. 5.03

Linz, Kathi. *Chickens may not cross the road and other crazy (but true) laws.* Boston: Houghton Mifflin, 2002. 9.13

Lünig, Johann Christian (1662-1740). *Vade mecum juridicum, oder, Der sich selbstrathende Advocat.* 3 vols. Basel: Johann Rudolf Im Hof, 1750-1752. 9.09

Marchant, François (1761-1793). *La constitution en vaudevilles: suivie des Droits de l'homme, de la femme & de plusieurs autres vaudevilles constitutionnels.* Paris: Libraires Royalistes, 1792. 9.01

Marinoni, Giovanni Battista (d. 1647). *La sferza de bruti e delle cose insensate.* Pavia: Giovanni Andrea Magri, 1636. 6.11

Mascambrone, Lorenzo. *Degli asili de Christiani ragionamento.* Rome: Camera Appostolica, 1731. 10.03

Mason, George Henry. *The punishments of China: illustrated by twenty-two engravings, with explanations in English and French.* London: Printed for W. Miller by S. Gosnell, 1808. 6.08

Matthaeus, Antonius (1601-1654). *De judiciis disputationes septendecim.* 3rd ed. Amsterdam: Johannes Janssonius van Waesberghe, 1665. 1.13

Maximae juris celebriores, deductae ex jure canonico, civili, glossa. Trnava: Typis Academicis, S. Jesu, 1742. 1.04

Meurer, Noe. *Tractatus juridicus de successione ab intestato, oder, Vollkommener Unterricht von Erbschafften, und Erb-Gerechtigkeiten.* Nürnberg: In Verlegung Johann Albrecht, gedruct bey Johann Ernst Adelbulnern, 1730. 5.13

Nakamichi, Yuki, & Yamanaka Masahiro. *Osaru no tomasu keiho o shiru: saruyama kyowakoku no jikenbo [Thomas Monkey learns the criminal law].* Tokyo: Tarojiroshaeditasu, 2014. 8.12

National Biscuit Company. *Trade mark litigation: opinions, orders, injunctions, and decrees relating to unfair competition and infringement of trade marks.* 5th ed. New York, 1915. 7.10

Niccolò de' Tudeschi (Panormitanus) (1386-1445). 5 vols. *Lectura super V libris decretalium.* Basel: Michael Wenssler, Berthold Ruppel & Bernard Richel, 1477. 2.02

Nuremberg (Germany). *Reformacion der Stat Nüremberg.* Nüremberg: Fridrich Peypus, 1522. 10.06

Ochoa, Juan Eugenio de. *Manual del abogado americano.* 2 vols. Arequipa: Imprenta del Gobierno Administrada por Pedro Benavides, 1830. 10.11

Oettingen, Franz Albrecht, Count of (1663-1737). *Philosophia legalis, sive, Quaestiones dialecticae, physicae et metaphysicae, ad scientiam juris accommodatae.* Dillingen: Johann Caspar Bencard for Johann Federle, [1682?]. 10.10

Order of reference of the Supreme Court of the United States, in the case of the State of Pennsylvania, complainant, against the Wheeling & Belmont Bridge Company and others, defendants: with the proofs taken before R. Hyde Walworth, commissioner, together with his report and the report of the engineer. Saratoga Springs [N.Y.]: George F. White, 1851. 7.11

Pecchio, Francesco Maria (d. 1692). *Tractatus de aquaeductu*. 4 vols. Pavia: Giovanni Andrea Magri, [1673?]. 4.00

Phillips, Watts (1825-1874). *A case in bankruptcy*. London: D. Bogue, [18--]. 9.12

Piccoli, Luigi. *Le servitù prediali sanzionate dal Codice Napoleone*. Brescia: Nicolò Bettoni, 1808. 4.08

Prieur de Saint Pierre. *L'arbitre charitable: pour eviter les procez et les querelles*. Paris: Laurens Raueneau, 1668. 5.08

Quick search manual: being a complete collection of the analyses and cross references in the Corpus Juris-Cyc system. New York: American Law Book Co., 1926. 3.07

Repertorium aureum continens titulos quinque librorum Decretalium, sive Concordantiae utriusque iuris. Cologne: Heinrich Quentell, 1495. 8.00

Republic of Venice, Council of Ten. *Parte presa nell'Eccelso Conseglio di X ... in materia de banditi*. Venice: Rampazetto, 1609. 1.01

Rosenfield, Bernard. *Let's go to the Supreme Court*. New York: Putnam, 1960. 5.05

Russia (Federation). *Illiustrirovannyi Trudovoi kodeks Rossiiskoi Federatsii*. Moscow: Izdatelstvo "Mann, Ivanov i Ferber," 2014. 2.11

Russia (Federation). *Illiustrirovannyi ugolovnyi kodeks Rossiiskoi Federatsii*. Moscow: Izdatel'stvo "Mann, Ivanov i Ferber," 2013. 9.17

Sánchez, Martín. *Conspicua et adprime frugifera dividui et individui arbor*. N.p., 1538. 3.08

Saraiva, Denise Cardia. *Direito penal ilustrado: parte geral*. Rio de Janeiro: Edições Illustradas, 1999. 8.18

Scott, John Anthony (1916-2010), ed. *The defense of Gracchus Babeuf before the High Court of Vendôme*. Northampton, Mass.: Gehenna Press, 1964. 10.08

Selves, Jean Baptiste (1760-1823). *Au roi: La vérité sur l'administration de la justice*. Paris: Chez Le Normant, Libraire, rue de Seine, [ca. 1815]. 5.11

Serralde, Francisco A. *El crimen de Santa Julia: defensa gráfica que, sirviéndose de signos físicos encontrados en los cuerpos de las víctimas del crimen, presenta el Lic. Francisco A. Serralde, defensor del coronel Timoteo Andrade*. México: F.P. Hoeck y Compañía, 1899. 7.08

Sheppard, William. (d. 1675?). *A sure guide for His Majesties justices of peace*. London: John Streater for Henry & Timothy Twyford, 1663. 1.14

Sobel, Syl. *The U.S. Constitution and you*. Hauppauge, N.Y.: Barron's Educational Series, 2001. 8.11

Sonnenfels, Joseph von (1733-1817). *Ueber die Abschaffung der Tortur*. Zürich: Orell, Gessner, Fuesslin, 1775. 6.10

Stoeckley, Clark. *The United States vs. Pvt. Chelsea Manning*. New York: OR Books, 2014. 5.12

Taylor, Jefferys (1792-1853). *Parlour commentaries on the Constitution and laws of England*. London: John Harris, 1825. 8.15

The telephone appeals: 113. Amos E. Dolbear et al., appellants, v. the American Bell Telephone Co. U.S.C.C. Mass. [etc.]: Oral argument of Mr. Storrow on the Bell patents. Boston: A. Mudge & Son, 1887. 7.09

Tengler, Ulrich (d. 1511?). *Der neü Leyenspiegel vö rechtmässigen ordnungen in burgerlichen und peinlicher Regimenten*. Strassburg, 1514. 1.12

The Terry contempt. [San Francisco: s.n., 1888.] 7.00

Teutsches corpus juris publici & privati, oder, Codex diplomaticus. 2 vols. Ulm: Johann Conrad Wohlers, 1717. 1.05

Trial and imprisonment of Jonathan Walker, at Pensacola, Florida, for aiding slaves to escape from bondage. Boston: Published at the Anti-Slavery Office, 1845. 6.07

The trial of Governor T. Picton, for inflicting the torture on Louisa Calderon, a free mulatto, and one of His Britannic Majesty's subjects in the island of Trinidad. London: B. Crosby and Co., [1806]. 7.03

The trial of Lieutenant-Colonel Joseph Wall, late governor of Goree, at the Old Bailey, on Wednesday, January 20, 1802; for the wilful murder of Benjamin Armstrong, a serjeant of the African corps, July 10, 1782. London : Sabine & Son, [1802?]. 6.06

Trial of Professor John W. Webster, for the murder of Doctor George Parkman: reported exclusively for the N.Y. Daily Globe. New York: Stringer & Townsend ... printed at the Globe office, 1850. 7.06

The unabridged graphic adaptation iTunes terms and conditions. 2 vols. Birdcage Bottom Books, 2015. 9.15

Veridica descrizione, e ragguaglio distinto della Promulgazione delle colpe, e dell'abjura solenne, e della condanna di galera fulminata dal Santo Tribunale dell'Inquisizione di Brescia, contro Giuseppe Beccarelli da Vrago d'Olio, li 13. settembre 1710. Brescia: Gio. Maria Rizzardi, 1710. 5.07

Wassenaer, Gerard van (1588-1664). *Practyk judicieel, ofte, Instructie op de forme en manier van procederen voor hoven en recht-banken.* Utrecht: Jacob van Poolsum, 1746. 5.02

Werle, Johann Moritz. *Album juridicum.* Augsburg: Matthias Wolff, 1733. 8.04

Wm. F. Wernse & Co. Promotional brochure for the *American digest and legal directory.* St. Louis: Wm. F. Wernse & Co., 1888. 1.06

Woodhouse, Henry (1884-1970). *Textbook of aerial laws: and regulations for aerial navigation, international, national and municipal, civil and military.* New York: Frederick A. Stokes, 1920. 2.10

Youth & law: legal advice for youth. [San Francisco?: High School Committee, National Lawyers Guild, undated. 8.19

Index of Illustrators

Acknowledgments

We wish to thank all those friends and colleagues who have provided us with inspiration, advice, and support in producing this exhibition and catalogue.

MICHAEL WIDENER
& MARK S. WEINER

The late Hans W. Baade
Erin Blake
John Robinson Block
William E. Butler
The late Morris L. Cohen
Joe and Wanda Corn
Jason Eiseman
Marcos Galindo
Jolande Goldberg
Edward Gordon
José Calvo González
Ryan Greenwood
Eric Hilgendorf
Carole Hinchcliff
Valerie Horowitz
James Eric Jones
Akira Kamo
Farley P. Katz
Blair Kauffman
Susan Karpuk
Gernot Kocher
The late Guillermo Floris Margadant
Georges Martyn
Rosemarie McGerr
Teresa Miguel-Stearns
Christopher W. Platts
Judith Resnik
Nicholas Salazar
Fred Shapiro
Jennifer Sheehan
Stas Skarbo
Courtney Weiss Smith
Gregory F. Talbot
Szilvia Szmuk-Tanenbaum
Anthony Taussig
Irene Tichenor
Otto Vervaart
Fang Wang
Flynn Warmington
John Wei
Stephanie Weiner
Emma Molina Widener
Henry Granville Widener
Anders Winroth

I have acquired illustrated law books from each of these book dealers for the Yale Law Library's collection. I am grateful for their collaboration and support.

MICHAEL WIDENER

Librería de Antaño
Antica Libreria
Antiquariat Aix-la-Chapelle
Antiquariaat Forum
Studio Bibliografico Apuleio
Nick Aretakis
Asher Rare Books
Lorne Bair Rare Books
Librería Bardón
Simon Beattie Ltd.
Studio Bibliografico Benacense
Between the Covers Rare Books
Bibliopathos Rare Books
Bolerium Books
Libreria Antiquaria Bongiorno
Edmund Brumfitt Rare Books
Leo Cadogan Rare Books
Casanova Books
Rodolphe Chamonal
Charbo's Antiquariaat
W. S. Cotter Rare Books
Justin Croft Antiquarian Books
James Cummins Bookseller
Division Leap
John Drury Rare Books
Exhibit A Press
Joseph J. Felcone Inc.
Steve Finer Rare Books
Arthur Freeman Rare Books
and Manuscripts
Rodger Friedman Rare Book Studio
A. Gerits & Son Antiquarian Booksellers
Franklin Gilliam Rare Books
Michael Ginsberg Books
Libreria Antiquaria Alberto Govi
Libreria Antiquaria Gozzini
James Gray Bookseller
A. R. Heath Rare Books & Manuscripts
Jonathan A. Hill, Bookseller
Antiquariat Inlibris Gilhofer
Antiquariaat Matthys de Jongh
Keip & von Delft
Kevin F. Kelly Bookseller
Antiquariaat de Kloof
Konstantinopel Rare & Fine Books
Versandantiquariat Rainer Kurz
Michael Laird Rare Books
Lawbook Exchange
David M. Lesser Fine Antiquarian Books
Studio Bibliografico Lex Antiqua
Libros Latinos
Herman H. J. Lynge & Søn
M&S Rare Books
Maggs Bros. Ltd.
Jeffrey D. Mancevice Inc.
Martayan Lan, Inc.
Mayfair Rare Books and Manuscripts
MC Rare Books
Patrick McGahern Books
Bruce McKittrick Rare Books
Libreria Antiquaria Mediolanum
Katalin Meiwes
Mémoire du Droit
Meyer Boswell Books
Milou Rare Books
George Robert Minkoff Inc.
Musinsky Rare Books
Bernard Quaritch Ltd.
Palinurus Antiquarian Books
Albert L. Peters Bookseller
Philadelphia Rare Books & Manuscripts Co.
Pickering & Chatto
Libreria Antiquaria Pregliasco
John Price Antiquarian Books
Studio Bibliografico Paolo Rambaldi
Bruce Ramer
Richard C. Ramer Old & Rare Books
William Reese Co.
L & T Respess Books
Riverrun Books & Manuscripts
Robert H. Rubin Books
Savoy Books
E. K. Schreiber
Garrett Scott, Bookseller
Susanne Schulz-Falster Rare Books
Second Life Books
Sokol Books
Antiquariaat A.G. van der Steur
Librairie Ancienne Les Trois Islets
Antiquariat Uwe Turszynski
John Turton Antiquarian Books
Librería Urbe
The Veatchs Arts of the Book
Christian F. Verbeke Antiquarian
Law Booksellers
Vico Verlag & Antiquariat
Vivarium Books

THIS BOOK is set in *Linden Hill* (2010) an open-source digital font, based on Frederic William Goudy's *Deepdene* (1927), by Barry Schwartz from The League of Movable Type. Numerals are set in *Constantia* (2006), a font designed by John Hudson.

Interior design and composition
by VALERIE L. HOROWITZ
Cover design
by PETER LO RICCO